Alan Rowan is a ____ list and mountaineer. His first book, *Moonwalk ____ ____ night ____ vas ____ blished by BackPa ____ ____ bed the Munros three times and is curren ____ urth circuit, the Furths (England, Wales ____ reland ____ tt p ____ s) and the Corbetts. He lives in Carno____ ie on Scotlan 's sunn____ east coast. More information, including mountain bl gs, videos, photos and hill guides can be found at: www.munromoonwalker.com

He is also on Facebook, www.facebook.com/MunroMoonwalker and Twitter, @MunroMoonwalker

A MOUNTAIN BEFORE BREAKFAST

ALAN ROWAN

A catalogue record for this book is available
from the British Library

ISBN: 978 1 90943 025 9

Design by Shed Collective
Typeset by Laura Kincaid, tenthousand publishing services
Printed and bound in Scotland by MBM Print SCS Ltd

Cover picture by Alan Rowan © Munro Moonwalker

For Trevor,
Forever in the mountains

1
Sandra Bullock and
the Paps of Jura

7
Small Change

17
The Day the Earth
Caught Fire

27
Car Crashes and Bum Slides

37
National Treasures

47
Dai Hard

57
The Prince of Walls

67
Dubhs and Don'ts

77
Lost and Found

87
Ice Cold in Affric

97
Scorch Mist

109
Northern Lights

119
The Eagle and the Fox

129
Ard Day's Night

139
Winter Wanderland

149
Wizards and Lost Soles

159
The Place You Are Calling
From Does Not Exist

169
Lights Out

179
The Supermodel

189
North by Northwest

199
Barn Nights

209
The Isle High Club

219
Dolphin Salute

225
Glossary

227
Acknowledgements

CORBETT

The name given to Scottish mountains more than 2500ft (762 metres) high but below 3000ft (914.4m) and which have a defined drop of at least 500ft (152m) between any adjacent listed peak. These were originally listed in 1923 by John Rooke Corbett, a member of the Scottish Mountaineering Club and the first Englishman to climb all the Munros (peaks over 3000ft). Those who climb all 219 Corbetts are termed Corbetteers.

Sandra Bullock and the Paps of Jura

Fast and furious on the road to Jura; a touch
of New Zealand hospitality; the smallest
bathroom in the western world; things
to do in Islay when you're dead tired

I WAS setting off on a long journey across the country to tackle a tough hill circuit and my overriding thought was: I wish Sandra Bullock were here.

Not that I have a crush on the lovely Ms Bullock. No offence Sandra, but the desire to have your company on this adventure was purely practical.

My car was in its death throes and I had just received a particularly worrying phone call. The whispered voice had warned: "You'll have to keep the car revs high or the engine could blow up."

I had to check I was awake. Had I been thrust into a cheap remake of Speed with myself in the Keanu Reeves role? No, this wasn't mad bomber Dennis Hopper on the blower. It was a mechanic giving the verdict on the likelihood of my trusty Peugeot 206 Gti making it to Jura and back. The engine was finished. It was just a matter of days, and whether these days would be enough to see me from my east coast home on a 350-plus mile round trip was the big unknown.

But I had to go now. At the start of the year, I had rashly set a finishing date of June 28 to complete my ascent of all the Corbetts, the 219 Scottish mountains between 2,500 and 3,000 feet. I had just 20 left to tick off but to stay on track for the big finishing party with friends in Knoydart I had to get to Jura pronto.

You think I would have learned my lesson. Having set a finishing date for my first round of Munros, I found it just heaped on the pressure to try to fit in these hills between work and family duties. Despite saying 'never again', I was now careering round trying to find weather and opportunities to hit my deadline.

It takes a bit of planning to get to Jura. There is no direct ferry from the mainland, so first you have to get to Kennacraig on the Kintyre peninsula to catch a boat to Port Askaig in Islay, then get the wee cooncil ferry across the Sound of Islay to Jura. Once on the island, there's a 12-mile run up the main road – actually, the only road – to reach the start of the route over the three peaks known as the Paps.

A month earlier, I had failed to get there despite military-style planning. Three of us had stayed the night in Kennacraig. We had intended getting the early ferry next day, doing a circuit of the hills and then coming off the western side to make all the ferry connections. It would be tight but it could be done.

But when we arrived at the terminal we discovered the ferry had been cancelled because they were rebuilding the pier at Port Askaig and the boat couldn't dock there. Instead it would go to Port Charlotte on the other side of the island. This would add hours to the journey and meant we couldn't get back the same day, so we trudged off and climbed nearby Ben Cruachan instead. Not a bad substitute, but still disappointing.

Now it was time to go again, so despite the dire warnings of my car's health, I loaded up and set off in the early darkness.

The first part was no problem. The car was behaving, the roads were clear and the traffic was flowing. The trouble started after leaving Glasgow. The road up the side of Loch Lomond slowed me considerably and the car didn't like it. On a couple of occasions I saw steam or smoke coming from the under the bonnet, but it vanished as soon as I accelerated past the dawdlers.

The good people of Inveraray must have been shocked to see a rust-coloured car streaking through the streets with smoke billowing out the front, the driver's side window open and the sound of a screaming, cursing and often pleading madman at the wheel. I was doing *Fast and Furious* long before Vin Diesel's big baldy heid made it to the big screen.

The stretch down the winding road from Loch Fyne to Lochgilphead was a combination of clear driving and smoky, expletive-filled overtaking with the foot clamped to the floor. The suspension was also on the way out. Every bump and turn was felt through my tailbone. It was like guiding a bobsleigh over a bed of concrete.

When I pulled into the car park at Kennacraig, my backside felt as if it had been paddled with cricket bats, my back was sore, my face was sooty from the blowback and the steam in the car had brought on a bad hair day.

It had been a rough ride but the car had made it. There was still the return journey to contemplate but that didn't worry me. I could put my feet up for a couple of hours for the crossing of the Sound of Jura.

I got chatting to fellow travellers, and recounted the tale of my fractious journey. Sympathy was in short supply. "Hah! Sounds just like film, *Speed*. You should have had Sandra Bullock with you, mate. Know what I'm saying?"

I did indeed. But it was a non-starter. Sandra would never have made it over to Scotland at such short notice.

The Paps were looking good as we pulled into the harbour. I couldn't wait to get up there.

I got talking to a couple from England on the short ferry crossing to Jura and managed to blag a lift to the island's solitary hotel at Craighouse where I was staying the night. The plan had been to get a good sleep and then get going before anyone else was awake, but it was only mid-afternoon and my nocturnal brain started thinking about a change of plan. Why not just set off now? It would mean a quick grab and bag of the main peak only rather than the full round of three, but at this stage of the race that would suffice.

A quick check-in and change and I started walking north just after 4pm. It was only about three miles up the road to the Corran River start point, but the great thing about walking on the islands is that virtually everyone who passes stops and offers you a lift. Within minutes I was sitting in the passenger seat chatting to a local teacher. John was a Kiwi who settled in Edinburgh but soon found it too crowded. Of all the places he had stayed in Scotland since, Jura was the closest in character he had found to New Zealand's North Island.

His school was in Islay and every day he drove from his home where the road petered out at Lussagiven on the north-east coast down to the ferry and over to work. He was heading home after another day in class when he picked me up. He dropped me at the start of the walk, a stile into open grassland which was swaying as one in perfect harmony with the brisk evening wind. There was a path of sorts leading to the outflow of lonely Loch an t-Slob, the small lochan which sits under the horseshoe formed by the grizzled slopes of the Paps.

The round of Beinn Shiantaidh, Beinn an Oir and Beinn a' Chaolais is a classic, a punishing push through a maze of giant boulders and scree with a lot of ascent and descent. Time was against me though, so this was purely a bagging trip for the middle peak, the Corbett.

The white horses were galloping across the water, the breeze building in strength. There's a set of stepping stones to cross the outflow, the biggest I'd seen, yet I was almost blown off halfway over by the gusty wind.

The slanting ascent to the 'hill of gold' from here was simple, first up a grassy wall then into the fields of boulder chaos where a ramp took a rising line north and then zig-zagged west to the rocky confusion of the summit. Nothing to see here, the cloud that been blowing in owned the high ground.

I dropped fast, wind assisted all the way. The retreating light bathed the lower ground in an eerie glow and the knee-high grasses were bending in my direction. The faint path I used on the way in was lost but it was simple to run through the soft ground to reach the road as the near horizontal rain started firing bullets at my back.

Darkness overtook me on the road back to the hotel, the yellow eyes of deer shining like torch lights from the trees. Passing cars stopped to offer a ride but I was a muddy mess and didn't think it was fair to inflict that on anyone. I was back to my room by 10 looking forward to a shower and a pint. However, the room appeared to be bathroom-free. Strange, when I booked I definitely heard 'en suite' mentioned. I went outside and checked the hallway, but my room had no exterior connections. Another look round. Just a built-in cupboard and a wardrobe. I must be in the wrong room. But no, there was the key with the matching number. Then I opened the cupboard and, voila, the smallest bathroom outside of Tokyo was revealed.

Inside this cupboard/shower room, they had managed to fit a toilet, basin and a shower. The toilet was so close to the wall I had to sit side-saddle. Try to sit down normally and a plumber would have to be called to free you.

The shower floor area was about the size of a single large tile. I stepped in and pulled the curtain round. It fit like a sheath. No problem with the water pressure though. They must have borrowed it from an elephant house. When I turned it on I was blasted back into the plastic sheath and became cocooned, a giant slug writhing around under a steaming waterfall.

When I finally untangled myself, it was down to the bar. I arrived in the middle of a party, but then I suppose every night is a party here. Any pub crawl here involves simply moving from one end of the bar to the other. I didn't stay long, much as I wanted to. With mission accomplished it was time for bed at the end of another frantic day.

I had time to kill next day and I managed to fit in a bus tour of Islay. That ate up all of 40 minutes of the five-hour wait until the ferry but with a car at the other end a tour of the distilleries wouldn't be a good idea. Especially when your car could explode.

The drive home wasn't as frenetic as the incoming one. It was almost as if the car had decided to go quietly. Next morning it failed to start. It had passed away peacefully during the night. I gave it one final salute. It had got me where I wanted to go one last time and then checked out.

It had taken me all round Scotland, to the Outer and Inner Hebrides, to Knoydart, Torridon, Ardgour and all over Sutherland and Caithness in my quest to add a Corbetts 'compleation' to the Munros one I had finished nine years earlier.

Now I was on my own for the final leg of the journey.

1
Small Change

*Victim of a magnificent obsession; miracle
recovery from a boating disaster; final
party that turned into a wash-out;
knee-deep in snow at midnight*

WHEN you are battling your way up a mountain slope in the middle of the night through waist-deep snow miles from the nearest road, a few feet becomes fairly irrelevant.

The achievement in besting the elements and reaching the summit is all that matters. Munro or Corbett? It can be a difference of just one inch.

I am not an out-and-out mountain bagger. It may have started off that way with a desire to climb all the Munros, but that quickly passed. The more you are out on Scotland's hills, the more you want to get out. It's an addiction. You catch the bug, but it's not like having the flu. It doesn't disappear after a couple of weeks.

The same with my night-time excursions. I worked long hours on the sports desk at a national newspaper in Glasgow and I had decided the only way I would be able to fit in my mountain obsession was to start climbing them after finishing work around midnight. This got me round all the Munros in six years, but I was now hooked on night-time walking even though it mostly involved going some 36 hours without sleep. It was a habit I wasn't prepared to kick.

So just a few days after toasting the final peak of my Munro round with friends in the far north-west, I was back out in the middle of the night in a quest to summit all the Corbetts.

These are the 219 peaks in Scotland between 2,500 and 3,000ft. By the time I had stood on the top of my last Munro, Am Faochagach, I had 23 Corbetts under my belt. Most had been my local hills, climbed on days when the weather on the higher hills was foul or just when I fancied something different.

Some had been climbed out of necessity en route to Munros. For instance, Beinn Tharsuinn and Sgurr na Feartaig were easier to include than avoid during a circuit of the Munros Bidein a' Choire Sheasgaich and Lurg Mhor. Some were simply a more mouth-watering prospect than some of their bigger, duller cousins. Those with their eyes only on the main event often walk past these lower peaks. I know because I tended to do that at the start. But with experience comes the appreciation that these hills should be enjoyed and savoured.

The smart way is walk them hand in hand. That way you cover all your options. It's the same theory as linking Munros rather than picking them off piecemeal. You learn as you go along that this is the more efficient and economical way to climb.

There are some who look down on the whole peak bagging thing, saying the hills should be enjoyed simply for their own sake and not be the focus for list ticking. But I concur with the legendary mountain man Hamish Brown. He saw nothing wrong with having a target if it keeps driving you out into the great outdoors. Climbing every mountain may have become an obsession, but there's no doubt it is a magnificent obsession.

I didn't come from a mountain background but was a kid who walked everywhere. We didn't rely on car lifts from our parents for simple, short trips. We just walked. I was always going somewhere, preparing to go somewhere or coming back from somewhere. I still am. But I would never refer to this constant uphill journey through life as an odyssey. According to TV, no one seems to just go on a journey anymore; they are all off an odyssey. I blame Odysseus. Unless you are Greek, and go wandering the globe for more than ten years, wearing a toga, sandals and a giant pair of padded underpants, you are not on an odyssey.

So, a brief explanation of the Corbetts.

They are nothing to do with the smaller of the Two Ronnies. These are mountains catalogued by John Rooke Corbett, a district valuer from Bristol and a member of the Scottish Mountaineering Club. He completed the Munros and their Tops – the second person to do so – in 1930. He also climbed all of Scotland's hills over 2,000ft, and out of this vast experience came his list of hills between 2,500 and 3,000ft. But unlike Sir Hugh Munro's listings, Corbetts had to have a rigidly defined drop of at least 500ft between any adjacent listed hill.

Munro never completed his own list before he died so it was left to someone else to become the first Munroist. Likewise, Corbett never lived to see his mountain list put into action. His sister passed it on to the SMC after his death.

There were a few alterations. Relevant hills in Galloway and the Borders were added, for instance, but because of the clear definition of what constitutes a Corbett, the tweaks over the years have been minor. There is a constant debate over whether the Corbetts are harder to finish than the Munros, and both lists have their champions. This is merely a diversion born of a love of mountains.

There's no point in descending into a Harry Hill-style fight involving papier mache models of Ben Nevis and The Cobbler, rolling around the floor punching lumps out of each other. There is no definitive answer. It's like being asked to choose between The Beatles or The Rolling Stones, Pele or Maradona, Wilma Flintstone or Betty Rubble – you will never get a unanimous decision.

Munros are at the top of the pile, our highest mountains, and there are 282 at the last count. Corbetts are smaller and there are 219 of them. But size alone doesn't provide an answer. When I 'compleated' the Munros the first time it had taken me 150 days. The Corbetts took me nearly 180, and there are many reasons for this. Munros have no defined drop or re-climb between each one, which means you can tick off big chains of four, five, six and even seven in a single outing, but because of the minimum 500-ft clearance rule you have to settle for lower daily tallies with the Corbetts. The biggest outing is at Bridge of Orchy, a circuit of five. Quinag in the North-west Highlands has three Corbett peaks, as does the Rois-Bheinn round at Lochailort. Most of the rest have to be done as pairs or singles, and there are far more days out required to bag one Corbett than for the Munros. Therefore a five-Munro day could be an easier outing than that of a single Corbett.

The 150-metre rule also makes a difference. Some of the hills classified as Munros in the Eastern Highlands, for instance, would not qualify as separate peaks if that criteria was rigidly applied. The South Shiel ridge, which contains seven Munros, might also lose one or two, so the total number would come down. A great example of the rigidity of the re-climb rule can be found in Glenshee. Poor old Meall a' Choire Bhuidhe is almost six kilometres from the Munro of Glas Tulaichean and at 868 metres, easily makes Corbett height, but despite the distance and the accumulative metres of ascent and re-ascent between the intervening summits, at no point does it reach a drop of 150 metres. So it remains out in the cold, and there are many other fine peaks which fall between the lines. Corbett baggers should do the decent thing and climb this hill. It deserves to be recognised as an honorary member.

Most Munros now have good paths or tracks all the way to the summit. This is not always the case with the Corbetts. Often they have to be approached over rough ground, a more time-consuming and strength-sapping effort. There also seem to be more Corbetts which necessitate crossing other summits en route.

Two former Munros have recently been re-classified as Corbetts, having been shown to be short of the magic 3,000ft line, but Sgurr nan Ceannaichean and Beinn a' Chlaidheimh haven't suddenly become any easier to climb. They are still big beasts that require a lot of effort. When it comes to technical difficulty the Munros are clear winners. Apart from the final climb to the summit block of The Cobbler, there are few problems to match those thrown up by Skye's Black Cuillin or the Aonach Eagach ridge in Glen Coe.

Conditions strike harder on the higher Munros, but in a hard winter there's not really much difference in difficulty between a 3,000ft peak and one at 2,999 ft.

The Corbetts are more widespread, taking the walker to more of the islands and to other Munro-free areas, such as the Southern Uplands and the Ardgour peninsula, and there's a lot more in the wilds of Sutherland. The effort needed for travelling is certainly greater. I don't think anyone could put their hand on heart and say for sure that one round is harder than the other. It is entirely subjective. The Corbetts mostly tend to be tackled after the Munros, so even the later ages of summiteers could be a factor in any individual determining which is tougher.

They are certainly a more acquired taste. Many people who 'compleat' the Munros never move on to the Corbetts. Some would rather do the Munros again, and sometimes again and again. Some move on to other things, such as kayaking, especially those with troubled knees after all these mountain ascents. I found it harder to attract partners for my Corbett outings. Many of those who accompanied me over the years on Munro trips just weren't interested in so-called 'lesser' mountains. Even the brave souls who had occasionally ventured out with me on my Munro night walks were far less inclined to take the bait.

My two good friends from the early Munro days, Fergus and Malcolm, had long since gone on to other things. Fergus had stated right at the outset that night walking was not for him. We still met once or twice a year for hill weekends but the fact I was now aiming for Corbetts while he was trying to round up his remaining Munros, while also trying to juggle family life and work commitments, meant our paths crossed less frequently.

Malcolm, meanwhile, was living in the USA, having said goodbye to journalism and then sailed off into the sunset, heading across the Atlantic on the coat-tails of the trans-Atlantic race. He was a superb sailor and had found his calling. Sitting in an office was not for a guy like Malcolm. Even the misfortune which struck him in the States turned out to be a blessing.

He had only been there a year or so when the eastern seaboard was devastated by a massive hurricane. Boats in their harbours were smashed into matchsticks by the force of the storm and we were wondering how he had fared. Then we got the call. He was fine but it wasn't such good news about his boat.

The exorbitant cost of insurance in the US had persuaded him to take his chances. After all, he argued, why pay $100,000 insurance for a boat that was worth just $10,000? After discovering he had survived unscathed, the conversation turned to the boat.

"Bit of a disaster there, I'm afraid."

"Oh, was the boat badly damaged?"

"No, it was fine, not a mark on it really."

So what was the problem?

"Unfortunately, the wind lifted it up and dropped it on a million-dollar yacht. It didn't do so well. Going to cost a fortune to get fixed."

For most people this would be a financial disaster, but the bold Malcolm managed to come out of this on the bright side. It turned out the owner of the yacht was sympathetic to his plight. They agreed Malcolm would undertake a lot of the repair work himself. In addition, Malcolm would crew the guy's boat, taking out friends and guests on pleasure rides. They became good friends. Malcolm still works on boats round the Boston area and is a member of the harbour rescue team.

We have walked the hills just once since he emigrated. Unfortunately he brought a monsoon with him and despite our best efforts battling against horizontal rain and swollen rivers we had to abandon the attempt on the final Munro of my second round. We couldn't let the Champagne and cake go to waste though, especially when we had a guest all the way from the US, so we proceeded as if I had just triumphed. He left next day and the following day I crested Beinn Eibhinn in the Alder range to justify the premature celebration.

So my Corbetts quest became a solo event, the night walks exclusively unaccompanied. It was reminiscent of the early days of my first Munro round, lone treks in the hours of darkness. But there were some significant differences.

For a start, some of the walks were shorter than needed for the Munros. If there was a long journey to reach the start that wouldn't be a problem. But on shorter distances, outside of summer hours, that would mean walking in darkness from start to finish and with less trodden routes to follow that could be asking for trouble. On these occasions, instead of heading off right after work at midnight, I would go back to my flat, have something to eat, chill out for a couple of hours then set off around 3am.

The golden rule: Never go to bed.

I had tried that in the early days. I thought I could sleep for a couple of hours then get up and go. It hardly ever worked. Once in that pit of warmth, the chances of arising to head off alone into a chilly, empty night frequently proved to be beyond my ability. Then there was the need to get used to sleeping for a few hours in the car. I'd always found this next to impossible but I managed to get it into my head that because it was uncomfortable, I would be more likely to get moving and wouldn't have any problem rousing myself for the task ahead. This was vital as there were a lot of Corbetts which required the use of the Corran Ferry, whose first sailing wasn't until around 5.30am. The car parks in Glen Coe became a regular haunt for my nocturnal zeds and the ferry crew got to know me well.

I was also going round the Munros again. Normal service was resumed for these nights out, a handy diversion from the main event. Climbing a Munro or two at night now seemed almost therapeutic compared to the frantic events of the Corbetts chase.

So were they harder to 'compleat'? They certainly took longer than the Munros and seemed to involve more effort to get round, but whether they were physically harder or not I couldn't really say. I just know I enjoyed the experience of seeing all those wonderful mountains and wonderful places. If you enjoy the Scottish hills then size is an irrelevance.

That's why I had left work around 1am for the four-hour journey to the head of Loch Arkaig on a cold winter's morning. That's why I was prepared to once again drive along the road from Hell, 22 miles of single track unpredictability that ends at a windswept parking spot with no mobile phone reception. And that's why I was now struggling my way up the slopes of a remote mountain in deep, soft snow when all sane people were tucked up in bed.

The twins of Sgurr Mhurlagain and Fraoch Bheinn sit above the north shore of the loch. They are only a few hundred feet below 3,000 and bookend a pass which leads to Glen Kingie and Kinbreak Bothy. The drive in had been pain-free, the snow confined to the higher ground.

The initial ascent, however, was steep, possibly because my internal clock was reminding me I should be sleeping. Bears have the right idea. Winter is a time to curl up, conk out and dream sweet, sweet thoughts of spring. And honey, of course.

This was now my 12th year of nocturnal walking but there was still this internal rebellion, a constant battle of the body and mind, a voice insisting normal people didn't do this. Walking in winter is also more tiring. You wear more and the weight adds to the effort. There's all the extras in your rucksack, such as crampons, ice axe, spare clothes, spare food for emergencies.

The terrain is harder for progress. There's no consistency of footfall. The ground varies from soft and slippery to rock-solid with each step. One minute you are sidestepping patches of sheet ice, the next you are slithering backwards in a mixture of mud and melting snow. It's a case of one step upwards, one sideways and back and then one back. It can be wearying. It's harder still when you have decided to forego sleep after another hard night running the sports desk at a national newspaper. But once the back of the ascent is broken and the higher parts of the mountains are in view, the mood changes.

You can climb these hills in any order but I turned my sights on Sgurr Mhurlagain first. The light was approaching slowly, no blazing sunrise to greet me. The wakening day provided a sky of various hues of black and grey but it was clear and I could see the route ahead. When I hit the roof of the hill, the main summit came into view, about half a mile away on a horizon curving right then left. The contrast of the pure white skyline with the black and grey clouds was stark and glowering but it was a false threat and I was soon at the small cairn. This was when I was hit by that true feeling of solitude. I was surrounded by sheets of white, a giant, ruffled quilt cover with bumps and ridges in every direction. The oppressive weightiness of the black sky, the whispering of the wind, the biting cold of the higher air, all combining to remind me I was irrelevant, an intruder in a unending vastness that could swallow me in seconds. And this was why I was here.

Sgurr Mhurlagain is one of those hills whose translation is open to various interpretations. Some sources refer to it as 'rough-topped peaks' while other possible meanings are 'peak of the bag-shaped sea inlet' or 'peak of the wool basket'. To further confuse the issue, another Murlagan in Perthshire is translated as 'an abundance of reeds'. There is no such confusion with its neighbour, Fraoch Bheinn, the 'heather mountain', although on this morning of snow and ice I would just have to accept there was indeed heather in abundance. It is another fine peak, with the advantage of better views north and west to bigger things.

Descending was a case of finding little gullies and bum-sliding my way down at a decent rate with the ice axe serving as a brake.

The return to the car was without further incident although the knees were feeling the steep decline.

The day had now fully arrived in glorious black and white with every tiny shade change in between and to top it off, a pale pink wash. From halfway back down the road, pointed Sgurr na h-Aide took centre stage, reflecting into the still waters from miles away.

The frantic nature of the world of sport and what would be waiting for me at the office seemed a million miles away.

2
The Day the Earth Caught Fire

From perfect calm to a world of chaos;
a countryside off limits; the man who
managed to fall up a hill; a few pointers
on how to cross a river safely

I WAS sitting in the early sun having my breakfast on the summit of Beinn Mhic-Mhonaidh unaware that 3,000 miles away across the Atlantic the world was about to catch fire.

It was September 11, 2001.

While I was making my way up through the silent woods under a clear night sky above Glen Orchy, the clock had just ticked past midnight in New York. While I sat at the summit cairn having breakfast with the clouds rolling over the lower slopes in the light of the new day, millions of people were enjoying their last night of peace for a long time.

And as I made my way back to the car after another calm and mind-cleansing early morning stroll, those who would bring horror and fiery death to so many were getting ready to board the planes they would use as missiles to devastating effect.

If there is such a thing as being caught between two worlds, this was it.

The first hint that anything so beyond our comprehension was happening came as I drove back towards Glasgow down the side of Loch Lomond. A breaking news report on the radio said a plane had struck one of the towers of the World Trade Centre. Then came a second report that another plane had struck the other tower. There was confusion as to what precisely was happening.

Then as reports started coming in of the crash at the Pentagon and the grounding of all flights as a state of emergency was declared, reality dawned around the world at the scale of this carnage.

By the time I got to work, all attention was on the 30 or so television screens around the office. The tension on the whole floor was all-encompassing, the only sound coming from the disbelieving commentators on the screens. The sports schedule was forgotten. It was as if the whole office, like every other workplace, house, bar or restaurant all over the world, was caught in a trance.

That dreamlike state was encapsulated in one surreal incident. As I looked away from our main screen over to the racing desk, I could see they were watching the racing from Newcastle. The world may have been coming to an end but there was still the small matter of who would win money on the 3.30. Eventually, we all gradually came back to the task in hand but the air of unreality of what we had just been witnessing cast a long shadow over the night, and would do for a long time to come.

It seemed incredible that just a few hours earlier I was sitting alone at the top of a mountain drinking in the solitude. I had come from a place of peace and serenity to scenes of madness and mayhem in the blink of an eye.

Fast forward nine years, and I am up early, getting ready for a walk in the Cairngorms. Days and dates tend to be irrelevant, the focus being on the joy of getting out on the hills with friends. No radio, no TV, no newspapers, just going through the motions of packing quietly so as not to wake anyone else in the house. Hours later we were on the plateau of Ben Avon in brilliant autumnal sunshine, blue skies stretching forever.

The main top is the wonderfully named Leabaidh an Daimh Bhuidhe (it means the bed of the yellow stag) and the summit is the top of a huge granite pillar. There are a few pillars in fact, and the main two are roughly the same height, so I have always scaled both. It was only when we were all on one pillar or the other and I mentioned we were standing on the Twin Tors that it clicked what day it was.

The Twin Tors on September 11.

There was silence for a few seconds. It seemed a collective shiver ran up our spines, as if everyone had suddenly flashed back to the enormity of that terrible day. It seemed a perfect place of peace and a perfect place in time for a moment of reflection.

The year that had culminated in fire and devastation had also started that way. The country was struck by an outbreak of bovine spongiform encephalopathy – mad cow disease to you and me – and the initial panic saw severe access restrictions imposed in the countryside. This didn't just apply to the movement of livestock. Many mountain areas were closed to the public.

It was a serious state of affairs but other countries had successfully managed to deal with it without resorting to such Draconian measures. It's understandable that farmers were worried about the spread of the disease but for some landowners, this was a great opportunity to keep walkers off their land, if only for a few months.

Many took a more sensible approach. They shifted access routes, provided good sign-posting and detergent footbaths to dip boots before going onto the land and put temporary restrictions in place on walking dogs. Some areas, such as the Borders, were particularly badly hit. My work colleague and occasional walking partner, Giles, had a two-week holiday booked in which he planned to cross the 212 miles of the Southern Upland Way, the long distance route which runs from Portpatrick on the south-west coast to Cocksburnpath on the east.

Suddenly he found most of it shut off. When he phoned to cancel his hotel and B&B bookings, he was faced with distraught landladies, some breaking down in tears, as they saw their whole business year collapsing in ruins. Quite a few never recovered, their livelihoods wrecked by something beyond their control. The cost to the whole country was catastrophic.

I had made a low-key start to the year, snowy conditions in January keeping me reasonably close to home. There were simple Corbett ascents such as Auchnafree Hill, Meall na Leitreach, the Sow of Atholl and Monamenach, although the couple of hours needed for the latter were dwarfed by the hours it took me to dig the car out after the early sun had melted the top snow and helped the car sink a few extra feet. The effort needed to extricate it also exceeded the energy expended on the walk.

I managed to fit in Benvane in the Trossachs before the curtain came down, a miserable, cold morning under pallid skies, over sheets of ice and wet snow and limited visibility. The farm where I parked lay silent in the gloom, no sounds of livestock, no dogs barking. The four-hour walk felt more like some kind of punishment rather than pleasure, a mirror for the whole country's mindset.

I only managed one more outing in the next eight weeks, a combination of behaving responsibly regarding where to walk and the prospect of not wanting to travel any great distance only to find an unexpected barrier and the possibility of confrontation.

When the rules were relaxed, many trips were accompanied by the stench of charred, rotten meat in the air from animal funeral pyres and the sight of smouldering cattle corpses, legs and horns jutting out obscenely from the mountain of burned flesh and hair. The constant cold, grey, snowy conditions just conspired to add to the air of depression. For our farmers, it must have seemed like the day of reckoning had arrived.

When the weather turned, as so often happens in our unpredictable climate, it seemed to happen almost instantly. One day I was battling through a white-out in deep snow in the Cairngorms, the next I was suffering from dehydration in a heatwave in the north-west Highlands.

The first days after the mad cow restrictions were eased felt like we had suddenly been unchained after months in a dark dungeon. There was a new-found urge to get back out and do some serious trekking. I was heading for Glen Feshie on the western side of the Cairngorms and was accompanied by Giles, a man needing some mountain tonic after the disappointment of his Borders debacle. We were doing a sweep of the Munro, Sgor Gaoith, and its satellite tops. It was a lovely spring day at sea level but the higher we climbed, the more the snow deepened.

The route up to the summit ridge of Sgor Gaoith is a constant, gradual slope, a complete contrast to the other side and its massive, plunging cliff faces. I was walking ahead, trudging through the calf-deep snow. Visibility was now down to almost zero and we could barely make out the horizon ahead. Giles was walking right on my heels. I was concerned about our lack of sight so I turned and said: "It would be better if you walked about six feet behind me and off to one side."

He looked at me quizzically.

"Why's that?"

"Because if I walk right over the edge of the cliff then you would likely just follow me straight over. If you are further back you would see me disappear and could go and get help."

The realisation of what I had just said hit him immediately. He looked at me with a mix of astonishment and fear. It hadn't occurred to him that there was any looming danger. He sank back and his demeanour changed. Now every step was a carefully placed foot, a pause for thought and then, and only then, movement. His winter skills resume had just been updated by a few grades.

Many people prove to be a contradiction when it comes to mountain walking. For instance, I can happily walk for 12 hours over multiple peaks and cover 25 miles, yet half an hour of walking round the shops in a town centre sees me struggling with sore hips and knees and in need of a long lie down. But I have never, ever met a contradiction like Giles.

There he was in a white-out, plunging through deep snow to an unseen horizon without a care. Yet put him in a boulder field or facing the prospect of a small hands-on scramble and he would be reduced to a gibbering wreck.

We once had to use our hands as footholds for him as he struggled to get down a short rocky step while two seven-year-olds scrambled nonchalantly past him. I remember how proud he was when he finally plucked up the courage to come up Buachaille Etive Mor with us and found himself enjoying it immensely. We thought then that the rocky back of the problem was broken, and persuaded him to come up Bidean nam Bian.

Unfortunately, he had seen the Buachaille rated as three stars for difficulty in a walking book, while Bidean was only rated two so he expected it to be much easier. It doesn't work like that. These ratings are always a matter of opinion so what worked once for him failed the next time and we were back to square one.

He was the only person I have seen fall UPHILL while walking downhill with poles.

We once stood back and watched as he performed a perfect triple somersault down the grassy slopes of one hill and then pick himself up, unhurt, to carry on. I wouldn't be surprised to hear that he suffered an attack of vertigo while trying out a new pair of boots on Tiso's rock path.

It has been suggested the Dutch Munros may be more his thing but his love of Scotland and its mountains is absolute, and his knowledge is second to none. It would just be better for his peace of mind if some government scheme could remove all the rocks from the hills. But you can't keep a good man down and Giles was a regular member of our party for the next few expeditions.

We slogged up the unrelenting slopes of Gulvain in a heat wave which saw every member of the party dive into the river at the bottom of the mountain to cool off. The following day we were on Creag Meagaidh, taking up Victorian photo poses in the unexpected snow bowl above The Window, the deep nick in the skyline that splits the corrie rim.

It was another day of blistering heat although I managed to get an unexpected soaking on the way down trying to outrun a sudden thundery downpour. I had taken the river rocks too fast and ended up slipping into the water. Luckily I wasn't far from the car. I've taken a few plunges during my many years on the hills but none too serious. Mostly it's down to over-confidence in drier conditions when you think you can do your own river dance, a few Michael Flatley moves across a series of stepping stones. In wetter weather when the rivers are in spate, you pay far more attention to their power.

I've never had a fear of water, but I do have a healthy respect. I learned to swim when I was young and regard myself as a fairly strong swimmer, but that would count for little in the freezing, raging turmoil of the rivers you so often encounter in the Highlands.

I was awarded a school swimming certificate at a tender age for being able to retrieve a rubber brick from a pool whilst wearing pyjamas. I don't know how much practical use that would be as it's highly unlikely I will ever be wandering any remote glens in a pair of pyjamas searching for underwater bricks. Although years from now, when my memory has gone and I and my wandering mind have managed to escape the care home ... who knows?

I have used custom-made waders – Drywalkers – for many years, basically a pair of plastic bags with soles attached and ties at the ankles and knees, but they are very effective. Instead of having to remove boots and socks and roll up your trouser legs, you simply pull the bags over your boots and tie them up. A steady walk across with the use of poles and you should be dry and happy at the other side.

They have proved invaluable, most notably in Fisherfield and the Rough Bounds of Knoydart, where the rivers take no prisoners. Bridges are often washed away. Some years, there are more deaths from drowning in these areas than from mountain slips.

Sometimes even these waders are of little help and a long detour upstream is the only sensible option. It's one of the basic rules of being a solo walker: most of the time your route plan should have the possibility of water hazards factored in.

I try to avoid any major river crossings during the winter months. A couple of hours' heavy rain or snow melt can mean a rapid rise in river levels and what was an easy passage on the way in may be an impossibility on the return.

Night walks were still proving elusive as we moved through May and June, a combination of work commitments and that I had simply got out of the habit. A switch to the more regular patterns of weather – wet and windy in the west, more benign in the east – in July got me back on track even if the Corbetts chase stayed on hold. I had big nights out in the Cairngorms, huge tidy-ups of Ben Macdui, Derry Cairngorm and all their current and deleted Munro Tops, a circuit of Lochangar and the Loch Muick summits and then another complete sweep round Cairn Gorm.

These huge walks set me up nicely for the resumption of better weather in the west and on a balmy September morning after the rain had swept through leaving every leaf and blade of grass dripping, I sat admiring the rear view of the Aonach Eagach's spires from the rocky top of Garbh Bheinn above Loch Leven. This is a much ignored peak, sitting as it does among some of the finest big hills in the country, but it's worth the effort. As the name 'garbh' suggests, it's rough and craggy. The views after you pass the halfway point are magnificent all the way to the summit. The only surprise was a party complete with guide heading up as I neared the foot of the hill around 9am. I imagine it was as much of a surprise to them to find someone already heading for home.

Eight days later, and I was sitting in perfect peace at the top of Beinn Mhic-mhonaidh, blissfully unaware of the horror that was unfolding halfway across the world.

We paid our silent tribute three days later. Fifteen of us lined up outside Davy's Bourach, the emergency shelter at the top of Jock's Road, as the sun turned the horizon into melted cheese. It was good to be with friends at such a juncture in the history of the planet, a buffer against the horrors that had struck out of the blue.

New peaks were few and far between: I spent the next few outings visiting old friends. A fast dash up Ben Nevis saw me emerging in the silent mist at the summit purged by the exertion. Then Tom a' Choinich, far up Glen Affric, gobbling up unclimbed tops with the voracity of a mountain Pacman while being treated to some unusual views of the empty and desolate back corries that take a series of huge mouthfuls out of the ridgeline.

Finally there was Stob Coire Sgreamhach, the second Munro of Bidein nam Bian, by the Beinn Fhada ridge which provided some interesting moments on loose, steep gullies – mostly avoidable as I realised on the way back down when I could see the correct line of the path – high above the Lairig Gartain before anyone else had risen.

It's moments like this when you realise just how alone you are in the mountains at this time of day. One slip and it could be all over, no one to even hear you scream.

There was one curious moment during all the excitement of this mini scramble. As I was clinging on to lumps of unstable earth and grass wishing I had hands and claws like Wolverine, I suddenly developed a terrible craving for a plate of baked beans.

It's often said your life flashes before you in times of danger. I think there must be something inherently wrong with me that the only thing that flashed before my eyes was a tin of beans. I had previous, though. Years before when we were lost in a blizzard on Ben Challum not knowing which direction to move, my main concern was whether I had remembered to set the video for the night's episode of *NYPD Blue*. There was a serenity that made any threat of danger so matter of fact. Maybe it's a kind of defence mechanism, think nice thoughts and nothing bad will happen, slow down time and give it time to sort itself out. Whatever the reason, it worked.

The last few months had seemed to have passed in slow motion, every mountain top I sat on surrounded by a heavy silence. Even the weather seemed to be have been struck dumb.

It was if a much-needed calm had been restored after this year of fire.

3
Car Crashes and Bum Slides

*Slip sliding away on a mountain road; an
offer I just had to refuse; a country and
western night out in darkest Perthshire; why
you should never buy a GPS from a drinker*

I'M halfway up a steep mountain road covered in sheet ice when
the car refuses to go forward. The wheels are spinning and my
normally reliable Astra is starting to slide alarmingly, first sideways,
then backwards.

I let it go a bit and then try accelerating again on a clear patch.
It moves forward then catches on the ice again and spins off
further than the last time. Then it catches. Now I'm heading
upwards again. Except the ice cover is heavier here. The car slides
back again.

I'm in no man's land, can't move forward, can't go back for fear
of losing control completely. It's 4am on a December morning.
There's no one else around and I'm stuck fast. I have to try one last
push to get myself out of this mess. So I accelerate. The wheels
just spin. I'm going nowhere. And then the car starts to slide back
again, faster this time.

I manage to pull on the hand brake but all that does is help the
car slew sideways, closer to the drop on my left-hand side. It stops
again, perilously close to the edge.

I decide to get out and have a closer look at my predicament.
I nearly take a tumble as soon as I step out of the car. The road is
like a sheet of glass and all I can see ahead is thicker and thicker ice
cover. There's no way I'll get up there, so retreat is the only answer.

I get back into the driver's seat but as I soon I start to reverse I realise I now have no control. The car could go over the edge at any second.

I make a decision. If the car is going over I'm not going with it. I get out and let it continue the downward slide, driverless. Strange thing is it doesn't seem any more out of control than when I was at the wheel.

I stand and watch helplessly waiting for it to disappear over the edge. It will be a long walk to anywhere and then a costly business to retrieve the car but at least I won't be mangled along with it. Then, after a slide of around 20 feet, it stops. It has run off the ice cover and reached a point of relative safety. I still don't trust it. I watch for a few more minutes.

It seems to have stabilised so I gingerly climb back in and start to reverse further down the road. A couple of minutes' later and I'm back on level ground, safe. I take a deep breath, a massive sigh of relief. This is not the best start to climbing a mountain in the middle of a winter night.

It was entirely avoidable. That battered warning sign I had seen off to the side of the road at the start of the incline. Road closed: Ice. That must have been genuine. I thought it looked like an old sign that hadn't been removed. The road looked clear and I had managed to drive all the way from Glasgow to Tweedsmuir without any problems. Okay, I was now on the unclassified road which runs from the A701 to the A708 past the Talla and Megget reservoirs but it still didn't look like any bother. I was wrong.

As I took the corner which leads steeply up to the Megget Stone, I noticed the danger sign out the corner of my eye but took no heed. Now after half an hour of anxiety I was back down at the corner parked up and ready to walk. What? You didn't really think I was going to the small matter of a near-death experience stop me from going up a mountain.

Now safely back on terra firma I was walking up the ice-covered road to reach the start of the walk up to Broad Law. Three hours later and I had done my circuit and was back at the car. It had turned into a beautiful morning. The waters of the Talla were motionless, the hillsides yellow and bright. It was far too nice a day for a disaster. Maybe I had just dreamed it.

The biggest problem with going up mountains in the middle of the night isn't the walk up the hill – it's the drive to get to the start. There's many times I would have gone for it had I not been worried about condition of the minor roads.

Skidding off a remote road in winter conditions could see you lying there a long time waiting for help to arrive. Normally when I do venture out at this time of year I take the slow, cautious approach. But we had been having one of these beautiful cold spells, accompanied by bright sun and blue skies. There hadn't been any sign of snow yet, and maybe that was the problem. Icy roads can be far more treacherous than snowy ones. That invisible covering that shows up as just a sheen in the right light often catches drivers unawares. Especially if they can't read simple road signs.

Just a week earlier I had sat on the summit of Beinn a' Bhuiridh in the Cruachan range having my breakfast, watching the sun shining down in nuclear fashion on a sea of thin cloud. But then the approach for this hill came from the main road and I had stretched out my journey, chilled out listening to Michael Chapman's 'Rainmaker', a perfect anthem for night driving but probably not a good one if you wish to keep the weather gods onside. You have to be certain of your forecast. And, undaunted by my Broad Law misadventure, the winter hits just kept coming.

First it was Creag nan Gabhar and Ben Gulabin in Glenshee, two fast ascents with a short drive between the starting points. Despite hitting the heights of the ski road, the surface was dry and clear of snow on a grey December day, a bonus for me but not so good for the ski centre where all the equipment was all geared up with nowhere to go.

I then braved the heights of the B847 off the Kinloch Rannoch road to climb Beinn a' Chuallaich in sometimes waist deep snow but the reward was stunning views of Schiehallion. Carn na Drochaide in the Cairngorms was next, again from the minor road round from Braemar to Allanquoich and then a wind-blasted day on Cam Chreag from the road in Glen Lyon, neither presenting any threat to driving.

Then came one of these incidents when you can see disaster unfolding in slow motion despite the reality of it being just a few seconds.

I was travelling to Crianlarich on a dark, icy morning in late February. We had just seen Berti Vogts unveiled as Scotland boss and the mood was generally upbeat. After all, he was German and a World Cup winner. We were on the march with Berti's Army, the paper had been put to bed and I had set off in a good mood.

The first clue that this would not be a normal night, however, came when I pulled in for petrol near Dumbarton. I was the only customer on the forecourt and after filling the tank for £24 I went in to pay. The attendant was sitting crunched in a tiny space behind the counter with a huge pile of boxes stacked up behind him.

I didn't have change, just two £20 notes. When I handed over the money he asked: "Do you want your change or would you like 16 boxes of tumblers?"

"Pardon?"

He pointed to the boxes. "Tumblers. Six to a box. You can have 16 boxes, £1 a box."

Now maybe he had mistaken me for a passing publican or possibly the real night attendant was lying tied up in a back room and this guy was taking the opportunity to try to flog his ill-gotten gains, namely, tumblers.

"No, I think I'm okay for glasses just now thanks. The change will be fine."

He seemed stunned I could turn down such an offer of a lifetime. I took my change and made my getaway before the tumbler offer became mandatory.

A few miles up the road, I wondered whether I had just been the victim of another night-time hallucination brought on by my body dropping a massive hint that it would prefer to be home in bed sleeping. Twenty minutes later, I turned off the main road at Tarbert on to the winding section of road that twists and squeezes round outcrops along the side of Loch Lomond, I felt the car slide. I was only going about 25mph at the time but I slowed down right away. The surface ahead was black and shining. A thin covering of rain had frozen and the road was now more suited to Torvill and Dean. I immediately cut my speed further.

As I crawled along under 20mph, headlights appeared behind me. Then they were right at my back. I slowed further but the car behind was tailgating, obviously frustrated by my progress. This went on for a mile or so until we came to a straighter stretch. The car swung out violently and accelerated at high speed. I wanted to warn the driver but reckoned flashing my lights would just suggest I was annoyed at his behaviour and wouldn't have any effect.

At the end of the stretch, the road curved to the left and there was a crash barrier on the corner above the loch side. The car roared down the straight but instead of taking the corner kept going straight on, smashing into the barrier, ricocheting back and then spinning round to a halt in trees at the edge of the road.

I gently came to a stop; I thought I would find a badly bloodied casualty fighting for life. Instead a young guy got out, dazed but otherwise okay. My concern now turned to anger. He had escaped injury but now I wanted to injure him. He tried to engage me – "bit slippy there, mate" – but I told him where to go and drove off before I lost the plot completely.

The attempted ascent of Beinn nan Imirean seemed tame after that and I felt my interest waning fast as I struggled through deep snow trying to stay away from the minefield of deep hollows waiting to see me sink in up to my neck. I pulled the plug after a couple of hours, my heart not in it any more. The normal adrenaline rush had been used up on the road.

The trend towards thin ice cover rather than any good lasting dump of snow gave me a real headache a couple of weeks later. Considering the time of year, I had rather ambitiously planned to try to climb the round of five Corbetts at Bridge of Orchy.

It was bitterly cold but clear as I set off up the steep slopes of Beinn Odhar with the light still struggling to wake. The books tell you to follow a track which leads to an old mine but it seemed simpler to go straight up. Besides, one of the last places you want to venture near in the dark is a mine.

I topped out, sweating despite the chill, with the sun now coating the summit area with its rays. It's a steep drop to the next peak, Beinn Chaorach, and then a big re-climb, but that wasn't what was bothering me. Although the front of the hill had been clear and dry, its back slopes were coated with frozen grass and massive patches of hard snow. And I had left my crampons in the car. Without them, trying to descend steep gully-riven slopes holding so much snow and ice was near suicidal. I did, however, have my ice axe. Rather than turn back so early into the walk, I decided to go for the bum-slide option.

This involves sitting down on the slopes and making a controlled descent using the ice axe as a brake. The trick is go down short sections at a time. Slow and steady with plenty of stops. Take off too fast and you run the risk of losing control of your descent and having the axe ripped from your hand. The result would be catastrophic.

I saw an incident recently in Glen Coe that highlighted the dangers of uncontrolled slides. I was walking up Stob Dubh, the main peak of Buachaille Etive Beag. It's a steep ascent at times, but in summer conditions no real problem. There were still some huge banks of snow to cross, and the path was buried in places. Several sets of footprints went up one section as if everyone had chosen their own carefully, sensibly not trusting to follow where others had gone.

When I neared the top of this stretch I met a young couple. We stopped to chat, then the guy started heading down on the clearer ground to the left. The girl, however, decided she would sit down and slide over the steep snow field. Bum slides are fine when you have an ice axe to use for a brake. She didn't. Before I could say that this might not be a good idea, she had taken off. She picked up speed quickly and about halfway down she realised she was having trouble stopping. Her squeals of delight suddenly turned to those of panic. If her boots hadn't then caught in the snow and slowed her, she might have continued to hurtle down uncontrollably.

She may have escaped unscathed. She may have hit the rocks at the bottom of the run and ended up with a broken bone or two. A few feet over to the right and she could have gone right over the edge of the slope and plunged hundreds of feet down the mountain face. My descent was less dramatic but I would have never made it down safely without the axe.

The route onward to Beinn Chaorach was straightforward but slow because the water that had been running through the grass for the past year had solidified and it was hard work avoiding the worst of the booby traps.

I descended Chaorach and climbed to the top of Cam Chreag without resorting to any more bum notes but the realisation was beginning to dawn on me that five hills in conditions like this was out of the question. I had lost a bit of time and the last peak, Beinn a' Chaisteil, is fronted by massive cliffs and I didn't fancy the walk along the top with tired legs and invisible icy banana skins lurking along the ridge.

My decision was quickly shown to be right. The descent of the west slopes of Cam Chreag resulted in a few unplanned slides, one that gave me a real whack in the tailbone. I was a relieved man to reach the main track and be able to drag my complaining carcass back round to the car unscathed.

If all these tales of woe were starting to sound like a bad Country and Western song, a midnight jaunt into the heights of Perthshire gave them even more credence. I had decided to tackle two separate hills in the same trip. They were short walks and only a few driving miles apart, but sometimes events in the office that day could hold the key to whether it was going to be a good night or a bad night on the hills and with that in mind, I felt this could turn out to be a disaster.

We had just watched the first Scotland match of the Berti era, and it hadn't made pleasant viewing. The Vogts wagon crashed at the first bend – a 5-0 hammering from France – and already the excuses were being trotted out. Suddenly we had a manager who had discovered we didn't have players as good as the Germans. The insight was blinding.

Meall nan Subh is not so much a hill as a series of bumps and crags with a high point hidden somewhere in the middle. This involved a drive via Killin into Glen Lochay and then an unclassified road over a high pass leading down into Glen Lyon. In winter, this would be impassable and any attempt could lead to another abandonment of the car or maybe even worse, but it was now allegedly spring and the road should be clear.

There were patches of snow and ice on the way up but nothing too forbidding. Anyway, I was more worried about the descent of the other side. An icy stretch there might be fun. Most likely not.

I parked at the high point of the road and set off onto the dark, misty slopes of Meall nan Subh, 'the hill of the soo (raspberry)'. I was dressed in black and I was heading for a hill named Soo. How much more C&W could you get? I reckon Johnny Cash would have growled his approval.

I was back at the car within two hours. I came, I saw nothing, I conquered. It was worrying that stumbling around a featureless, sodden lump in darkness while everyone else was asleep was becoming my lot in life. It didn't even feel unpleasant any more. There was even a film called Insomnia doing the rounds. Everyone was finally getting it.

I made it into Glen Lyon without any skids then took the next unclassified road from Bridge of Balgie over by the Lawers range to begin my attempt of Meall nam Maigheach. There was a glow all around as the dayshift started in earnest. Not unsurprisingly the one parking space was vacant and I was soon following a wall uphill to reach another featureless summit. I didn't even notice the views. I was more interested in a bacon roll and coffee in Killin, and a seat watching the mesmerising sight of the Falls of Dochart doing what they do best – fall.

The whole night seemed to have passed in a blur.

I was snapped out of my reverie by a trip to Ardgour via the Corran Ferry. It's always the best feeling to see the sunrise while gently sailing to another horizon, the sparkle on the water bringing life to another day. I had managed to perform a minor miracle by dragging along Robert, Fergus and Neil, a coup that would never be repeated for Corbett duty. We were heading for the magnificent Garbh Bheinn and while Fergus was excited by the chance to use his GPS, I stuck to map and compass and Robert and Neil stuck to not really bothering where they were or where they were going.

GPS can be a great help on the hills and is now widely used by mountain rescue teams but I have lost count of the amount of times I have met off-course walkers wandering about with their little handset sending them all over the place.

"You're heading straight over a cliff."

"Well, that's where it's telling me to go."

On longer walks, there can also be problems with battery life and if you don't have a spare set you may suddenly find your route-finding mate just dying and leaving you (literally) high and dry. As with most technology it's only as good as the instructions you feed into it, and I suspect on this occasion that Fergus had fed in a wrong number as the little man on the screen was weaving around on a bizarre route like a Saturday night drunk.

Fergus looked perplexed.

"Hmmm, don't know why it's doing that."

It wasn't the time to suggest that a wrong number or digit had been keyed in so I suggested: "Maybe the wee guy's been at the sauce."

This was a good out for Fergus.

"Could be. The guy I bought it from certainly enjoyed a few small sherries of an evening."

So here's a tip – when buying a second-hand GPS, always ask about the original owner's wine consumption. It could save you a real headache.

A couple of weeks' later and I was in Strathconon as the morning rose, striding up grassy slopes in stifling heat trying to stay a step ahead of the midges. I was on the 'little hill of the lambs', Meallan nan Uan, within a couple of hours, well ahead of the beasties. As a breakfast spot it was unrivalled.

My next target, Sgurr a' Mhuilinn, was just a short hop over the corrie to the north, but further to the west were the peaks of Sgurr a' Ghlas Leathaid and Sgurr a' Choire Rainich, twin spires that are regarded as the highlight of the circuit. Today, however, they seemed a million miles away.

I told myself I would be back here one day and that they could wait even if felt like a false promise. The thought of all that extra climbing in growing heat and then a four-hour journey back for work just didn't appeal. I had convinced myself tired.

4
National Treasures

Heatwaves, midges and karaoke hell; why
I felt I had to pay my apologies to Rob Roy;
referee in a long-distance bun fight; early
morning sunbathing on a rocky deckchair

THERE is no doubt travel broadens the mind. Most of the time, however, it usually only goes to emphasise to me how lucky we are to live in such a beautiful country.

I love going abroad but I have lost count of the times I have visited a foreign landmark and come away underwhelmed. You see the picture postcards, you buy into the myth and the hype – and then you see it with your own eyes. What we have on our own doorstep is often far more impressive.

I was standing at the highest point you are permitted to reach on Vesuvius, trying to peer through the heat and smog haze that smothers Naples. The walk up had been on a driveable track, the views of the lower mountain slopes just scrub and trees, limp and lacking greenery in their constant battle with the heat. The black river of consolidated lava that once poured down the side of mountain still lies on course but you only catch a glimpse.

From the air, on a clear day, the view down into the empty, hollowed-out belly of this still active volcano is impressive. Problem is when you are at the vandalised and graffiti-covered trig post that marks the high point for tourists this view is unavailable for most of the year.

Looking down into the giant crater is impressive but it's a restricted view. Maybe if you could gain access to the highest point of the rim it would help a little but then there are safety reasons for blocking further access.

There's no doubt Pompeii is magnificent but it would help if there weren't lines of stalls selling all kinds of tat at the main gate and, of course, the obligatory McDonald's. Maximus Mac and fries. Kind of kills the romance somehow. It's the curse of progress and big cities everywhere.

That smog-laden atmosphere stretching for miles across the Bay of Naples brought into sharp contrast the pin-sharp views I had found among our own national treasures that year.

Sgurr nan Ghiubhsachain is one of our most iconic peaks. You may not be familiar with the name, but you would recognise it instantly. It dominates the view down Loch Shiel from the National Trust centre and monument at Glenfinnan, deep in the land of the Jacobite, its soaring rocky ridge rising in two huge strides from the waterline.

Just one week after standing at frozen Loch Etchachan in the heart of the Cairngorms as the last snows melted from surrounding slopes, I was pulling into the parking area at Callop off the Mallaig road at 3am in balmy conditions.

I had come straight from a busy night of football. Celtic had made it into the UEFA Cup final with an aggregate win over Boavista and would now face another Portuguese side, Porto, in Seville for the trophy. There were a lot more busy nights to come but for now I was concentrating on the climb ahead.

The heat was oppressive. It would be midge hell out there. This was a day (or night) for getting ready in the car and then exploding out of the door and walking away like you had left a bomb primed to go off. Don't stand still long enough for them to find you. Even worse, telly karaoke 'talent' Gareth Gates was sitting at the top of the charts with a version of the old Norman Greenbaum classic 'Spirit in the Sky' and I couldn't get the song out of my head. Being eaten alive suddenly seemed preferable to being taken for a fan of the spiky-haired serial song murderer.

It was already light as I headed along the track by the loch side. Ghiubhsachain's thrusting chest was in sight above the remnants of the fir trees which give the hill its name. The way up is steep but straightforward, a series of dodges round rocky outcrops until the first platform of Meall a' Choire Chruimm is reached. The western faces of this hill falling down towards the water are intimidating and intense.

A look back down the ridge showed the Glenfinnan viaduct as a fixture from a miniature rail set as it shrank with every upward movement. I was lashing with sweat when I reached the large summit cairn. Breakfast was once again reserved for one, a picture window with a view stretching forever. From here I could see all the Corbetts still to be conquered; ahead was Stob a' Bhealach an Sgriodain and the wilds of the Cona Glen, south of that the Strontian peaks and to the west over Loch Shiel the Beinn Odhar Bheag group with Rois-Bheinn and An Stac rising behind.

Moments like this always made me resent having to go back to work. This was the true downside of climbing in this manner. No matter how good the day, or how good the view, I would have to leave it all behind because of time restrictions. Still, there was another Corbett to climb today and if I really had to get moving it was fitting that it was on to Sgorr Craobh a' Chaorainn, 'peak of the branch of the rowan'.

The descent was a case of picking my way through slabs and steep grass, then a long, rising line to reach a rocky nose. The way ahead was simpler than it had looked and it ended on another fine rock platform. I stayed high on the ridge passing over the subsidiary peak of Meall na Cuartaige before dropping off to pick up a good path over the bealach and through the trees. There were now a few other cars beside mine, day trippers enjoying a break beside the gently babbling waters. Despite having spent seven hours in the outdoors, the prospect of having to go to work meant I still envied them.

The Americans were storming Baghdad but it was all quiet on the western front as I reached the head of Loch Etive in rising light. It was 3am and I sat watching and listening to the dark waters lapping against the giant pebbles and skeletal remains of the pier. I was underneath another national treasure, Beinn Trilleachan, a mountain famed for its giant boiler-plate slabs. These seem to burst straight out of the loch into the sky, making Trilleachan seem a much bigger mountain than its 840 metres.

The name could refer either to sandpipers, 'drilleachan', or oystercatchers, 'trilleachan'. Either would seem at home here along the edges of the loch with its mix of salt and fresh water. You may think you need wings to reach its dizzy heights but the reality is a bit simpler. There's a muddy path, an old cross-country route which links this loch to Loch Creran, leading up by the edge of the forest for about a kilometre before turning on to the main ridge. It's then just a case of keeping to the line with just a minor top and some re-ascent along the way. The view from the summit cairn draws the eyes down the full length of the glassy slash of Loch Etive towards Oban and the south-west.

The return was a retracing of my steps but with the Etive and Glen Coe peaks laid out across the horizon, this was no hardship. It was warm enough for a spot of sunbathing, a slight breeze from the water keeping the midges at bay. It didn't pay to linger, though. I could easily have dozed. It wouldn't do to sleep in for a lunchtime start. I arrived back in the office to see the images of Saddam's statue being toppled.

Two weeks on and I was at the head of Loch Lyon on a subdued morning, one of those days when dulled skies provide enough light to walk without a torch but which seem to leach every drop of colour from the landscape. I walked under the shadow of the dam before open slopes beckoned with a steady plod on grass towards the top of Meall Buidhe. The flat summit held three cairns in a triangle and I visited each one. I hated the thought that I would later discover I had missed the correct one.

The saving grace of this walk is the extensive view north over the wastes of Rannoch Moor to Ben Nevis, its scimitar ridge shape dominating the skyline of mightier peaks than the one I was standing on.

The route to Sron a' Choire Cnapanaich, 'the nose of the knobbly corrie', involves a few twists and turns – knobbly, right enough – that could lead to confusion in poor weather. This summit gives a good view of Loch an Diamh and little wooded islands which from above look like a couple of soul patches. It also provides a good link to the Munro Stuchd an Lochain, but I had already decided I would opt out. It wasn't only the colour that had been sucked out – my enthusiasm had gone the same way.

I decided to put some colour back in my life in the oasis of The Trossachs. Deep in the green heart of Rob Roy country lie two fine hills, Meall an t-Seallaidh and Creag Mac Ranaich, and I decided on two separate walks. I approached the former from Balquhidder, along the right of way from Kirkton Glen, with a short detour to seek out the grave of our most famous outlaw and offer apologies for Liam Neeson's awful attempt at a Scottish accent.

Once clear of the forest it was a sharp right turn up typically rough slopes of grass and crag to the ridgeline. On a clear morning it's easily seen why this is the 'hill of the view'. I could have carried on and traversed Creag Mac Ranaich but it seemed less complicated to return by reversing the route, and besides, I would welcome another venture into this terrain from a different direction.

I came at Mac Ranaich's crag from the old Glen Ogle railway line, my walk along the grassy ramps in the mist greeted by hundreds of rabbits dashing to and fro across my path like some sort of bunny rush hour.

The word 'ranaich' can also be read as roaring or crying, so some translations suggest this is the 'rock of the son of the roarer'.

According to legend he was a fearsome robber. He certainly wouldn't have been an easy-going type if he spent his time around these slopes – this is rough, tough territory with a rough, tough history. Family's 'Burlesque' was a good soundtrack for the triumphant drive out, Roger Chapman's rolling and tumbling voice a metaphor for the day I had just had.

I ventured further into the interior with an early morning jaunt from the end of the road at Inverlochlarig, through the farm and up by the river on to the steep grassy ramparts of Stob a' Choin to enjoy a sensational inversion with a light so bright that it washed out the photographs. It's a mountain your knees will remember for a long time.

The wisdom of combining Corbetts and Munros was highlighted during a trip to Blair Atholl. Beinn Mheadhonach was the main objective but it made sense to keep on going further on from the summit cairn before dropping down steep heather slopes and heading over wet ground and peat bogs to emerge on Carn a' Chlamain. This is a mountain better suited to winter conditions when the ground is encased in a deep freeze. The traverse over the bogs was enlivened by the rash of hares shooting out from under my feet every few seconds as if they were auditioning for a Cadbury's Caramel ad.

When it comes to ancient landscapes, there isn't anywhere finer in the world than Skye. A group of us had hired Sligachan Lodge for a week but the weather didn't quite play ball. The consolation was that I would feel no compunction to attempt any Black Cuillin peaks, instead sticking to mopping up Corbetts.

We left in convoy, but one of our group had his whole family turn up to wave him off, tears and all, as if he was heading for two years at the South Pole. Mind you, it was Skye. There was a good chance it could be even colder there. He only lasted half the week, and most of that time he was on the end of a mobile phone, settling domestic disputes from 250 miles away.

On the first day, we were doing a circuit above Loch Ainort, over Belig and then round to Garbh-bheinn. I had emphasised how important it was that we all stick close and keep an eye on each other. At one point I turned round to make sure he was doing okay and he wasn't there. I shouted but there was no reply. No one else had seen him. I went back up the ridge and found him sitting on an outcrop chatting away on his phone. Another family 'crisis'. Something to do with who could have a biscuit and who couldn't.

Somehow I just couldn't picture Sir Chris Bonington unclipping himself from the rope on Everest to officiate in a long-distance row about his kids' supper. Okay, we weren't on Everest but then he wasn't Sir Chris. It doesn't help your concentration if you are having to referee a domestic bun fight.

We spent a blustery day with a short burst up Glamaig. The uphill was a chore but the downhill was a fast slalom on sheets of scree. It was a short outing of three hours. It's hard to believe that in 1899 a Gurkha took just 55 minutes to do this same route barefoot.

Day Three and we were provided with yet another variety of weather, this time a low, clinging, impenetrable mist. We were optimistic in trying for Sgurr nan Eag and became confused in the rocky chaos of Coir' a' Ghrunnda. I suppose the clue was that everyone else was heading down as we were heading up. We eventually found the loch after a couple of attempts but couldn't even see the water, never mind the other side. We agreed to cut our losses and drop back down before we took a seriously wrong turn.

The relief that we had made it back down safely was emphasised when we hit the pub. We ordered six drinks and six plates of scampi and chips. We were still there five hours later. It takes a lot of alcohol to kill that adrenaline rush.

When we got back to the house the furniture was cleared from the living room for the wrestling to begin. One or two of our party had seen this scenario before so ducked off to bed quickly. Those who stayed had to fight. It was messy.

Our week was also enlivened by having our own mistress of mayhem present. Georgia had laid down an earlier marker by dropping a pile of plates while unloading the dishwasher. She then challenged Robert to a race as we came off Sgurr nan Eag, a contest that ended early when she went headfirst down the gravel path, skinning face, hands and knees. Then came the piece de resistance. During our day's rest, she and Rebecca went for a drive round the island. At one bottleneck on a single-track road, a testosterone fuelled petrolhead in a flash car started gesticulating at the girls to pull in and let him past.

Georgia was having none of it. She gesticulated back at him to give way. The gesticulating went for a bit and became more heated. Eventually, realising that the girls were not giving in, he slammed his car into gear, reversed at a furious high speed straight into the front of another car. At that point the girls thought it might be a good idea to leave the scene. We thought it might be an idea for Georgia to head home before the island was hit by a tidal wave.

One of the outstanding memories of my early days of night-time walking was being decked by a tree as I tried to climb through a pitch dark forest from the Mile Dorcha car park on the Arkaig road. Now I was back at the site of that sneak attack, ready to go another round.

I was aiming to circuit two Corbetts, Meall na h-Eilde and Geal Charn, on the hottest night of the summer so far. These were the type of conditions when night walking came into its own. I could be down and out by the time the temperatures were starting to soar.

There were no surprises this time, no sucker punches. I was up through the trees and then over the remains of the bridge before I knew it. At 5am I was sitting on the 'hill of the hinds', Loch Arkaig whitewashed by the sun, the summit rocks and cairn washed black in shadow and everything in between looking as though it had melted as in one of Salvador Dali's masterpieces.

The ground shimmered beneath my feet as my shadow preceded me up Geal Charn, a drink every second step, the background a sea of shifting shapes, the mountains bobbing leviathans under the spell of the blinding sun and its power to create a moveable feast of moods. This was a hotspot which would have been the envy of the Med, a rock deckchair to drink in the warmth. It was a long, hot drive back to Glasgow, a few pitstops along the way to replace gallons of lost fluid.

The heatwave walking continued with an ascent of the wonderfully named Streap. It means simply 'climbing' and just to make sure you get the message, the peak next to it is Streap Comlaidh, 'climbing adjoining'. They don't chuck spare words around in this neck of the woods. Streap is a wonderful hill, steep ridges soaring to its apex, every bit a match for the Munro neighbours of the Corryhully Horseshoe, and it makes you work hard for your tick.

I reached Callop around 1am, mellow after a Steely Dan-filled play list, including the rather apt 'Midnite Cruiser', and promptly dozed off for a few hours.

A short way up Gleann Dubh Lighe I cut off to the left heading for a gap on the ridge. This was hard going, first through waist-deep ferns and then walking over the side of steep slopes, having to traverse up and down to circumvent the huge boiler plate slabs angled across my route. The reward when I hit the ridge was an airy walk skywards, with soaring peaks on each side, to the little platform which housed the summit cairn. I had time to spare on the way back to work so I stopped in Glen Coe to drink in the views in the remaining time.

I found myself back in the same neck of the woods not long after this with the promise of another night ascent in stifling conditions. The circuit of hills to the west of Loch Shiel had always looked appealing and I was ready to see them at close quarters. Or so I thought. As I left Fort William I also left the clear skies and was swallowed up by a grey pea-souper. This was not in the script.

I also made the mistake of not wearing waterproof trousers and after a creep through a tunnel under the rail line and a plod through knee-deep grass I was soaked. My first target was Beinn Odhar Mhor which despite its name – Mhor or Mor is big, Beag or Bheag is small – is the lower hill compared with its sibling Beinn Odhar Bheag. It is however bulkier, the equivalent of a taller, slimmer brother being called Shorty and the shorter, stouter brother Lofty.

The grey stuck with me on the long push, a sightless slog which left me a bit confused when I reached a cairn. I had been walking for over two hours and thought I should have been at the top of the Corbett peak so retraced my steps in the clag to see if I had missed anything. Ten minutes later I was back at the cairn and decided to push on where, around half an hour later, I found the summit I was looking for. In clear weather this would not have been a problem, but here I seemed to have been walking for ages.

By contrast, the swing round on to Beinn Mhic Ceididh, 'hill of the son of Katie', was without hesitation. The drop down the rocky north ridge involved a few dodges to avoid crags and huge slabs. By the time I hit the road, the sun was finally out.

I took advantage of the cooler hours of this continuing summer scorcher to tick off Creag Mhor in the Cairngorms as part of a big circuit with one of my night-time favourites, Bynack More, and sweeping up a whole heap of tops along the way. Ben Rinnes went the same way, an hour and a half rise on a superb path, and then a drive down the road to tackle Carn Ealasaid to make the long journey seem worthwhile. I even managed to make it to the top of The Cobbler.

It was August and I was closing in on 100 Corbetts. Nothing could stop me – or so I thought.

5
Dai Hard

*Helicopter rescue in Wales; dinner gongs
and a formidable woman; the mountain
guide who conquered by bluster; how
to do 20 peaks on ten pints a night*

MY mountain ambitions took a setback in the autumn of 2003 when I found myself on crutches after a tumble in Snowdonia.

I had been involved in a couple of near things before, once coming off the back of Buachaille Etive Mor when a ledge collapsed and again when I fell on an icy February day during a round of the Glen Rosa peaks in Arran. Both times I had escaped shaken but unscathed. This was the first time I had sustained an injury that left me needing assistance to get off the hill.

I had been descending Tryfan with my friend Trevor when I came to grief. We had ascended the north ridge, a constant 3,000-foot scramble, without any problem. But on the way down the other side en route to Bristly Ridge and a round of the Glyders, I jumped from a rock only to notice at the last second someone sitting underneath. I tried to adjust my footing but when I landed I felt my foot and ankle go in opposite directions. There was no snap but I thought I had broken my ankle. My foot was flopping around.

After the initial shock and a few minutes massaging my foot, there was no pain so I tried to stand. My ankle collapsed. I tried again. Same result. I had wrecked my ligaments. I would not be walking anywhere.

I could have descended on my own. It would have been a long, slow process but I could have crawled and dragged myself to the bealach and then made my way along the approach path to the road. But as Trevor and I sat there weighing up our options, one of the Ogwen Valley Mountain Rescue Organisation team came along. He was fully kitted out in assistance mode complete with radio. He had passed us earlier and turned back when he noticed our problem.

He explained that members of the team regularly patrol the two busiest mountain circuits at weekends. Our friendly local rescuer suggested that he and Trevor try to walk me off the mountain. One on either side, and with my arms round their shoulders, we set off. But as soon as my foot scraped the ground – and it is almost impossible to completely rein in the need to try to walk – my ankle collapsed and we were back to square one.

I was immobile. We were going to have to get help. But to take a casualty off the hill on a stretcher would need at least six, possibly eight, rescue team members. I was beginning to feel like a burden and was cursing my clumsiness. By this time, another couple of team members had arrived. They suggested calling in a helicopter. I was aghast. It seemed over the top for such a simple injury, but it was explained there was a major mountain and sea rescue exercise going on down the coast involving an RAF Sea King helicopter.

"They are just dropping dummies into the bay and then picking them up. They might as well come and get the real thing." He was kind enough not to say 'a real dummy' but I couldn't have argued – that's exactly how I felt. He also told us: "Anyway, good practice for the pilot – it's his first real flight." He didn't really have to tell me that.

There's often a little bit of friendly friction between the MRTs and the helicopter teams: the MRT guys think they do the work and the fliers get the plaudits. Cue two of my rescuers to lapse into their Statler and Waldorf routine.

"We better call it in before the weather changes."

"Yeah, they don't like coming out when it's cloudy."

"Or when it's windy."

"Or when there's something good on the telly."

Soon we could see the big yellow bird heading our way. One of the team set off a flare to guide it in. It came up the valley, getting closer and closer to the billowing red smoke and the real-life dummy. Then, at the last minute, it veered away up another valley to the right. This sparked Statler or Waldorf back into life. I could picture Fozzy Bear at the copter controls.

"How the hell did those guys ever find Iraq?"

Minutes later we could hear the thunder getting closer, the chopper appeared above us and a guy rappelled down to my side. He introduced himself: "I'm John and I will be your rescuer for today." The chopper had swerved off again. John explained it could only stay hovering for 90 seconds so he was off to do a circuit by which time I would be harnessed up ready to hoist into the belly of the beast. I had a harness behind my knees and one under my armpits. My RAF rescuer had also clipped himself to me and when the copter reappeared we were ready to go.

The biggest surprise was that the lift was so smooth I didn't even realise I was off the ground until we were just under the doors. The difficult part is getting over the lip and into the chopper but even that went without a hitch. I was strapped on to a stretcher and handed a set of earphones. The noise was horrendous – I had to wear them. What was more horrendous to me, however, was there being no noise. If I am in a big flying machine I prefer to hear it is still in the air so the earphones came off.

While all this was going on, I had thrown Trevor my camera so he was snapping away all the time, recording it all for posterity. Then came the bombshell. He had assumed he was also getting a ride in the helicopter and when he was told he would have to walk down himself he was like a wee boy who had just been told his birthday party had been cancelled. Adding insult to injury, he also had to carry my rucksack with his own.

When we touched down in the hospital grounds at Bangor, we were met by a medical team who switched me to one of their stretchers and wheeled me inside. I was taken to a ward where I lay still wearing my slightly ripe hillwalking gear. All around was the usual hospital chaos – bodies everywhere, all types of alarms and call systems going off, nurses rushing here and there. Despite all this, I seemed to be the centre of attention. Every nurse in the place wanted to come and say hello.

"Oh, you're the guy who arrived in the helicopter," I was asked more than once.

I felt it was only fair to point out it wasn't my helicopter.

When things settled down, a male nurse with a strong Scottish burr came and introduced himself. He was delighted to discover I was a sports journalist – and with his favourite paper. Being a Saturday afternoon, he kept popping in to keep me abreast of the unfolding football scores north and south of the border.

I was there for a couple of hours, before it was confirmed it was only ankle ligament damage so I was strapped, handed a pair of crutches and set free. Trevor was waiting with my car and I hopped into the passenger seat. I called my wife Alison to tell her what had happened.

"Had a bit of an accident on the mountain. Been to hospital, now I'm on crutches."

There was silence for a few seconds. Then she started howling with laughter. She passed on the message to my daughters and now there were three of them in hysterics, unable to speak. So much for the sympathy vote. Never mind, I got a small measure of revenge when I told her she would have to travel to Glasgow and pick me up because I was now unable to drive home.

The weekend had been a bit surreal, but it was typical of the scenarios you found yourself in with Trevor. He was a mini-tornado of mayhem, a ball of perpetual motion. The two of us had set off on a wet and windy Thursday evening from Glasgow, destination Snowdonia. We had a stop-off into Manchester's so-called Curry Mile, a starter in one café, main course in another and then a sweet from a takeaway, before we hit the road again.

There was no doubt we were now leaving England and driving deeper into Wales. With every passing road sign another vowel would disappear, replaced by two or three consonants.

Double d's without a Pamela Anderson or Katie Price in sight, an 'ell of a lot of l's and more y's than the most inquisitive toddler can provide in a day.

By the time we reached the car park at the Llanberis Pass, the combination of the curry festival and the decision to sleep the night in the car was looking like a bad mistake. The wind was rocking the car as we tried to sleep. It was rocking in the car as well.

We wandered into the Pen-y-Gwryd Hotel at 7am looking for breakfast. We were staying there for the next two nights after all. It wasn't open to non-guests yet but the wind was howling and the rain lashing down, so the owner took pity on us and gave us tea and toast. She also tried to talk us out of doing the Crib Goch ridge in these conditions but we wouldn't be swayed. This was Dai Hard, with a vengeance.

The conditions on the ridge were tough, gusting winds and driving rain, and we were soaked through but the scrambling was great. We were in our element, albeit a very wet element. We were glad of the respite the restaurant at the top of the mountain provided for a hot drink and something to eat. By the time we were walking out the weather had settled into a fine autumn mood and we were looking forward to a hot shower, a comfy bed and lots of food and drink.

The Pen-y-Gwryd Hotel is one of a kind. This is where the 1953 Everest expedition was based, and it has the feel of a museum with mementoes from their stay everywhere, from some of the old boots and gear to their names etched into the wooden ceiling.

Nowadays, of course, this would likely be regarded as vandalism. The local buses, known as the Sherpa service, also add to the historic grandeur of the area.

The hotel boss was also one of a kind. She ruled with a rod of iron, a female Basil Fawlty. Dinner was served at 7.30 sharp, no stragglers, no excuses. To make sure everyone got the message, she sounded a large gong bang on time. Everyone was there, half-dressed or still dripping from the shower. Pity in a way, I would love to have seen what happened to transgressors.

After dinner we descended into the common room where there was a snooker table and a table tennis table – yes, table tennis in a pub – for relaxation. We enjoyed rather a lot of relaxation with the other guests, so much so that we fell off to our beds around 4am.

By the time we headed out next day to climb Tryfan and the Glyders we were probably in a worse state than the morning before. I could have sworn the mountain was moving. But we set to our task and headed up the continuous hands-on ascent which the north ridge provides. The place was heaving, bodies all around, all working out their preferred routes.

There's a hiatus about halfway up before the final steep slopes are assaulted. While we were pulling up the superb dry faces we were passed by members of the Scottish Ladies Mountaineering Club, climbers as graceful as ballet dancers, who seemed to be hardly touching the rock as they moved ahead quickly.

Then we heard a booming voice which seemed to echo all over the mountain. This was Michael, a huge Irishman with a shock of white hair, Father Jack Hackett in Scarpas, who was leading a rather nervous party up ahead. "Davie, watch you don't fall there. You don't want to fall there. Margaret, watch your step, there's a huge drop. Careful now, this bit is dangerous." And so it went on. This group had arrived on the first ferry from Ireland to Bangor that morning for a weekend's scrambling with Michael as their guide.

He was dragging himself up by sheer brute strength, a total contrast to the dancing ladies we had met earlier, and he was carrying a pair of walking poles. We asked him if the poles weren't more of a hindrance on this route. "They give me confidence," he told us in a low conspiratorial tone. "To tell you the truth I'm scared shitless up here but I don't want the rest of them to know that or there will be mass panic." And off he went, bellowing out instructions, the scared leading the very scared.

Coincidentally, I was to meet Michael again the following year. I was over in Ireland to join a party for a tour of all the country's 3,000ft peaks. I was chatting to another mountain guide, also called Michael, outside a pub when I recounted the tale of meeting an Irish guide on Tryfan.

"Ah, that'll be Michael. I'll give him a call."

Ten minutes later I was going round for round with the two Michaels. I managed to do six days' mountain walking in a row, taking in around 20 peaks and was at my fittest in a long while and yet I must have put on about two stones with the Guinness. That's Ireland for you.

Tryfan's summit with its two matching blocks, Adam and Eve, was mobbed and there was a queue to climb up and make the leap from one to the other, a leap that is said to give you the freedom of Wales. Either that, or a very big fall. I didn't need Adam and Eve to help me fall. I did it all by myself just 15 minutes later.

Now we were heading north again, Trevor driving and me with my crutches in the passenger seat. A change of clothes would have been a good idea but we were racing against the clock. It was now early evening and with helicopters and hospitals taking up much of the day, we hadn't eaten since breakfast. I was in Trev's hands, his knowledge of the Manchester area from his years working there meant I could rely on him to find us sustenance.

I found myself in an up-market Indian restaurant in Altrincham on a busy Saturday night, still wearing the clothes I had on when I fallen down a mountain hours earlier, struggling around on crutches.

The place was huge and it was packed. Bright young things all in their finest party gear enjoying their Saturday night out. The two smelly old guys were packed away in a corner as far from civilisation as possible. We were totally out of place but Trevor was in his element. He enjoyed being the odd man out and I'm sure he was enjoying my discomfort. He was also desperate for a shot on my crutches.

Some intensive physiotherapy had me back on my feet within ten days but it was more than three months before I ventured out on the hills again. The injured ankle was heavily swollen and to this day is still bigger than the other one. It is also stronger. The body is a remarkable piece of machinery.

My reluctance to get back on to the mountains was based on the fear that any small knock could lead to a recurrence of the injury. I felt it would be irresponsible to go out and possibly have to call for help again. Better to sit it out until I could have the comfort of company. My first walk came at the start of the following year. I met two friends at Dalwhinnie and we set off up The Fara, a long ridge which sits above Loch Ericht. It's an easy climb but the inactivity meant it was a day of struggle with little movement in the ankle.

We came in from the north and on the lower slopes a lot of the tree cover had been felled. The ground was an awkward assault course of grassy potholes and uneven runnels between tree stumps, but it was a good work-out.

Another four weeks passed before I got up the courage to go solo, this time an easy round at the ski centre in Glenshee where I figured there would be plenty of people around if anything went wrong. Exactly five months to the day of my accident, I climbed

Beinn Mholach, going in from the A9 along the shores of Loch Garry. It was a 12-mile yomp, my biggest walk since the lay-off, but it passed without any problem. My confidence had been restored and so had my speed. However, my next big mountain day served as a reminder that I had been right to have a healthy dose of caution about going out solo again.

Fraochaidh sits hidden in the shadow of the Beinn a' Bheithir massif. It doesn't see nearly as many visitors but the 'heathery hill' is bulky and it takes a fair bit of effort on a long, contorted ridge to reach the summit. The total climb is more than that needed for many Munros, and it's about four hours from the road. I hadn't seen a soul all day since setting off, but as I neared the end of my walk and my car in Ballachulish, I met a woman standing on the track.

She asked if I had seen her husband. He had set off to do the same hill but was now at least two hours overdue and she was getting worried because he was making a bit of a comeback after a recent heart scare. I never heard any further news so I assume he eventually turned up. But it made me think that one little injury or bout of illness could see you lying a long time in such lonely country before anyone would find you. The Corbetts see much less traffic than their Munro counterparts and in some of the more remote areas you may be the only person to have visited in weeks. If you were lying injured on the trade routes on Beinn a' Bheithir for instance, it's likely someone else would soon be coming along. On the likes of Fraochaidh you could be in for a long wait.

Much is made of the cost of sending out a helicopter to rescue injured walkers and climbers by those who are too lazy to try to understand how it works. It's an old chestnut, an easy target to whip up taxpayer fury at this supposed waste. The facts are hardly mentioned. Helicopter crews are not just sitting around waiting for mountaineers to call. Rescue missions are valuable training. In my case, the helicopter was there already on exercise.

A few years later, we were crossing the Horns of Beinn Alligin in Torridon when we noticed a figure shadowing us. We stopped for a lunch break and he caught up. He was an RAF helicopter pilot who had flown many missions to aid mountain rescuers, and he always wanted to see some of the terrain at ground level. But as he made his round the mountain he became a little intimidated and had started to simply follow our tracks. He said he hoped we didn't mind.

I then told him my tale of being plucked from the side of Tryfan and my gratitude for the crew of the helicopter. I said he could follow me any time he liked. I also told him my now constant worry about having to call anyone again.

"Don't worry about that, mate," he said. "Anytime. Keeps me in a job."

I like to think I paid off part of my debt that day by helping out an RAF hero in his time of need.

6
The Prince of Walls

*Tragedy that left us numb; an emotional
day out on the Buachaille; a fitting
farewell to a treasured friend; tears and
fears that shaped the way ahead*

MY FALL in Wales was a reminder of just how easily things can go horribly wrong. Mountaineering can be a dangerous sport, one second of miscalculation ending in tragedy. I had got off lightly; some damaged ligaments, a couple of weeks on crutches and a badly bruised ego. I was wary of going out on my own on the hills for a few months afterwards, but the recovery was complete and I was back to business as usual, the pain of that momentary lack of judgement pushed to the back of my mind.

I had survived my first serious spill on the hills, but what was to follow would make my tumble pale into insignificance. It would leave all of us numbed, horrified beyond words. It would rob us of a good friend, a real adventurer, who lived life to the full. It would bring it home all too painfully how fragile life is.

And it would see some of our hillwalking friends drift away from our outings forever.

Yet, as everyone who has experienced tragedy says, it started just like any other day, one of normality and routine, a day in which we were preparing for a party and a grand outing surrounded by friends in Glen Coe on one of our finest mountains.

Many years earlier I had decided I would like to celebrate my birthday with friends and colleagues at the top of Buachaille Etive Mor. This became an annual favourite and there was an open invitation for anyone who fancied taking up hillwalking or joining our gang. It was the ideal starting point for newbies – they were safe in a large group, it wasn't too long a day, the pace was more leisurely than normal and, because it was July 7, the chances of having major weather issues were remote. Had my birthday been in February, for instance, we would never have started this tradition. The Buachaille can be deadly under snow and ice.

There have been plenty of fatalities over the years. But in the summer months it's the perfect mountain to get you going. From the road leading into Glen Coe it looks like the archetypical peak, a perfect pyramid of rock soaring into the sky. If you asked a child to draw a picture of a mountain, this is what they would produce.

The walk up the jumble of rock that litters the spectacular Coire na Tulaich is sharp but short and there's the feeling of a real mountaineering day for those unused to mountain walking. It also meant we could sound out potential recruits, see just how fit or otherwise they were and whether they would be able to come on some of the bigger trips. If you don't fall in love with the mountains after a day on the Buachaille then perhaps this sport is not for you.

The 2004 ascent was to be a special one. It was my 50th birthday and a larger than usual crowd had signed up. So many that we decided to hire a coach. It meant we could enjoy an after-climb party in the Kingshouse Hotel bar without anyone having to worry about driving.

At first, the walk took place on July 7, the actual day of my birthday. But after a couple of years we moved it to the nearest Saturday so that more people would be able to come along. My birthday had been on the Thursday, so were heading up two days later. It was shaping up to be a party to beat them all. Then tragedy struck, something we could never have contemplated in our darkest nightmares.

On the Friday morning, Trevor failed to appear for work. This was most unusual. He was in charge of one of the features departments and he never missed a day. His staff were puzzled. There were a lot of youngsters on his desk and he would never leave them in the lurch. He was also due to hand over a car he was testing in his role as motoring writer to a colleague on another paper that morning. He would not have ignored that responsibility. It just didn't make sense.

After Trevor had been overdue for about an hour, one of his colleagues came across to ask me if I knew where he was. There was no panic, in fact he was smiling, thinking that Trev had possible got up to a little mischief the night before and was sleeping it off somewhere. My reaction was the same. We shared a few laughs about possible scenarios and then decided to wait for Trev to turn up somewhat the worse for wear so we could give him a hard time. By lunchtime a few concerns were being raised but still nothing too serious.

We had been calling his house – no reply.

We tried his mobile – it went straight to voicemail.

Now there were the beginnings of a growing sense of unease.

We took a trip down to his flat, but no reply. We feared he might be lying inside, injured or ill, so we called the police. They managed to get a set of keys for the house and we accompanied them inside. No sign of Trevor. No sign he had been there in last 24 hours and no clue as to where he could be.

We headed back to the office, a mix of puzzlement and creeping dread fighting it out in our heads. Then a chance remark from another colleague who had just arrived at work changed the focus. He had been speaking with Trev the day before and said he had made a passing remark about possibly heading up a mountain during the night. Two and two suddenly became four.

We asked if had mentioned the Buachaille. Yes, that was the name, our colleague said.

Now it was full alert. The local police contacted their colleagues in Lochaber. But one of the problems was that no one knew the registration of the test car he was using. Another hour or so passed by which time we had tracked down the car make and number. Then came the news we had dreaded. Police had found the car among the dozen or so parked in the layby at the foot of Buachaille. Now it was a full-scale mountain alert and the Glen Coe Mountain Rescue Team was called out.

There is that moment in times of stress when you believe that this cannot be happening, that everything will be all right, it will all be a big mistake and that Trevor will come through the door with that trademark grin on his face, puzzled and amused by our consternation.

One phone call killed that hope. A body had been found by mountain rescuers. A formal identity would take a while but there was no doubt in our minds it was Trevor. The way everything now tied together meant it could be hardly be anyone else.

It seems horrible that you keep hoping it is someone else, someone you don't know, someone who has never done you any harm, but you do. Anything rather than face up to the stark reality that your friend has gone. You think back to the last time you saw him. What was the last thing you discussed? What was on his mind?

The atmosphere in the office was unnatural, the silence deafening. We couldn't wait to get to the pub, where we could draw strength from numbers and friendship, to breathe out after what seemed like a never-ending day of tension.

The bar was packed, everyone seeking solace and possibly answers to what had just happened. We went over the events of the day and, as so often happens, ignored the maudlin side and instead told tales of our madcap pal. This is the response to the realisation that the night ahead will be a lonely one.

At this point, no one had mentioned the following day's plans. Then I made up my mind. There was only one place I could be, one place to drink in every emotion and one place to say goodbye. I was going up the Buachaille.

The first reaction wasn't incredulity or horror but fear. The fear that our favourite mountain had turned into a monster, that one friend had already been lost and that another could easily follow. But slowly they came round. First one stepped over that line in the sand. Then another and another until we were eight. This was the backbone of the group, the regulars.

There would be no party now, and it was no trip for those on the periphery.

This was group therapy at 3,000ft for Trev's oldest friends.

We met the bus at the office next morning and made our way to Glen Coe. Instead of a party of around 35, there were just eight on the coach. Everyone took a seat on their own, plenty of space from the others, a skeleton crew with a reverential discussion level, no loud laughing, no raised voices, no shouting down the aisle. We set off in silent, single file heading into the maw of the mountain which had claimed our friend. But the mountain was the same as it ever was; it was we who had been changed. It stood as it has for millions of years, watching people come and go.

It always feels warm in this corrie; it's only when you hit the ridge that the temperature changes. But it was different this day. When we hit the top of the climb where we always have a moment of rest before the final push to the summit, it was still, not a breath of wind, clouds hanging steadily like free-floating balls of cotton wool. Everyone unconsciously drifted away a few yards in different directions for a moment of contemplation. There was silence.

One of the girls summed it up: "Even the weather is holding its breath."

Twenty minutes later we were at the summit and two hours later we were down in the Kingshouse with a toast to our absent friend. It may seem strange to some but we had a sort of birthday celebration. There was a cake and a card but it was in the lowest key possible. After all, a lot of people had gone to a lot of trouble and Trevor had died while trying to pull off the biggest birthday surprise of all.

Ever the party animal, he had set off up the mountain sometime after midnight with the intention of planting a card and a bottle of Champagne at the summit where I would find it when we arrived there next morning.

But he wasn't going to go up the Coire na Tulaich walkers' route. He had always fancied the trickier Curved Ridge, a scramble up steep rock faces on the eastern edge of the mountain where all the best climbing routes are. For a climber of his ability, that shouldn't have been too big a problem. But whether by accident or by design, he had strayed on to Crowberry Ridge, a much more serious proposition, one that shouldn't be tackled without ropes.

We will never exactly what happened but I can always picture Trev going up Curved Ridge and thinking: "This is too tame," and then heading for the more exciting looking route further over. He fell a long way. The only possible consolation is that it would have been over in an instant.

Robert told me his wife, Jane, had made a special cake for my birthday. It was in the shape of a yellow helicopter, a joking reference to my rescue in Wales the year before. When she heard the news about Trevor, she tossed it in the bin. There was nothing to joke about now.

I spent time with Trevor's parents and his brother, Alistair, as the following week unfolded. There was a massive collection for the Glen Coe MRT from individuals as well a huge cheque from the company. They carried out their work with the usual dignity and professionalism which accompanies every tragic event they have to attend.

It took a week to formally identify Trevor. The funeral took place while I was in Switzerland. The holiday had been planned for a long time, and it would have been selfish and unfair on my family to have cancelled now. Besides, if he could have had a say, the wee man would have been giving me pelters for even thinking of cancelling. Eddi Reader made an appearance at the service with a poignant version of Wild Mountainside, a song so fitting for one who loved life on the wild side.

The humanist service also highlighted that Trevor would be forever young and that we would also remember him that way; no gradually fading away, no pains of ageing. I think there's a certain nobility to that. Growing old is like being one of the survivors of a shipwreck, treading water until we slip under the surface one by one, left, if we are lucky, with only distant memories of what we were. At least Trev was spared that fate.

A few weeks later we accompanied Trev's family to the Buachaille for a short service and a scattering of his ashes in the stream that runs down the corrie. The annual walk has since changed from a birthday one to a memorial one, and every year myself and a couple of others pour a dram into the water to remember our friend. I hope he's counting, because that's 12 drinks I've bought him now. He'll need deep pockets to reciprocate by the time I join him.

Trev's death had a huge effect on us all. Some of the group drifted away, some immediately, some gradually. Some had suddenly become too aware of the fine line between life and death on the mountains, while some had just lost their appetite for a hobby which had claimed the life of their friend. The weekends away that were just a bit of fun would carry the shadow of death with them for a while. Some just thought the dynamic would never be the same again.

Just a couple of months before, he had been the life and soul of the group during our annual big outing. We had stayed in chalets at Kinlochewe, and Trevor had pulled his usual party trick of conjuring a three-course meal for the whole group, all the little flourishes you would expect in top restaurant.

One night he managed to build a fire in the middle of the river for an impromptu picnic, bottles of beer being cooled by hanging down on a pulley system in the cold waters. One picture makes him look like a fiery spirit stoking the flames. As one of the last images we have of him, it has seared itself in the memory.

On another occasion I met him at Wasdale in the Lake District and he handed me something wrapped in tinfoil. It was a tattie scone with black pudding and bacon inside, still warm.

"Never mind your porridge, get that down you," he said.

I certainly needed it. We did a circuit of Scafell, Scafell Pike, Lingmell and Great Gable, and I was having to run to keep up with him. On our way up Scafell we saw a sign saying there had been a huge rock fall in Lord's Rake and advising another route. Trevor just looked at me, grinned, and then set off up the rake, ready to dive out of the way if the huge boulder jammed ominously at the top suddenly decided to head our way. What was the challenge in skirting round it, he would argue.

I can understand why some people decided to call it a day after Trevor's death but I believe that giving up something you love out of fear is the wrong way to go. I lost count of the times people asked me: "Ah, you'll be giving up the hillwalking now then," and then being amazed when I said I was carrying on. Why would I give up?

There's an acceptance among mountaineers that it can be dangerous, and most people I know have lost friends or have known someone who has died in the hills. Many sports and hobbies are dangerous. You can always be unlucky but you can cut the odds markedly against accidents by good practice and experience.

Death is viewed as a price that is occasionally paid for doing something that is exhilarating, healthy and life-affirming. If one of the gang dies then celebrate their passing rather than running away from it.

I know that if the boot was on the other foot Trev would have carried on. It's happened, it's sad, now get over it. I'd hate to think that if anything happened to me, my friends would suddenly turn tail and run. My fall in Wales left me cautious for a while but I soon got going again. Walking down the street can be dangerous – you just have to overcome the fear factor.

Many years ago, a young climber was killed in a fall. Fellow members of his club were devastated but no one thought of quitting. Then the man's parents got in touch saying they wanted to give his mates a lasting memorial to their son.

They were thanked but told not to bother. The parents were insistent however and soon a wooden bench seat with an engraving arrived at the club's hut. It sat outside all summer, never used. During a freezing winter spell, the club members who were braving the cold in the hut took it inside and chopped it up for firewood.

That may sound heartless but that's exactly what their son would have done. No room for sentiment, the bench was put to practical use.

Our group made one last visit together before it all changed. We met at the Three Sisters car park in Glen Coe and handed over the cheque to the MRT leader John Grieve. After the short ceremony, we had a beautiful sunny day on Bidean nam Bian. There were plenty of laughs. Then we descended to the pub in Kinlochleven where the drinks flowed unstoppably, a real drowning of the sorrows. It was as if all the contrasting emotions of the past few months were being unleashed.

The next day was wet and windy and most of the crew had hangovers. We set off up Mam na Gualainn, a long mountain above Loch Leven requiring the use of cars at both ends. It was to be my 100th Corbett but it was clear to see that many people didn't have the heart for another walk.

The trip and the era had ended in the sunshine yesterday, and this became a trudge. Conversation was muted and the party became fragmented. A few tempers flared as the route finding became difficult. I had taken off ahead, running up the mountain, keen to find my own space, to clear my head. When we finally regrouped and found the summit we stood in a circle round the trig point as if at a prayer meeting as the rain drizzled down unabated.

After a few seconds of silence, one of the guys broke the spell.

"Congratulations to Alan on his 100th Corbett. Now let's stone him to death."

That did the trick. It was the realisation that it was a miserable day and that the walk hadn't been the best, but also that we couldn't keep wallowing in misery. The mood was lighter on the descent, and we hugged and gave our best wishes until the next time, knowing that for some there would not be a next time. We had spent a week in Kinlochewe just a few months earlier, and a weekend in the Lake District not long after. These trips now seemed like distant memories, and for some, these memories would now be painful ones waiting to be triggered.

Three years before Trevor's accident we lost another good friend to the mountains. Tim was a superb climber and, when I was starting out, an inspiration, the perfect sounding board for a rookie. He had that same devil may care, what will be will be attitude of the mountaineer.

He had just completed an ascent on Ben Nevis and had packed away the ropes and slings ready for the walk back down. As he descended he failed to notice his crampons had balled up with hard-packed snow and he slipped.

His partner watched in horror as he tried desperately to plant his ice axe while picking up speed on the slope. Then he hit a rock, lost his axe and went a long way down out of control. He was alive for a week but there was no chance of recovery. His family took the heart-breaking decision to switch off life support.

It seems ironic now that later that year Trevor and I had sat in blazing sunshine with a group of pals at the South Top of Gulvain looking over to the Ben and toasting Tim's memory. A mere three years later and we would be doing the same for Trevor.

7
Dubhs and Don'ts

Rising through the pain barrier; a season
of spectacular inversions; chance meetings
in the middle of nowhere; from winter
to summer in a matter of minutes

IT'S part of human nature that you look for positive signs of regeneration in the most unusual places, something that gives you hope.

We had just suffered a horrendous loss with Trevor's death and for some it had proved too much. Our trips were finished until the spring, a six-month gap that provided everyone with space to breathe and take stock.

Some would never return, either spooked by the closeness of tragedy and the thought that it could have been them. It certainly would never be the same again without the wee man. My idea of therapy was to get my head down and show the mountains they didn't frighten me. Physical pain often always help overcome psychological pain, so tramping up hills in the middle of night at a rate of knots was the ideal tonic.

I was where I would always find my sanctuary, alone with my thoughts and the whispering sounds of the wind and water. We were all hoping for a new dawn, but my last night climb of the year served up a truly sensational one. It was a freezing mid-December night, the sky was filled with a sea of stars and the trees along the roadside were glistening with a frost so translucent it felt like driving along a hall of mirrors.

I didn't have a Corbett to hand, so I was heading for Dalmally and the Cruachan range just off the A85 west of Tyndrum to climb the Munro twins Beinn a' Chochuill and Beinn Eunaich. Here the cloud was right down to the road. The track from the farm was frozen hard as rock but it was remarkably ice free. As I rose out of the cloud base coated head to toe in white rime, the dawn arrived in a riot of colour. Streaks of pink, purple, yellow and blue jostled for position above the inversion.

Trevor had always been a great supporter of my nocturnal ramblings and I liked the idea that this was a fireworks display organised by him from above, a spectacular nod to remind me to keep chasing the dream. This morning sky seemed to draw a line under any doubts I had harboured about doing the right thing.

It was the culmination of a series of spectacular inversions I had experienced at the tail end of a difficult year. Over a few weeks through October and November, I had sat above the clouds on half a dozen occasions watching the higher peaks sticking up through a sea of cloud. First there was an afternoon where I found myself alone on Beinn Dorain and Beinn an Dothaidh at Bridge of Orchy. That was followed by an unseasonably warm night on An Caisteal and Beinn a' Chroin, dipping in and out of the thick mists that swirled around the hillsides creating giant grey creatures that afforded a spectral guard of honour.

Similar weather conditions helped Beinn a'Ghlo live up to its name as the 'mountain of mists' as its three Munros vanished and reappeared in the biggest game of hide and seek I had ever played. Then after another day of upside down cloud on the Lawers range came that spectacular fireworks show to close the year.

The start of 2005 was a typical Scottish winter of freeze/thaw – two rival siblings of Mother Nature doing their worst to win her attention. One week it was blasting bitter winds and driving snow piling up, the next blasting balmy winds and heavy rain to wash away the snow. The result of this clash of opposites was a few calm days in between while the atmospheric bruisers took a breather at the end of each round.

If you are going up mountains in the middle of the night in winter, it's often better to pick ones that involve simple navigation. Stob an Aonaich Mhor is one such hill. It sits above the eastern shore of Loch Ericht, and there's a track running all the way from Bridge of Ericht at Loch Rannoch to the power station nine miles in. The approach is often described as 'long and uninteresting' but there's little chance of getting into trouble and the track makes for fast walking, even in snow. Weighed down by heavy winter clothing and a bigger pack it's good training for tougher days to come. The final compensation is the setting of the summit cairn, which provides views up and down the length of the loch for the coming dawn.

I then had a short run up via Aberfoyle into the wild country between Loch Lomond and Loch Katrine on a freezing morning when even the moon appeared to be shivering. The sky providing the backdrop to Beinn a' Choin was black and threatening in sharp contrast to the carpet of white on the slopes above Loch Arklet, but it remained dry and calm. Standing alone at the summit in this dark silence made me feel as if I had somehow wandered on to the surface of an alien planet.

The return of the snow provided an interesting ascent of Beinn an Lochain's narrow and craggy north-east ridge before I was back in cold, dry, inversion weather for an early start in blistering sunshine on the Ben Inverveigh circuit at the foot of the Black Mount. That was the turning point. Spring stayed put this time, the winter gear was discarded and suddenly it was as if my heels had sprouted wings. It was time to start putting in the road miles and heading farther afield.

Glen Etive houses some of our finest views, from the back of the Glen Coe giants to mighty Ben Starav and its kin. But the Munros don't have the monopoly on good looks here. Bristling for attention are some magnificent mountains that don't quite touch the 3,000ft mark but are every bit as spectacular and tough.

Stob Dubh, the 'black peak', is a great example. Black beast may be a more accurate description. Its near vertical rise from the floor of the glen to summit cairn with nary any relaxation in angle suggests an air of impregnability. On closer inspection it's a bit of an impostor, but still an unrelenting brute of a climb. Starting this hill in the relative coolness of darkness is a good idea. In the heat of the day you will find your water supplies depleting fast.

There's no finesse here – just cross the waters of the Allt Ceitlin and take a vertical line. There are crags – they are responsible for the 'black' part of the name – but they are of no real threat. And as on so many occasions with a Corbett sitting bang in the middle of bigger hills, you find the summit provides a spectacular 360 degree panorama of unrivalled beauty, with even Ben Nevis getting into the action.

Sitting out the back is a second peak, Beinn Ceitlin, worthy of getting its own show rather than just being an extra to the main event. I suspect many people never reach this point, being happy with what they have. It's a shame, it doesn't deserve to be ignored. It's not all about soaring, pointed peaks and narrow ridges though. These are the features that grip the imagination and invite fear and awe in equal measure, but most seasoned mountaineers would rather face this in wild conditions than vast rolling plateaux.

Navigation is simpler when you have a definitive point. Any mountain can be dangerous in foul weather but there's nowhere deadlier than the Cairngorms. The open spaces attract the highest wind speeds in the country, making it impossible to move at times. The consistent depth of snowfall can be immense. Every step becomes a trial of strength, a battle through waist-deep drifts, with the constant danger of a deeper hole lying in wait to pull you under.

The huge distances to be covered mean that one small error in a bearing can lead you miles off course. Horizons become blurred, merging into one background with the sky, and massive cornices hide the true lines of safety from plunging cliff faces.

Yet they are ideal for night walking in benign weather, the long approaches providing a good workout under cover of darkness and then good paths leading across the summits easily picked out by moonlight.

Early March, and with snow still blanketing the higher tops, I was having a couple of hours' snooze in the car at Achlean in Glen Feshie. The clocks were still on winter time and I had arrived earlier than planned. It wouldn't be a long nap though, too nippy for that. I was psyching myself up for a walk that would notch up around 30km over two Corbetts, Leathad an Taobhain and Carn Dearg Mor.

The best way to tackle these two was to walk past the latter and head further out to the col between the two which overlooks the Minigaig Pass. I would be on good tracks for the early part of the walk which would make fast progress. Leathad an Taobhain means 'slope of the rafters' because of the ribbed effect of the snow on the folds of the hillside and it is one of the higher Corbetts, at 912 metres just two short of Munro height. It also covers a vast area, a series of giant mounds in which there are more than a dozen 'summits', but with the track rising to within one kilometre of the trig point the navigation is relatively simple.

Now it was just an easy descent back to the col and then the steeper pull-up to Carn Dearg Mor. But just as I hit the lowest point of the traverse I felt something tweak in my groin. Suddenly I was struggling to stand, never mind walk.

I had to decide whether to cut my losses and follow the track back out leaving the second hill for another day or hobbling on and completing the circuit. I stared up at Carn Dearg Mor longingly. The idea of turning my back on it after all this effort would be like swallowing poison. Injured groin or not I was going for it. Besides, I already had enough children – the groin could take a break for a few weeks.

The uphill push didn't seem to make it any worse. As long as I took it slow and steady I should be fine. The summit cairn was as good as a painkilling injection. Once again, ambition had triumphed over pain. The route down was pain-free. I had walked myself back to fitness.

Two weeks later came another test. It was time for our annual week away, and this would be our group's first big get-together since Trevor's death. We had a house on the shore at Glenelg but although we had a good turn-out there were some absentees.

I had travelled up a day earlier to net a couple of remote Corbetts above Corran at the head of Loch Hourn as a prelude to the big week's walking.

It's a long journey from the east, three and a half hours to Glen Shiel and then over the steep pass of the Mam Ratagain and down the length of Glenelg to the road end. That's more than five hours of driving and the cloud cover wasn't giving anything away. The landscape had disappeared. I needed some help from above, some music to lift the soul on this black night. Step forward The Reverend Black Grape. Hallelujah! Shaun Ryder's skewed gospel provided the ideal soundtrack to every twist and turn of the wheel. I was now joyful and triumphant.

By the time I arrived, darkness had been and gone. It had left behind threatening skies of battleship grey, a sheen of wetness on the road and droplets of water clinging to every hanging leaf. It wasn't raining but it may as well have been. There was a dampness in the air that quickly transferred to my clothing.

Sheena's Tea Hut stood silent, the doors of the famous shed yet to open for the day. A couple of stags looked up from their lunch on the beach. Empty boats in various states of decay lay scattered along the pebbled shore.

I headed east along a track quickly leaving behind the smidgeon of civilisation dotted along the shoreline. Within minutes all traces had disappeared and I plodding up the infant slopes of Beinn nan Caorach with the shyer face of The Saddle looming on the horizon. Caorach could refer to sheep or rowan berries. Easy to confuse the two. I often get them mixed up as well. The higher I rose, the more Glen Shiel's peaks were unveiled; the South Shiel ridge, the Five Sisters and, beyond that, the Affric regiments gathered on parade.

The ridgeline took me north, then a short descent and a stiff ascent brought me to the top of Beinn na h-Eaglaise. This is the 'hill of the church' and refers to the place of worship in Arnisdale far beneath my feet which was founded by Celtic missionaries. Unfortunately, the mist had closed in and despite my prayers it refused to move. I should have brought the Reverend Black Grape with me.

The descent took me into the steep confines of the Bealach Arnisdail, the pass which divides Beinn na h-Eaglaise from the Munro Beinn Sgritheall. It had been some four years since I had last been here and I was dismayed by the level of erosion. The path had virtually disintegrated in places, leaving sections of boot-sucking mud and running water. It was almost a pleasure to get into the waist-high trench further down.

I emerged at the start of the row of houses and started walking back along the road. A car passed going the other way, then stopped and reversed. I heard my name being called. I turned to see a grinning face leaning out of the passenger side window. It was an old newspaper colleague I hadn't seen for years yet here he was, on an unclassified road in the back of beyond. It turned out he and his wife were staying in a cottage just a mile or so down from where we were based.

Strange to think that a minute or two either way and we would have continued blissfully unaware of the other's presence. It also brought to mind the strangest coincidental mountain meeting I had ever heard.

An old colleague told me he had been walking in the Blair Atholl area and decided to take a different route than that of the rest of his party as he wanted to see the house where he had been evacuated to during World War II. Later in the day, as he made the long trek towards the A9, he decided to try and hitch a lift back to his car. Dozens of cars passed him until, after about 20 minutes of trying, a Range Rover pulled up and the driver offered a lift.

They got chatting and the conversation got round to where my colleague had been walking. He explained that he had stayed in the area during the war years. The driver said that was a coincidence, because he too had been evacuated here. Then my friend mentioned the name of the house. The driver looked stunned – it was the same house.

Then they exchanged names, and stared at each other in astonishment. They had been playmates in the same house more than 50 years ago but hadn't seen, or heard, from each other since. One diversion, one car out of many, that happened to stop at that very minute and a reunion that neither could have imagined in their wildest dreams.

There were no more coincidences that week although we did experience one of the most rapid seasonal changes of all time.

Our first day on the hills was on Sgurr Mhic Bharraich, a rocky peak which sits above Shiel Bridge and Loch Duich. We started off in sunshine and light gear but by halfway up the rain had arrived, then higher up the snow. By the time we were on the top we were attired more for an Alpine winter adventure than a Scottish May.

Out of the gloom came that one ray of sunshine that changes the mood. As we sat eating our sandwiches at the soggy summit, the cloud parted like a pair of cinema curtains and we were treated to a grand picture, a view all the way down to the loch. The next day we made the long, wet slog up Gleann Choinneachain to keep the Munro-baggers happy for an attempted assault on A' Ghlas Bheinn and Beinn Fhada.

The first problem was putting the navigation in the hands of two map rookies. They were certainly keen. It was stop-start all the way as we fixed positions from one tree or rock to the next, a constant stopping to check the map to see that it was the right tree or rock. Eventually it was suggested they forget individual features and fix a line to the Bealach an Sgairne. That got things moving for a bit.

In hindsight, it would probably been a better idea to do the navigation experiment on a clear, dry day. Standing around in pouring rain with no visibility doesn't do much for body and soul. They both had previous when it came to route-finding it has to be said. One time when I asked Rebecca where we were going she said: "Eh, I think it's left of north."

And Susan, having been shown how to find her route round a corrie in clear conditions, then asked the classic: "But how would you know which direction to go when you can't see?"

The next problem was trying to cross the thundering waters of the Allt a' Choire Chaoil. The stepping stones were hidden under a wall of foam so the sensible option was to head upstream. I found a crossing point above a series of waterfalls and made it over, and a couple of the others did too. Then we had a near disaster.

As Crawford was making his way over, he slipped off the rocks and went into the water. He managed to scramble to safety but he was shaken. A foot or so more and he would gone right over the waterfall.

We reached the bealach without any further incident but as we ascended the snaking steps in the grass leading up A' Ghlas Bheinn the rain switched shifts with the snow. It never let up and the group picture on the summit looks like a holiday snap from Antarctica. We decided to leave Beinn Fhada for another day.

May 9 and the snow was still falling so we decided to stick to a short walk. We settled on Sgurr nan Airgid above Loch Duich. If we got lucky the views from the summit would be wonderful, if we didn't, well, it was short and sweet. This is the 'peak of silver' and legend suggests wealth of some kind, perhaps even a hidden trove of money hidden hereabouts by the Spanish who laid siege to Eilean Donan Castle and fought at the Battle of Glenshiel in 1719. We didn't find any dosh but we did find treasure in another form. This was the day winter said goodbye and spring arrived, and it all seemed to happen instantly.

One minute we were ploughing our way uphill in full winter gear, the next we were stripping off as the clouds scurried away and the sun came out with all guns blazing. It was the fastest seasonal turnaround I had seen. From battling snow and icy winds, we were now coping with a heat wave.

Next day we took the little Kylerhea Ferry into Skye and had a t-shirts and shorts day on Bla Bheinn and the following day took our red faces and red legs along the seven Munros of the South Shiel ridge.

Kingdom of Heaven was the big cinema release at that time. It seemed rather fitting that we had found our own in the north-west of Scotland.

8
Lost and Found

The mountain I couldn't find; days
of mist and island peaks; deer dodgems
on the Road to the Isles; the hill that
was worth a thousand ascents

THERE are hills which prove problematic and not always for the reasons you might think. There are hills that throw up technical difficulties, such as the Cuillin on Skye. There are hills that can be a navigational nightmare in the wrong conditions. And there are hills which turn out to be a nuisance for the most innocuous of reasons. For instance, Ben Challum, the Munro near Crianlarich, is not one of the most challenging but I have twice been forced to turn back just below the summit because of appalling weather.

But how about a mountain I couldn't even find? Creach Bheinn sits above the shores of Loch Creran, a sprawling mass of a hill covered in its lower reaches with forestry. You'd think it would be difficult to miss. But on a dark January night that's exactly what I managed to do. It wasn't all my fault. The last time I had been down in this direction was ten years earlier when Malcolm and I had climbed Beinn Sgulaird, a higher neighbour immediately to the north. We had no problems finding that, so I wasn't anticipating any snags.

But that was in daylight and this was now the middle of the night. Oh, and someone had built a bridge over the loch in the intervening years. This was not on my map. So, instead of following the old route of the A828 right round the loch, the bridge now cut five miles off the journey. All well and good but because it wasn't on my map I wasn't expecting it and ended up driving over the bridge. I realised soon I come too far and backtracked, again across the bridge. The darkness didn't help.

Never once did I think that the road had been dramatically altered.

Never once did I think to cut off and drive under the bridge and along the old road to my destination. I just figured it had to be somewhere back up the way I had come.

So I found myself taking the most likely forestry track and heading uphill. Then along a bit. A good bit. Then down again, and so on until I covered a good few miles going in circles.

By now the light was up and everything was becoming clearer. Then I saw where I should have been, a few miles off to the north-east. It looked a good mountain but having wasted a good couple of hours or so I had no time to start again. It would have to wait for another day. My night-time drive had given me a couple of hours' walking on the Gleann Dubh forest tracks, and now I was heading for an early bath.

Maps can often be years out of date. Buildings that are marked are now little more than ruins suffering from the ravages of time, covered in vegetation, invisible from any distance. Slopes marked as clear could now be covered by ranks of forestry and vice versa. Even rivers may have changed course.

My mistake would be rectified five months later, but again I would spend part of the day in confusion. This time the confusion was glorious. If there is an afterlife I would imagine this is what it would be like for hillwalkers.

I found the correct start point at Druimavuic House and headed uphill through dripping trees and bushes by the stream which quickly soaked my trousers. I turned south and took to open slopes with the landscape covered by a diaphanous mist which danced and swirled in the light wind. There was an ephemeral visibility which allowed me to see contours and images as if through a veil without revealing the full extent of its beauty.

This cover stuck with me all the way on to the high parts, a confusion of knolls and outcrops which kept the true character of the summits well hidden. The sky was a clear blue and the sun was blazing now but it only seemed to make the wisps of white shine even brighter, keeping the hill's secrets locked away.

I kept waiting for the big reveal but it was taking its time. It was just a case of keeping to a compass line until I hit the summit. There was almost a feeling of disappointment when it finally appeared, a jolt back into reality.

Breakfast was served with Loch Linnhe and Mull prominent in the massive picture window. I wanted this day to go on forever. I managed to draw it out as long as possible by descending over the peak of Creag na Cathaig and then down a steep dip and up on to Beinn Sgulaird. I had spent a good part of the morning lost but I had found a great feeling of peacefulness. The good mood lasted for the drive back and carried on through my shift. Sleep came quickly that night, picking up on the dreamlike state that had lasted for 24 hours.

Getting lost on the hills is an occupational hazard. We all do it every so often. The trick is to turn it to your advantage or, using the buzz phrase of politicians, incompetent management or TV newsreaders, 'learning lessons'. It's the great get out of jail card. Anything goes wrong, just say: "We've learned lessons."

Life is now just one giant school, with every Tom, Dick and Harriet constantly learning lessons but it seems, never actually learning lessons, if you know what I mean. Coupled with the constant upward inflection at the end of speech, it is one of the great irritants of modern communication.

Mistakes in route finding keep you alert, and a little error can have a positive long-term impact helping to vanquish over-confidence.

My next night outing would certainly be one to keep me on my toes, a combined route at Loch Rannoch that would take in two Munros and a Corbett during a circuit of the massive Coire Eigheach, one of the biggest corries in the country.

The route over Carn Dearg and then Sgor Gaibhre is straightforward enough but there's a little kink in the ridge near the second summit which can often lead to confusion. Walkers often get led astray on the next part of the traverse towards Meall na Meoig, being pushed over to the wrong side of the ridge by crags and then being faced with an almost mirror view of the area they should be heading for. It's unusual for any fatalities here but the wrong turn can lead the unwary to a spot miles from where they want to be.

Meall na Meoig itself is only one summit on Beinn Pharlagain, a series of knolls, false tops, dead ends and diversions, a giant puzzle in mist or poor visibility. I enjoyed my traverse but I was especially glad I managed it without incident.

I missed my initial target again during a round of the Rois-Bheinn peaks out in the wilds of Moidart but was able to adjust my plans quickly and keep the day on track. This circuit of three Corbetts sits off the road to Mallaig, the route starting behind the hotel at Lochailort where the road splits. I had arrived fairly chilled with a combo of the laid-back Southside Johnnie and the Ashbury Dukes and then some head-banging from Ash to fire me up in the final stretches.

The wilderness experience kicks in just minutes after leaving the car as you take a good path through broken rocks and trees clinging on to giant slabs for dear life. The emergence into the grassy lower part of Coire a' Bhuiridh comes as a bit of a disappointment, but I was expecting great things from the secrets that lay hidden in the cloud all round so managed to keep my cool.

The suggested route is to head for a lochan and then climb on to the ridge to reach the first peak, Druim Fiaclach, 'the toothed ridge', which is reputed to the finest on the circuit. I did what was asked but there seemed to be two or three patches that could have been lochans that were now lacking in one vital ingredient, namely water. So I picked a possible former lochan and pushed up into the mist.

I emerged somewhere on the ridge, guessed I wasn't quite where I should be and backtracked for a while. Then I picked up the path and continued in the other direction again. I found the cairn but if this was the finest summit on the ridge I would just have to take their word for it. All I could see was rocks on either side of a path.

The coming day brought a little more light to the subject though and brought me easily to the first Corbett of the day, Sgurr na Ba Glaise. They were big on cattle in these parts and this is reflected in the name 'peak of the grey cow'. The fact that this animal was deemed worthy of note could have been the fact that it would have stood out among the mostly red and black beasts in the herds. Either that, or it had some special talent. Probably safer to go with the first explanation.

The cattle connection continues as you follow the remains of an old wall up on to Rois-Bheinn. Depending on where you look and how you interpret the spellings of this hill, it either means headland, horse or showers. One letter can make a big difference.

Magnificent though the summit is, a short walk out to the western top provides an even better view out over Loch Ailort to Eigg and Rum.

The final hill, An Stac, is exactly how it's described – a steep, rocky, conical peak that can be likened to a sea stack with a line of sight akin to a craw's nest. The view over the spread of alternating land and water from here is almost hypnotic, and once again Eigg and Rum stand proud on the horizon.

I had just endured the pain of seeing Dundee United suffer yet another Scottish Cup final defeat. This one didn't seem so bad, because they had massively overachieved by setting up a Hampden date with Celtic and no one really expected them to win. The fact we only lost 1-0 was encouraging, the fact we had just one shot on goal in the whole game, not so. The fact that I then had to relive every kick to organise and edit a pull-out on said game on the Sunday only rubbed salt in the wounds. By the time it was put to bed, I was heading for the hills.

A desert island would have been good, and the recent views of Eigg and Rum had fixed this idea in my mind. However, the islands were too far after an exhausting couple of days so I plumped for the next best thing – the Corbett twins of Cruach Innse and Sgurr Innse. They sit like a couple of islands to the east of the Lairig Leacach pass above Spean Bridge. It was not too long a drive and the darkness would be gone just as I arrived.

I walked down the stony track into dancing veils of mist, brilliant sunlight hiding just above, the mountains keeping themselves under the covers, grabbing an extra few minutes of a lie-in before rising for the day. As I came up Cruach Innse, I rose above the mist. Suddenly I was on an island, a chunk of rock peeking out of a sea of rolling white. Some two kilometres to the south lay the other island, Sgurr Innse. I felt I could swim to it from here. I was lost again, this time in a sea of tranquillity.

From one oasis to another; the drive back to the office was accompanied by the Gallagher Brothers' latest anthem 'Lyla' and breaking news that Martin O'Neill had resigned as Celtic boss for family reasons with Gordon Strachan already being ushered in as his replacement. It was shaping up to be another busy few days.

The summer was filled with the build-up to Wimbledon and The Open, and a revolution at Hearts, with the colourful Vladimir Romanov providing screeds of copy to fill the back pages and the promise of great things with the unveiling of George Burley as boss and a flurry of exotic signings.

The Corbett chase had been put on hold but that didn't mean I was slacking. From the start of June until December I managed to rack up around 30 Munros, including a few night owl trips and a trip to Italy and a climb along some of the peaks of Monte Baldo above Lake Garda.

Winter saw me back among the Corbetts, Farragon Hill and Ben Vuirich followed by the double act of An Dun and A' Chaoirnich, started in darkness and finished in darkness. The new year was only three days old when I was sitting at the top of Meallach Mhor staring down the trench of the Gaick Pass towards the last two summits of the previous year. Continuity was the name of the game.

The easy peaks kept tumbling through a mix of freeze and thaw – Geal-charn Mor in flurries that couldn't decide whether they were rain or snow, Corryhabbie Hill, where the cairn was buried under six feet of the white stuff and then Creagan na Beinne, where it was summer on the ground and winter on the top.

The first big journey of the year came in early May, a long journey from Glasgow to Assynt with Ullapool a sleeping community on the way. This wasn't exactly moonwalking. The moon was out while I was driving and was clocking off from another shift when I arrived at my destination, Quinag, a multi-topped mountain with three of these tops designated as Corbetts, a rare treat in this list of mostly singletons.

Quinag means 'milk bucket' or 'water stoup' due to its shape and it is pronounced Coon-yak. It's a dramatic mountain, soaring rock prows on every face, stacks of rocks of every size pancaked together and deep corries biting into its complex topography. It's also a quick ascent from the road and then a comfortable round on decent paths. I came down feeling reasonably refreshed, buoyed no doubt by the realisation that I was staying in the area for a few days so did not have to tackle the long, long drive back just yet.

I managed to fit in Cul Mor and Sail Mhor despite the weather turning wet and windy, Ben More Assynt and Conival and then a day circuiting Scotland's finest mountain, An Teallach, and all its tops. Not a bad tally for a few days away.

Two weeks later, having spent a day suitably entertained by the first of Hearts chief Romanov's fall-outs with the Scottish football authorities, I took off at midnight towards Mallaig and the wonderfully evocatively named Braigh nan Uamhachan, 'slope of the caves'. It's a long mountain running south to north between Loch Eil and Loch Shiel. There are two main ways of approach and I took the Gleann Dubh Lighe track to the west as it seemed to have the advantage of less forestry and crags to weave through, an important consideration for climbing in the dark.

The latter part of the drive was spent dodging deer on the road. There was a strange pink light backlighting the blackness and it gave the deer the appearance of otherworldly creatures, horned demons snorting steam.

It was 4am when I set off walking. I started climbing just past the bothy on open slopes. Navigation was simple once on the ridge, and I spent a lot of the time merely following the line of a wall along the crest. To the west Streap and the Corryhully Horseshoe Munros lay under a blanket of cloud but to the east Gulvain stood in all its glory, the clarity of the air allowing me to pick out every rock. Two sides of a ridge, one hidden, one in full view. Our weather hardly ever fails to serve up something for everyone.

I never found one cave. I think whoever named the hill was at it. The track seemed harder on the way out but perhaps that was the morning finally catching up with me. Confirmation of that was the fact I stopped for a snooze at a layby in Glen Coe and then had a coffee stop at Tyndrum. It's not always easy walking at night.

The pull-outs had been done, the previews all wrapped up, now it was time for the action – the 2006 World Cup was about to kick off in Germany. Unfortunately Scotland were not involved, but recent results had been so bad it almost seemed a relief not to have to face the world's big guns with Berti at the helm.

There was a double-header to get us under way so that meant a later start at work. And that meant I could fit in a mountain the night before and have plenty of time to play with before reporting for duty.

Ben Tee is the impressive pointed peak that dominates the skyline on the drive from Invergarry towards Loch Lochy. It's another 'fairy hill' and shouldn't be confused with Ben Hee, which is located in the far north. If you get these two mixed up then you really shouldn't be allowed out on your own, although the thought of having the two in proximity would raise a few laughs. Tee-Hee, if you like.

Ben Tee was known locally as Glengarry's Bowling Green despite the lack of greenery at the top, but fairies were said to be partial to taking part in the games and were particularly welcome as they were prepared to race down the slopes for bools that had gone astray.

Access is by a sharp left turn after crossing the Caledonian Canal and then a short drive down towards Kilfinnan Farm. For years the farmer here had been charging walkers £2 for parking. Then it was revealed that he was only allowed to charge if anyone parked over the bridge on his land. If you park before the bridge, it's free of charge. Anyway, there's a good, flat grassy area for cars there. Cross the bridge and you would probably need to replace your suspension with the battering it would take on a boulder track.

This should have been a simple ascent on a lovely morning. Every route description I've ever seen for this hill says: Do not take the path to the waterfall.

I took the path to the waterfall.

I later convinced myself I wanted to see the waterfall. I'll let you into a secret – I didn't want to see the waterfall. I still don't know why I took that path but the one I should have taken zig-zagged through high ferns and was hidden from view, it was the middle of the night and I was possibly still half-asleep. Or maybe it's the equivalent of seeing a big red button which says Do Not Press.

Whatever, I ended up climbing a ridiculously steep, vegetated hillside looking down into a deep gully. I saw the waterfall. Wasn't worth it.

A hands and knees scrabble up loose slopes got me back up to a fence after a few interesting moments and more level ground. Then I found the real path at a stile over a fence and from there it was a dawdle despite the stifling heat.

I hadn't brought any bowls with me so I just stretched out for a rest at the top for an hour or so and had a leisurely breakfast. The descent was enlivened by the thick band of mist lying statically about 300 metres above sea level making it look as if the landscape had been torn in half.

I suppose if you want to be sure of avoiding the chances of taking the wrong route you could always follow in the footsteps of Richard Wood. This remarkable mountaineer had climbed Ben Tee a grand total of 1,048 times during his days of living and working in Invergarry before he moved to live in Cannich.

Richard was one of the first 100 people to 'compleat' the Munros having finished his round in 1969. Since then he has scaled more than 6,000 Munros and climbed and walked all over the globe including in the USA, New Zealand, Norway and the Alps. He was also partial to the occasional night stravaig, heading out in the hours of darkness during his early days in Perthshire and the east coast. It would nice to think that just once he had gone off course on Ben Tee.

9
Ice Cold in Affric

Deep freeze sleeping and mudpacks;
racing the storms as winter sweeps in;
following in the footsteps of Bonnie Prince
Charlie's milkman; run-in with a Cyclops

IT's a freezing mid-November night and I am the lone occupant of the car park at the head of Glen Affric. I have taken nearly four hours to get here from Glasgow, hardly another soul on the roads.

The driver's seat is in the recline position, as far back as it will go. I am in full winter mountain gear, including hat and gloves, and I have a jacket and a travel rug draped over me. I am freezing. Around five minutes after parking up, the warmth of the heater seems like a distant memory.

My toes are starting to feel cold, even through the double socks and walking boots. My ears and nose are starting to sting with the numbing temperature.

I toss and turn, unable to find a comfortable position, my body too long for the space available. My throat feels as though someone has burst an ice pack in my mouth and shards have gone everywhere.

The moon and the vast canvas of stars are cutting through the trees, providing a beautiful but annoying light which is preventing me from believing it's really dark.

You can't fool your body into sleeping, no matter what time of day or night. It's time to get up and go. But if I thought it was cold in the car, the first step outside provides a real shock. You wouldn't survive five minutes stranded out here.

It's also like a skating rink. The rain earlier in the day and the lack of cloud cover now has coated the ground with a thin layer of ice, invisible until the light strikes it at the right angle. In these conditions it is often safer higher up. The chances of slipping and breaking a bone or two would seem more likely the lower I remained.

Teeth chattering, I make the final adjustments, checking all my kit before leaving the car park and taking the forestry track on the south side of Loch Affric.

The two hours or so of misery in the car have served one purpose though – the light is beginning to rise. The two hills I am about to tackle form a complex and often pathless horseshoe which would provide a challenge in the dark. I need some light for this one.

The sky is a shade short of black, a dark, dark blue, the static bundles of cloud on the horizon appearing a mix of yellows and oranges, a trick of the rising light behind them. A small marker cairn on my left signals the start of the ascent. The frozen mud crunches and snaps under my feet as I rise by the side of the fermenting waters of the Allt Garbh.

The path sometimes vanishes among gnarled, twisted trees, now stripped bare of their foliage as they bed down for the winter. The banks of the stream seem to be getting steeper. I begin to think I have missed a crossing point further down in the darkness, but with the way the water is running it may have been impossible anyway. I arrive in a deep rocky little gorge where the waters run level amid huge boulders. This is the best bet for a crossing – it looks much steeper further on and I don't want to backtrack. This is a Corbett walk after all, the marked path could just be a figment of a map-maker's imagination.

A bit of judicious boulder-hopping gets me across with dry feet, and a few minutes later, after a hands and knees scrabble up a steep, loose bank, I locate the path again. The first target is to find a way up the steep crags of Na Cnapain. Looking up from the path, this prow looks mightily impressive, a mix of rock and vegetation, little sign of any chinks in its formidable armour. Its optical bark turns out to be much worse than its bite and, despite slushy patches of wet snow, I am soon on the ridge watching the early light wash over the loch.

By the time I have strolled along to Carn Glas Iochdarach it looks like the sun has decided to have a day off, the sky dulled to a grey wash with streaks of pink. I would lay odds that Caravan got the inspiration for their album, *The Land of Grey and Pink*, from a similar viewpoint.

Now I was at the point where reality kicks in, booting my optimism and enthusiasm into the long grass. I had thought I would be able to extend the route to take in some of the Munro tops of nearby Sail Chaorainn but the plod along to the first Corbett of the day, Carn a' Choire Ghairbh, took longer than I expected and the muddy, slippery ground was only highlighting how tired I was. It was becoming obvious that a couple of hours' non-sleep in a motorised icebox was just not enough.

My second Corbett was Aonach Shasuinn and it lay 6.5 kilometres and a further 450 metres of ascent away round the massive horseshoe ridge. There were a lot of rises on the way so I thought it wise not to add any more to the day. Tempting though they were, I managed to turn my back on Sail Chaorainn's Tops and swept under the connecting peak of Carn a' Choire Ghuirm to gain the ridge beyond. Now it was just a case of staying on the rollercoaster for a couple of hours. By the time I reached the stacked cairn I was shattered.

Aonach Shasuinn is the 'ridge of the Saxon (Sassenach)' and is thought to be a reference to English troops who were ambushed and killed in this area during the years of searching for Bonnie Prince Charlie after Culloden.

It was a weary near three-hour walk back out and I was ambushed several times, not by Jacobites but by the boggy terrain.

After one fall I was cheered by the sight of a heron taking flight as I struggled to extricate my feet and legs from the glaur. No doubt it was having a good laugh at my plight.

The car park was busier when I stumbled back in looking like the creature from the black lagoon. I sat for a while, a November picnic, while I contemplated peeling off every muddy layer from my exhausted body. The mudpack must have provided some extra insulation because when I did strip down the cold hit me hard.

Maybe I was still in state of brain freeze when I decided I would vary my route back by a taking a 'shortcut' over a series of B roads from Fort Augustus to Daviot. I had some time to spare so thought it would be good to see somewhere new. That's always a good thing – except when you do them in a blizzard. At first it was a pleasant drive on the opposite side of Loch Ness by a series of lochs I had never visited. A couple of stops for a coffee, pictures and a leg stretch, all very civilised. Then it started to snow. Heavily. Now it had changed from a pleasure drive into a battle against the elements. By the time I hit the A9 for the 'faster' run home the visibility was nil, the car was sliding all over the road as the white stuff piled up and traffic was down to one lane. It would seem that the art of making life easier for oneself is one I had yet to master.

Like most constant walkers, I have learned to rely on weather windows. My next Corbett outing was one such effort, a short period of remarkable calm between two massive storm systems.

The office had been rocking as the winds roared in over the Clyde, moaning through the vents and air-conditioning system, tossing branches and concrete around like confetti at Godzilla's wedding. The window panes sounded as if they were being hit by a constant hail of bullets as the wind-driven rain came in volleys. At one point there was talk of evacuation as the river level threatened to spill over, submerging the underground car park.

So when I announced that I was going to head out for a walk later that night, I was probably one phone call away from being sectioned. But that's the beauty of weather windows. This would be blown away in a couple of hours and we would be in the eye of the storms. There was a good 12-hour gap before further mayhem arrived.

The worst of the devastation stayed hidden in the darkness as I drove up the A9. By the time I started my walk into Glen Strathfarrar the light was rising. The locked gate across the glen was of no consequence. I didn't need someone to give me a pass for access. I was only going to climb Beinn a' Bha'ach Ard which sits right at the entrance to the glen and is a prominent sight for travellers across the Beauly Firth.

As I set off from the car, the extent of the damage became evident; the road was covered in rubble and broken branches, the water had swollen and poured over its banks, creating little islands and isolating trees. There's often an eerie silence after a huge storm, but this one had left a little behind. There was a ripple on the water and a bracing breeze swooshed through the trees causing them to bend back and forward like a team of synchronised contortionists.

Just past the little power station I left the road and headed west on a track, dodging round and over fallen trees. Then it was north straight up the hillside, a tough push, pathless over a series of heather and rocky knolls, all the while boggy and insecure underfoot.

The walking became more solid with height and despite a coating of snow I was at the trig point summit within three hours. Mindful of the possible margin of error with the weather I dropped down quickly to the north to continue the circuit and got my best view of the day. From this angle Beinn a' Bha'ach Ard was a perfect pointed peak standing against a pink and violet sky, the snow-basted slopes glinting and winking in the low light.

The round covers three more minor tops and then drops down to Loch na Beiste, a small oasis in an idyllic sheltered setting. Beinn a' Bha'ach Ard means 'mountain of the high byre' and with a lochan of the beast alongside suggests this was fertile ground for cattle.

The heavy rain returned about halfway back down the road and by the time I was back at work around five hours later the winds were storming in again, and the building was shaking again. The heads were shaking as well at the thought of my 14-hour round trip between storms to climb a hill.

The Groundhog Day feeling was back the following week with another opportunistic dash into the high country. This time it was to climb Beinn Bhan from Glen Gloy above the Caledonian Canal.

There was renovation work going at the previously derelict house of Inverskilavulin but a good path took me round the property and on to the open hillside. The climb was steep but fast on grass and I hit the top just as the sun was breaking into its full morning glory, setting the summit aflame in a golden glow that was painful on the eyes.

Beinn Bhan is a common mountain name, one of many white or fair hills in Scotland, often because of pale rocks or features, but the reason behind the naming of this one is a little different – it is said that snow lies here earlier than any other hill in the area. If there was any lurking at the moment it was well hidden.

Loch Lochy stretched ahead, its flanking hills dotted with cotton wool wisps, and rolling, lazy tidal waves of cloud off in the far distance. It was hard to believe that a few hours from now it would be hidden under a pall of greyness and precipitation but the evidence was presented on the drive back as I aquaplaned down the road.

There was still no sign of snow by December 23 as I dodged Christmas shopping duties and made the short jaunt up the Munro Meall Chuaich. January was well under way before winter got its act together. A couple of outings on my local hills had come and gone with just the merest hint of the white stuff. Then it hit with a vengeance.

Early morning and I'm on the Mallaig road, a black line through a landscape of pure white. The trees are laden, the sky clear and bright, the deer at the roadside looking for scraps. This is the most notorious road I know for playing deer dodgems. They are everywhere, standing on the road when you come round a bend or dashing out at the last minute, startled by the headlights. It's like a videogame and the car is your console. No points for hits though, just a huge bill for damage to the car. I rear-ended a stag here once. Luckily I was already alert to the dangers and had killed my speed by the time he loomed right in front of me, a classic case of a deer frozen in the headlights. A small shunt and he and I escaped damage-free, apart from a few hairs plastered to the bonnet. His, I might add.

Now it was time to scale Sgurr an Utha, the 'peak of the udder', so named because its shape was said to resemble that part of the cow. Personally, I don't think it's too obvious. Sounds like it's the work of someone with a bovine fixation, although it is recorded that a companion of Bonnie Prince Charlie was able to get milk for him while he hid out hereabouts on the hills. A note to the milkman for an extra pint would have been a dead giveaway.

This was a deep snow walk from the start, ankle deep, then knee deep, thigh deep and finally even chest deep on the way down a deep gully. It was well worth the effort though, a perfect view in every direction from the big cairn, including the blue slice of lonely Loch Beoraid off to the west.

Three days later and I was hoping for a repeat performance but instead I travelled slowly up the A9 in a convoy of vehicles with a police escort. By the time I was halfway there I was questioning the wisdom of this outing but it seemed harder work to leave the procession and turn back. Conditions didn't get much better as I left the procession and headed over to Laggan. The minor road to

Garva Bridge was snowy and icy, and beyond that I seemed to be on a bobsleigh track with no chance of turning round. The only option was to keep going.

I did find a place to stop near the foot of the hill. Maybe the sensible move would have been to retreat at this point but it seemed a long way to come and a lot of effort to get here to then not do the hill. If I got stuck here so be it – at least I would have another tick.

I headed further up the Corrieyairack Pass on foot, then took to the white-out terrain. Progress was a series of stumbling, sinking and rolling and not always in that order, but I made it to the buried cairn where I had to prop my poles just to add some colour to the picture. I made it back to the car in a round trip of 3 hours 48 minutes. Not that I was counting. There were lots of deer on the road on the way out but even they seemed too cold and hacked off with the weather to make any pretence of running away.

It was a pleasantly surprising trouble-free sleigh run back out to the main road, the only roadblock being a mass crossing of sheep at one point.

Rather appropriately for this time of year, my next target was Carn a' Chuilinn, the 'cairn of holly', near Fort Augustus. It's unclear whether this is so-called because holly could be found here or whether the mountain's shape is thought to resemble the spikes of the holly leaf. Whatever the reason, it was the season to be jolly. Pity no-one thought to tell the Grinch we met on the way out.

This isolated hill sits in Glen Doe, where work was under way on a massive hydro-electric scheme. I had checked to see that access was okay before I set off on my chosen route and been told it was fine. I also checked the signs at the entrance which warned of heavy plant and suggested the best way to proceed.

As I got ready to set off, another walker appeared. He had been concerned at the work going on and whether he could walk there. I reassured him and we set off. We stayed off the main track at the start, cutting across country to avoid the huge lorries and earth-moving machines. Eventually we had to walk on part of the track until cutting off over heathery ground to the mountain. So far, so good. But on the way out we started to meet some of the workforce.

As I was talking to a couple of guys, a car screeched to a halt beside us and a very angry man with one eye got out. He identified himself as a foreman and proceeded to have a rant.

"You can't walk here – this is restricted. Anyway, this is a private estate. You shouldn't be on this land."

Where to start.

Well, first I pointed out to this Cyclopean madman that we had followed the advice on the route.

Then I pointed out we were now just 20 minutes from the car. What were we supposed to do – stay up on the hill for the next six months until all the work had finished?

And finally, if he was in charge, then why was he so unaware of the access laws in Scotland?

He took all this in and then backed off a bit.

"Well, it's health and safety rules."

And then he pointed to his missing eye. "It's dangerous. How do you think this happened?"

I really had no idea but before I could ask, he turned, got back into the car where a blonde woman was in the passenger seat, and sped off. Ah, that explains a lot. He was flexing his muscles to try to impress a member of the opposite sex.

The rest of the workers were rolling their eyes and sniggering.

One said: "Just ignore him. He's full of crap. And the eye thing? Nothing to do with work. He was playing with fireworks while drunk at a party and managed to fire a rocket into his face."

It certainly wasn't rocket science to realise that he was not well liked.

The snow returned with a vengeance and the Corbett chase was put on hold. I did get out for some hills though. We had to retreat from the summit slopes of Ben Challum in an almighty blizzard, the second time that has happened to me on that hill. I knew it was time to give up when I turned to my companions only to discover them on all fours trying to find something to hold on to as the wind blasted across the ice-scoured slope.

There was more success with a long walk from Glenshee to Lochnagar on a windswept landscape in temperatures well below zero and an icy round of the Glen Lyon Munros.

At the first sign of a thaw, I managed to do two of the Corbetts called Carn Dearg near Roy Bridge, then a long and featureless walk to the long and featureless top of Carn na Saobhaithe and finally a disappointingly misty summiting of Meall a' Phubuill in the early hours after a walk over a wasteland of mantraps and felled trees that looked like the aftermath of an intensive aerial bombing campaign. That's dedication for you.

10
Scorch Mist

High and dry in wettest part of Scotland;
a morning amongst islands in a foaming
white sea; ferries, goats and wind; the
wrong way to train your dog

THERE are good Munros and not so good Munros, good Corbetts and not so good Corbetts. This can apply to any list. But there are a handful of special mountains which transcend any parameters. Height, or the lack of it, does not matter a jot. Ben Aden is one of those mountains.

It sits in the Rough Bounds of Knoydart, a tough, threatening conglomeration of rock in the heart of some of our wildest country which deserves every superlative heaped on to its broad shoulders. It won't go down without a fight.

Then there's the approach routes. Whichever way you come at it will prove a long one. It has the feel of a true mountain expedition, involving high passes, rivers that can rise alarmingly fast, a lack of paths and bridges.

If you attack from Sourlies at the head of Loch Nevis you first have to do the long walk in from Loch Arkaig and then after an overnight stop at the bothy, a tough tramp up by the unpredictable River Carnach before tackling complex slopes.

An approach from Barrisdale in the north is also a fine way to come in, but again that probably means a stay at a bothy and then a long, strength-sapping push round towards Loch Quoich before finding a safe way up. I decided to come in from the Kinloch Hourn road.

Winter was well and truly put in bed and we were in for a scorcher. I left work just after midnight but it was light for most of the journey – moonwalking not required. Four hours later, with the heat already rising and scarcely a drop of wind, I set off among the peat hags, bands of rock and oozing channels of run-off from the recessed waters of the loch, round the nose of Sgurr nan Eugallt and on to a decent path sticking to the shoreline.

The dreaded Abhainn Chosaidh was crossed with little more than a boulder hop but the tide marks high on its banks confirmed I had caught it on a good day. At times of spate this is impassable, a raging torrent that would sweep you away in seconds.

After two and a half hours' walking and the humidity building, I reached a small dam. Ben Aden dominates the skyline immediately above, a haughty ruler peering down on its subjects. The route now heads into one of the roughest corries in the country, Corrie nan Gall, with Sgurr na Ciche and Garbh Chioch Mhor dead ahead in the chaos of rubble. I spotted a flash of red up there, someone wild camping. It doesn't get much wilder. This is hardly a tourist hotspot. You don't wander in here by mistake, you have to want to be here.

Even now Ben Aden is not easily conquered. First there is the small matter of heading up its satellite peak, Meall a' Choire Dhuibh, easy at first, more complex higher up, massive slabs lining its slopes. The traverse to its bigger, meaner brother took longer than I thought in the heat. It's an intriguing route though, weaving in and out boulder fields, finding rents in the most unlikely places to push ever upwards, all the time aware of the isolation of my position.

Then I was at the top, with its revelatory views in every direction. Loch Quoich looked a long way off, an S-shaped patch of blue stretching away to the horizon.

It had taken more than five hours of hard graft but there was no doubting my lunch perch was a million times better than a plastic seat in the canteen.

Ben Aden is the anglicised version of Beinn an Aodainn, 'hill of the face', a likely reference to the mountain's features as seen from the Carnach side. Whichever angle you look at this hill, it is ruggedly handsome. It was hard to tear myself away but it was 11am and there was a long way to backtrack. I knocked about an hour off the return despite feeling dehydrated. I was tanking gallons of water but it seemed there was never enough.

I was having visions of ice-cold pints of lager and cider dancing across my eyeline. It spurred me on. I had to turn this to reality very soon. I knew that when I hit the car I was only about 30 minutes away from the Tomdoun Hotel. Never has a pint tasted so good.

Heatwave walking is hard work. No one likes to walk in blistering temperatures. But since I had spent most of the last five months bemoaning the lack of sunshine, it hardly seemed fair to complain.

I was sitting having breakfast on the summit of Sgorr an Diollaid in Glen Cannich as the heat wave swept on unabated. I say sitting, but I was reclining on rocks which formed a perfect deckchair. Three hours was all it took for this hill, with an hour's sunbathing on top. It seemed a long way to come so just to make sure I grabbed a sunspot before someone put a towel down on it.

As I approached the summit I spotted a couple sitting over to the left. They waved but their dogs were not quite so happy to see me. They came running over to me snapping and snarling, but their owners seemed oblivious to their pets' behaviour and made no effort to call them off, not even the usual platitude: "Don't worry, he/she won't harm you." Maybe they just assumed I wouldn't mind having my legs chewed.

While I was growling at the neighbours and laying out my towel on Sgurr an Diollaid, the political landscape in Scotland was changing dramatically with Labour's towel being whipped away from under them as the SNP swept to a historic victory and control of the Scottish Parliament.

It seemed the season for incredible events. A female police officer was suing for £1.5 million compensation for being hit on the head with a pineapple during a demo down south, even though it had probably counted as one of her five a day. Even more incredibly, Scotland managed to win a football match, a 2-0 victory over the mighty Faroes. The world was going mad. Escape was, as usual, the only answer.

The last time I had tackled Corbetts at the head of Loch Arkaig, I had to battle my way upwards in waist-deep snow in the middle of the night. This time looked like being the complete opposite, an ascent against the heat in bone-dry conditions. The biggest problem would be the dreaded midge.

The great forecast had also made me ambitious. I wasn't coming all this way just to do a Corbett. No, this time I was going to take in a Munro, Sgurr Mor, and then another Corbett, Sgurr an Fhuarain, to complete the circuit. Three birds with one stone, a more efficient way of ticking the lists.

I reached the Mile Dorcha car park around 1am and pulled in for 40 winks. I woke three hours later, somewhat bemused as to my surroundings. I soon recovered. It wasn't as if this was a new experience. I was surprised to see so many cars when I reached the end of the road. There were also splashes of colour everywhere, tents zipped up tight against the midge swarms, but no signs of life yet despite the wash of early light.

The track walk was done in sunshine, then as I rose north on a good path for Druim a' Chuirn, I disappeared into low mist. The change in temperature was dramatic. I had been walking in a short-sleeved top but the moisture in the cloud brought an instant chill. It was short-lived. Once I hit the ridge I rose above the cloud again and the sun was with me right round the horseshoe to the summit of Sgurr Cos na Breachd-laoigh. This tongue-twisting name translates into English as 'peak of the hollow of the speckled calf' and suggests a shelter in which deer would hide their young ones.

The bank of cloud I had passed through midway was settled into every glen to the north and east, cutting off the peaks like islands in a foaming white sea. To the west, there wasn't even a hint of a cloud, just blue sky with a few jet trails as far as the eye could see.

To get to Sgurr Mor involves a walk over at couple of minor peaks and then it's a long pull up to the massive cairn on the highest point in the area. The final hill of the day was Sgurr an Fhuarain. It's one of the higher Corbetts but it looked fairly insignificant from Sgurr Mor and it proved an easy rise along a gentle ridge.

So it made my decision to turn my back on it all those years ago during my first round of Munros even more puzzling. It would not have added much to the day, but my sole goal at that time was the Munros and I headed off happily having bagged Sgurr Mor. Why would I want to climb another hill when I didn't have to? Hindsight is a great thing, but experience has taught me to take your opportunities when they arise.

The other curious thing was that I been struggling badly after about an hour of walking, recovered remarkably by the end of the second hour and then was striding out to the car after nearly ten hours. Maybe my body was still protesting at the lack of sleep at the start and then decided I wasn't going to give it any more rest until the finish so it might as well hurry things along. Just to prove that I treat my body like a temple, I bought it a fish supper on the way down the road. Not exactly health food but sometimes it's just what you need, especially after torturing yourself for hours on end.

I suppose I shouldn't get so hung up about a guilty pleasure once in a while, but it's scary just how many bad diets are out there. As a nation we seem to have gone down the American route: over there one half of the population are fitness fanatics and the other half fatness fanatics. There doesn't seem to be a middle ground and it's worrying that the same now seems to be the case in Scotland.

Poverty is a major contributing factor, of course, as are laziness and ignorance. But one of the biggest contributory factors is the decline in sporting activities at school and the amount of physical exercise for kids. When I was at school there were teachers who ran sports teams after hours, but budget cuts and health and safety liability have put paid to much of that. The big supermarket chains don't help much either. The only items they ever seem to discount heavily are fizzy drinks, crisps, sweets and junk food.

I was in a supermarket recently when I was suddenly aware of an awful smell. Then, over the Tannoy came an invitation to descend on a certain aisle to sample some new barbecued spare ribs. All of a sudden, from nowhere, came the rush. No one appeared to be weighing in at less than 400 kilos. It was like a Sumo open day. Some were even in mobility scooters, taking corners on two wheels to reach the goodies.

As I stood transfixed with my basket, I was nearly trampled in the rush. There was a sea of obesity all around me, being encouraged to chow down on junk food, but I remember my overriding thought was: these people can move fast when they have to. It was depressing and hilarious in equal measure.

I managed just one more Corbett before the heatwave faded, a short trip to Arran to climb Goatfell. Or Goat Fell if you prefer.

It means goat hill. Or maybe it means windy hill from the Gaelic for wind, gaoithe. There are certainly maps from the 1600s which suggest the former. Most people prefer goats to wind, so we'll go with that.

One of the lovely things about the Arran hills is that most of them can be done by bus. Since all the hills are in the middle and the road runs right round the island that's hardly a revelation. But there is something particularly appealing about a mountain which involves coming in by ferry, then catching a bus to the start.

There were no goats but a very strong wind on the climb but I was up and down in three hours. I would have stayed and explored the ridge longer but despite the dry conditions the higher points were covered by cloud. I decided a cool drink and a lounge by the shore was a better way to spend the rest of the trip before I took the ferry back.

I got chatting to a fellow walker as I enjoyed my pint. Unfortunately, he was a really nice guy. Why unfortunately? Well, he was the spitting image of the late actor Peter Sellers; same square face, same hair, same light moustache, same smile and grin when he spoke.

I was sitting having a drink with Inspector Clouseau. Rude though it may seem, I just could not concentrate on a thing he was saying. As he chatted away I kept pleading internally: "Say minky, say minky, say minky." He didn't say 'minky' and luckily for me the ferry pulled in before I lost the plot completely.

My fears were confirmed on my next outing, an ascent of Beinn Bhan near Applecross – the heatwave was well and truly gone. I spent the whole four hours wandering around in thick mist, the magnificent corries I had admired many times from afar now invisible at close range. I am keeping a return visit until the next clear weather arrives, reckoned to be sometime in 2025.

There is something more relaxed, decadent even, about using public transport to reach your chosen mountain. Ferries always provide a sense of adventure, that feeling of sailing off to foreign lands like an ancient explorer. And a combination of trains and mountains? Heaven. I once sat and tallied up how many Munros and Corbetts you could access from the West Highland Line and was surprised to find it was somewhere around 90.

Most people alighting at the lonely Corrour Halt are heading into the Alders range or doing a through walk along one of the Rannoch ridges. Beinn na Lap is also a popular choice, but it's a short day and the wait between trains is long.

First time I came in to climb this hill I bought a one-way ticket then walked out along the historic Road to the Isles. Once again I had ignored a Corbett in close proximity. Now I was here to climb the wonderfully monickered Leum Uilleim – 'William's leap' – and I would take in Beinn na Lap as part of Munro round No.2 to flesh out the day between trains.

The early sleeper which picks up at Crianlarich, Tyndrum, Bridge of Orchy or Rannoch is a happy little train. The staff are engaging and relaxed, the passengers likewise. No problem with drunks or rowdies (unless, of course, you happened to be on the one that brought the Trainspotting guys north) – nearly everyone on this train has a reason to be happy.

The station platform at Corrour is short so all the walkers and climbers are in the one carriage. Routes and ambitions are exchanged and discussed, there's an atmosphere of children with their train set.

In the winter months it can resemble the refugee train from Doctor Zhivago, everyone huddled in that carriage, either heading into, or away from, the cold conditions, yet still they all have smiles plastered on their faces.

The train clickety-clacks along the single track across the empty moor, passengers glued to the windows hoping for a glimpse of the deer hiding in plain sight, one sudden movement giving away their position. And in the distance, a tiny speck of white in the midst of sea of yellows and browns, the station house, getting closer all the time.

There's that moment of activity when the train stops, everyone piling off on to the platform, and then it's off again, vanishing into the distance. Silence settles again as the disembarked peer down the now empty track to moorland and mountains, as if mourning the loss of their ride and experiencing the fear of will it ever return to pluck them back off this desert island. Then suddenly, everyone is snapped out of their reverie and dispersed on their mountain quest.

I was the only soul heading for Leum Uilleim and after the initial bog trot on a waterlogged path, higher ground provides a more pleasant walk. The large cairn on the summit marks the centre of a huge circle of mountains, the Nevis range, the Mamores, Glen Coe, and I spent my brunch time playing Guess the Peak. But when it comes to finding out who William was or why he was leaping, that's a different matter; it remains lost in the mists of time.

Another train journey, another Corbett opportunity. This time it was the line from Inverness to Kyle of Lochalsh and a stop at Achnashellach to climb Fuar Tholl. This mountain is part of a grand circuit of peaks which make up the Coire Lair horseshoe and the route starts straight from the station.

Again I missed out Fuar Tholl first time round but there was a good reason on that occasion. I had managed the Munros of Beinn Liath Mhor and Sgorr Ruadh but had been walking in zero visibility from 4am. I decided I had had enough and bailed out early. Fuar Tholl is probably the finest of the three however, and was well worth a return visit in good conditions. Don't let the translation 'cold hole' put you off; it is more often referred to as 'Wellington's Nose' because of its profile from Loch Carron.

The Munro/Corbett combination worked out well again the next day, An Ruadh-stac being swept up along with Maol Chean-dearg. In dry weather this is a delight, long stretches of slabs mean you can run up quickly with friction as your new best friend. The way down is slower however, and in wet, greasy conditions care must be taken.

There is a note of caution about using the train. It is not unheard of for a weary traveller to fall asleep on the home journey and miss their station. My former mountain buddy Malcolm and his Munro bagging dog, Scoop, managed to combine to bring an unusual twist to this story.

Malcolm's car history was chequered at best and after a weekend on the hills his latest jalopy had given up the ghost. After a good kicking failed to achieve any result, there was a frantic dash to catch the train back to Glasgow. Making it with seconds to spare, he settled down into the seat nearest the door with Scoop lying at his feet. All now well in the world he dozed off. The train pulled into Irvine, and everyone who was getting off headed for the exits.

As the train was pulling out of the station, a half-asleep Malcolm glanced out of the window to see Scoop staring back in at him from the platform. The dog had seen the crowds getting off and obviously decided to go with them, then realised his master wasn't coming along. Too late.

Malcolm sat immobile for a minute or two, stunned. Now he would have to get off at the next stop and take the train back to scoop up Scoop. Could this day get any worse?

The answer to that came in the next few seconds. As he was about to get up and alert the guard about his situation, the train shuddered to a halt. Now there was mumbling and grumbling from fellow passengers about another rail delay. Then a voice over the Tannoy: "ScotRail would like to apologise for the delay, ladies and gentlemen, but all trains have been halted due to a dog running loose on the railway line."

Cue further passenger outrage. Malcolm thought it better not to mention that he knew the canine culprit and slid back down into his seat. Eventually the train got moving again and he got off at the next stop. By the time he had caught a train back to Irvine, an hour or so had passed. When he reached the station there was no sign of Scoop.

He was walking around calling for the dog when one of group of kids spoke up: "Hey mister, are you looking for a dog? A black and white dog?"

"Yes, have you seen him?"

"He went home with Jimmy."

"And where does Jimmy live?"

He was given directions and half an hour later he arrived at the block of flats where Jimmy lived. When the door opened, he could see through to the kitchen where Scoop was tucking in to a free feed.

Thanking the family for taking care of the dog, he called out for Scoop to come. The dog looked at him, then down at the food, then back at Malcolm and then proceeded to enjoy his meal. Malcolm could wait – after all, he had left him alone at the station.

11
Northern Lights

True rock stars and a Viking heritage; an
audience with the Queen; threats and
curses on a crumbling mountain;
red sky at night was our delight

THOSE chasing Munros are afforded a brief taste of the wild lands
of Sutherland but it's the Corbetts which provide the main course.

The four 3,000ft peaks north of the line between Ullapool
and Lairg are heavily outnumbered by their lower neighbours, and
anyone who has stood on the summits of Ben Hope, Ben Klibreck
and the Assynt pair cannot help but fall under the spell of this
ancient landscape. Impossible shapes thrust up from every corner
of the land, rock dinosaurs moulded by tectonic events millions
of years ago. Viking names dominate, a Norse code for tales of
bravery, exploration and adventure; Foinaven, Arkle, Suilven,
Canisp, Breabag, strangers in a strange land.

The area is home to Scotland's Geopark and rock groupies
flock here to study some of the oldest – the Lewisian gneiss in the
area is dated at 3,000 million years old – and grandest terrain on
the planet. Geologists have long been fascinated by the intricate
and unique puzzles thrown up by the Moine Thrust. This is an
area which runs from Loch Eriboll some 120 miles south-west to
the Sleat peninsula on Skye over two vastly contrasting rock belts
with complicated layers which went head to head in the ultimate
smackdown.

Its discovery in 1907 was a milestone in the history of geology
as it was one of the first thrust belts discovered and it provided

further proof as to the formation of the landscape with Scotland being squeezed between two competing tectonic plates. There's certainly a feeling that you are being squeezed at times as you drive along these roads, the mountains rising up from nothing on each side of you, their sudden appearance often belying their height and bulk. Every mountain here exaggerates, like animals puffing up to appear more frightening, a geological version of Deimatic behaviour. The emptiness of the surrounding land merely adds to that illusion. This is a land before time and is all the better for it.

Lairg has the feel of an outpost, a last vestige of civilisation before the rough stuff starts. Once you leave the gardens, greenery and houses behind and pass through the other side, the road splits into the A838 and A836, which take opposing lines north until they meet again on the loop right round the top of Scotland.

Despite being single track, progress is generally speedy with only the occasional need to pull into a passing place. The more you drive these roads, the more you become part of the inter-vehicle ballet with avoidance techniques and timing that means no one ever seems to have to pull over.

I left the office in the middle of the night, delighted I had a few days' R&R to recover from punishing shifts of up to 12 hours, a necessary evil when we were hitting holiday time. I had a rest stop near Aviemore, a stroll round the car under a clear sky with wall to wall stars. I prayed this was an omen for the days to follow.

The few other vehicles thinned further after I left Inverness, the compass set on a far north bearing. Lairg was fast asleep when I arrived and I tiptoed through it quickly to emerge at the start of the perfect blackness leading on from the single track sections. I was making good time, helped by the fact I could see oncoming headlights miles away until I pulled over at my destination. With first light opening its eyes, I set off from Carbreck on a track heading for the twins of Beinn Spionnaidh and Cranstackie.

Once past the house at Rhigolter, it's just a case of heading up to the col between the two and then choosing which one you want to climb first. This is often a case of which obstacles are in your way and how you avoid them, and I felt myself being drawn over to the right on the way up the corrie so Cranstackie won the day.

This was a typical example of my decision-making process on solo hill expeditions. No matter how logical I am in everyday matters, when it comes to the mountains I have a one-track mind but so many times that track has two trains running on it, heading towards each other at a great rate of knots. The resulting collision can be messy – it probably explains some of the more questionable decisions I have taken when faced with choice. Never mind the path, just go straight for it. Not always the more sensible or popular option but I always get there in the end.

The summit area is a huge boulder field – Cranstackie means 'rugged hill' – with a prominent cairn right on the prow of the cliffs. Clear blue skies provided a 360-degree panorama. The bulk of Foinaven dominated the skyline to the south, the pale grey rocks of its long multi-topped ridge shining almost white in the sun, while to the north, Beinn Spionnaidh stood up, the last high point on the way to the northern coast.

The main feeling looking west was that of emptiness, peaty moorland spotted with little lochs and lone rock outcrops stretching as far as the eye could see, and to the east Ben Hope seemed a lone guardian of a similar landscape. Beinn Spionnaidh, 'mountain of strength', is only a mile or so away and the views are much the same as from Cranstackie. A lone raven kept an eye on me, switching peaks in the opposite direction, his staccato croaking call the only sound apart from the wobbling rumble of the huge boulders I was crossing in leaps and bounds.

I spent the night at the hostel in Durness which hosted only a few other souls at this off-peak time. I managed to pay another visit to the spectacular Smoo Cave. In the summer months at times of low tide it becomes one of the unusual concert venues in the country, a full orchestra taking advantage of the unique acoustics to perform classical music inside. Durness certainly likes its music. John Lennon used to holiday here as a boy, a perfect excuse to hold a regular festival. It's a long way from Abbey Road but it still manages to draw crowds.

I took a slow drive round the coast next day heading for Ben Loyal. On a beautiful morning this entails plenty photo stops, a stunning beach or inlet just around every corner. Reaching Tongue involves a twisting drive round the length of Loch Eriboll. There's no point trying to hurry; every other car keeps stopping to capture the scenery every couple of minutes. The loch wasn't quite so popular with the squaddies who were stationed up here in the 50s and 60s – they referred to it as Loch 'Orrible.

Ben Loyal is often referred to as the Queen of the Scottish mountains. Its striking outline is admired from miles around and it regularly garners rave reviews, so it was with some sadness I found it to be one of most disappointing climbs I have made. The walk in on the track from Ribigill was pleasant but ordinary, but as soon as I passed the deserted cottage at Cunside, things went downhill even though I was going uphill.

Squelching grassy terrain could be expected on the initial part of the ascent but the greasy mix of grass and rock on the rise to the ridge was unforgiving. Sodden, slimy lumps of earth seemed to slew off with every step and there was brackish water running everywhere. With the shifting ground, I needed to use my hands a lot and they came away covered in goo. It was if every slug and snail in the world had been here on their holidays this year. By the time I reached a decent height, my legs and boots were soaked and my enthusiasm had been severely punctured.

Sgurr Chaonasaid, the northern summit, is a fine viewpoint but with plunging rock faces all around it needs a lot of care. The granite tor of An Caisteal, the main summit, lives up to its name for it is a castle, a trig point perched above soaring faces which are breached on the west. The descent west off the ridge can also be problematic in thick weather as it depends on good navigation and route finding to avoid bands of crags. Still, it's infinitely better than descending into the pit of the slime creatures.

The next two days saw me back on the Munros Ben Hope and Ben Klibreck, but they had brought with them deteriorating conditions and the resultant lack of views. The consolation was that I was staying at Sleeperzzzz, a quirky hostel at the railway station at Rogart.

Accommodation is on one of two old first-class railway carriages which have been converted so every compartment has two beds and a long seat. There is a communal kitchen, dining room and sitting room and at the end of your stay you get a railway ticket (punched, of course) as a souvenir. It's a great place to take your kids. There's also a Romany-style caravan for hire. It has become a favourite over the years, as well as being handy for exploring the northern territory.

Ben Loyal may be the pretty boy or girl of the north, but the real star attraction is Foinaven. It's just a few feet under Munro height and every so often the rumour that it was about to be 'promoted' reared its head, with the result that there was a charge by Munroists akin to a Klondyke gold rush to stake their claim on this mountain. Recent satellite measuring has put paid to that, however, with Foinaven coming up even shorter than originally thought. It's still one of the most impressive hills in the land though and its ascent hasn't lost the feel of an old-fashioned expedition.

For a start, it's a long way in from the road, albeit mostly on a good track. The walker coming in from the south is then faced with a five-mile long ridge and a lot of up and down over the five summits on its spine. The thought of retracing your steps all this way is a non-starter for most people and the usual route is to drop down from Ceann Garbh at the end of the ridge, and walk out for more than three miles over undulating ground, dodging through channels to avoid water hazards. And finally there's the prospect of a long road walk unless you have done your homework and planned ahead at the start of the day.

The three main mountains in this area, Foinaven, Arkle and Ben Stack, lie on the Reay Forest Estate which is owned by the Duke of Westminster, and if their names seem to ring a bell even if you have never been on a hillside in your life, that's because they were also the names of three famous racehorses. Arkle was one of the best steeplechasers of all time with a series of big race wins, Foinaven famously won the Grand National in 1967 and Lord Ben Stack was also an equine of note. All were owned by the Duchess of Westminster.

The trip to climb these hills was sparked by my enthusiasm to explore more of this wilderness after the usual Munro expeditions. I was joined by Robert, Giles and Mark for the long trip north to the hotel at Rhiconich, our base for a few days. I drove one car with Giles in the passenger seat. At one point as we came round a corner on the dark road I noticed at the last minute a stag standing on the tarmac and swerved out of his way in time, before correcting my line to drive on.

"That was a close one," I said to Giles.

"Very impressive, you managed to miss both of them."

"Both of them?"

Turned out there had been another stag a few feet further down on the other side of the road that my quick correction had managed to avoid even though I never saw him.

A collision with a deer would quickly ruin your day. It's not uncommon to have your vehicle written off in a stag-car interface. That would often be a best-case scenario. In Canada, for instance, moose collisions are a common cause of road tragedies. A few years back in Torridon they tried an experiment in which wooden posts were placed along each side of the road through the glen on which wolves' eyes had been painted. The thought was the deer would steer clear of a possible predator. But it backfired. Deer have never seen wolves and their natural curiosity to check out what was going on was bringing more of them down to the roadside. The posts were soon taken down. Another area's effort to try to keep deer away involved spreading lion dung around but the smell from this was so foul that it was scrapped following complaints from locals.

We parked 10 miles down the road the next morning under promising skies and took the private track leading to the aptly-named cottages of Lone. On the way you pass through a curious rock feature. It looks like two matching halves of one giant boulder that have been split by a bolt of lightning from the mighty Thor, leaving enough room for the track to continue. It now climbs through a small pine wood to emerge after a series of zig-zags to follow the banks of the Allt Horn. Arkle can be climbed from this point but that was for another day and we continued on for another few miles until the track turned at the Bealach Horn. We left it here and headed north up grassy slopes with the first peak, Craig Dionard, the target.

The surroundings now looked more like the setting for One Million Years BC. Raquel Welch in a fur bikini would certainly been a welcome distraction as we slogged our way upwards under increasingly threatening skies, but with our luck we would be more likely to see her snatched away by a pterodactyl. Or worse still, be forced to listen to one-hit wonders Terry Dactyl and the Dinosaurs, a song that brought painful reminders of romantic angst from my teenage years. I'm glad they are now extinct – the band I mean, not dinosaurs. One my recurring nightmares is that they will be cloned Jurassic Park-style and we know how that turned out.

By the time we hit the first summit the gloom had descended. I've been in white-outs but this was the first time I had been in a grey-out. The cloud that had dropped merged with the pale grey quartzite of the ridge creating an eerie sight. Foinaven is covered in quartzite scree, and in misty, still conditions you can hear the mountain breaking up under your feet. Another few billion years and it will be gone forever so if you're planning to climb this hill I suggest you do it soon. Some translations suggest fair or whiter mountain. A more unflattering offering is 'wart mountain' based on the premise that it has three protuberances on its face. Nowhere does the word grey come into play but that is what we had today.

Our mood had changed, from the prospect of a day of fine weather and gorgeous views to a stinker of a walk on a shattered ridge. It didn't help that we had been going for about four hours and still had at least the same again to go before we were finished We reached Point 808m, where the ridge becomes much narrower and much rockier. From there, it's a steep drop on a path through broken rock. Giles was looking worried.

"Eh, where do we go now?" he asked.

"Dead ahead, down there," I said pointing to the drop.

"Would this not be a better way," he said pointing to a level grassy platform.

"No, that leads to a sheer drop."

This was Giles at his finest. He has walked in blizzard conditions and not batted an eyelid (mind you, they may have frozen open), but present him with any hands-on rock moves and he will have a meltdown. So, when I had insisted that the rocky descent was the way we were going, he looked past me to the other two and said: "Does anyone else think we should turn back now?"

We had been walking for more than four hours. Going back now wouldn't save any time. And there was always the chance the cloud would lift and rescue the day. We would be kicking ourselves if we retreated and then that happened.

Robert and Mark looked back at me for the reaction. They weren't disappointed.

"Giles, if you don't get your arse down there now, I'm going to ******* throw you down."

He decided it was probably safer to tackle the down climb.

The clag stayed with us until the end although it was dry. The route across the rough ground under the main body of water, Loch na Claise Carnaich, seemed to take forever, and when we emerged on to the road just north-east of the hotel a pint was definitely overdue. Foinaven's charms had lain hidden but at least it meant a return journey would be a certainty.

We sat on the terrace, tired but happy with the day's efforts. It seemed that someone, somewhere, decided we were due a consolation prize for our sightless day because we were treated to a spectacular sunset. As we gazed down Loch Inchard, the red sky on the horizon started expanding slowly, lazily washing down over the waters, filling in every square centimetre, until the whole landscape was drenched in a deep red. Then the dark curtain came down and it was gone.

The next day we took the same route in but this time cut off early and made a beeline for the near symmetrical horseshoe ridge of Arkle. The main summit sits less than a mile away across a curious flat bed of fissured slabs that resembles a high-altitude pavement. Foinaven was in full view all the way round, showing us what we had missed yesterday. It's a big brute. We could see the route up, the impressive length of the ridge, the place I had threatened to kill Giles.

Arkle seems to have had the Norsemen confused. It can be taken to mean either 'arc hill' or 'whale rock' but the most favoured is 'hill of the level top'. Robert, however, gave it another name. He had injured his knee on the way up and was painfully slow coming down. Until, that is, he discovered he could fool his joints by walking backwards down the hill. Arkle therefore became Elkra, 'the backward hill', in our book.

It was later that year when I was on holiday in Austria that I once again remembered how, despite their comparatively lowly heights, Scotland's mountains are real mountains. We were 8,000ft up and still in a meadow. You had a long way to walk to reach the real deal. But here we can stop at the roadside, get on our gear and within minutes we are in the centre of rock playgrounds that are the envy of the world.

Inversion over Glen Kingie from the summit cairn of Sgurr Cos na Breachd-Laoigh on a brilliant spring morning with Sgurr an Fhuarain, right, sticking out above the cloud

Looking along the snow-plastered ridge to the summit
of Sgurr Mhurlagan under dark, threatening skies

A skeletal tree stands alone as the morning
light starts to rise en route to Beinn Loinne

Sunshine on a winter morning above a sea of cloud on Beinn Loinne, with Ben Nevis rising highest amongst a jumble of peaks on the horizon

Boots and artefacts from the 1953 Everest
expedition in the Pen-y-Gwryd Hotel at Llanberis

A sign for the Sherpa bus service, left, but I had to use
a different form of transport after my fall on Tryfan

The inimitable Trevor Walls in a typical pose for the
camera on the rock known as The Cannon on Tryfan

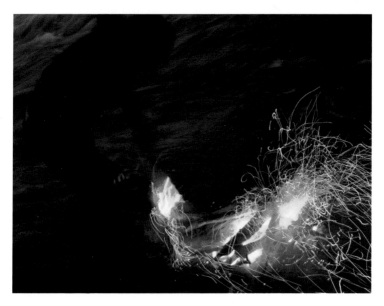

Trevor managing to stoke the party fires
in the middle of a river at Kinlochewe

An assortment of peaks make their morning entrance through
the mists from Beinn a' Bhuiridh in the Cruachan range

Blue skies and brilliant white at an early summit of Sgurr an Utha
with Streap and the Corryhully hills in the background

Above the snowline after an early push up Sguman Coinntich with Skye's Black Cuillin lined up on the horizon, complete with white caps

The view back down Loch Quoich from the summit of the remote
Ben Aden after a long, hot trek to the Rough Bounds of Knoydart

Wellington's Nose, the famous profile of the wonderful
Fuar Tholl catching the sun's rays near Achnashellach

Clear blue sea and skies stretching into the distance from the main summit of beautiful Ben Loyal in the far north

Sgurr Dubh, resplendent in Torridon's autumn grey, towers over the Ling Hut on a late autumn morning

The classic profile of rocky An Ruadh-stac, one of the
most beautiful and graceful Corbetts in the north-west

Cutting a lone figure on the summit ridge of An Ruadh-stac during
a dash over from the neighbouring Munro of Maol Chean-dearg

Peaks of the Flowerdale Forest, Beinn an Eoin and Baosbheinn, stand proud in a stunning landscape of lochans

Rolling mists clear to reveal the waters of Loch Hourn and
the Knoydart hills from the summit ridge of Sgurr nan Eugallt

Dangerous chickens ahead, left, while Rudolf
gets a festive makeover in Sutherland

Rays of early sunlight burst through a sea of grey to
illuminate the summit trig point on snowy Ben Hee

The popular bothy Shenavall which stands in the heart of Fisherfield
below the Corbett twins Beinn Dearg Mor and Beinn Dearg Bheag

Looking down Fionn Loch over Meall Mheinnidh just after
dawn from the climb to the summit plateau of Beinn Lair

The basic shelter at Carnmore in the heart of Fisherfield,
complete with earth floor, cattle skulls and indoor plant life

Above the early cloud on a circuit of the Rum Cuillin,
looking down on Hallival from the highest point, Askival

The safest phone box in the world, left, and a cool
customer watching over drinkers at Kinloch Castle

V for victory as I reach the summit of Beinn Bhuidhe in
Knoydart and the 'compleation' of my Corbetts round

Enjoying a well-earned rest on Beinn Bhuidhe at
long last, high above the waters of Loch Nevis

12
The Eagle and the Fox

A merciful death to start the day; eye
to eye with the master of the skies; the
dark secret of the rhinoceros; a fleeting
encounter with a black adder

THERE are many magnificent sights in the Scottish landscape but
nothing comes closer to making the heart soar than seeing a golden
eagle in full flight.

I have been fortunate enough to have encountered these elusive,
imperious wonders of nature on more than a few occasions: in
Assynt, on the Cruachan peaks, in the Fisherfield Forest and in
Torridon. I was once trailed along part of the Rum Cuillin ridge by
a curious sea eagle patrolling its territory.

Watching these huge birds effortlessly ride the thermals to
rise miles into the sky in a matter of seconds is always a sight
to behold. My most memorable encounter was on the rolling
slopes of An Sidhean, a mountain which sits tucked away in the
heart of the East Monar Forest above the northern shore of Loch
Monar.

The ascent of the 'fairy hill' is reasonably short and the walking
is simple but reaching it is another matter. There are paths coming
in from Strathconon in the north but the approach from the east
means an excuse to travel again through Glen Strathfarrar, our
finest glen. Timing is everything here if you are driving. There
is a locked gate at Inchmore, vehicle access is only allowed on
certain days, and the opening hours vary on a daily and seasonal
basis. Winter hours are often a better bet as you can gain access by

arrangement through the SMC. You can cycle or walk up the glen at any time.

I had driven up to the dam beneath Monar Lodge and then set off for the path which would take me round the house and then along the lochside. As I neared the lodge, I caught a flash of movement in the grass off to my right. Lying on its back was a huge frog, one leg missing and its insides hanging out, yet it was still trying to drag itself along. The flash I had seen was likely a raven. I couldn't just walk on and leave this creature in agony, waiting for the raven to return and finish the job. The only thing to do was put it out of its misery. I looked around and found a boulder. But even knowing this was the merciful thing to do, it's never easy to take that final step. There's always that second when you hope that some revelation will hit you, that you won't need to drop the rock. It didn't and I dropped the rock.

If the frog incident was still preying on my mind, some ten minutes later the scourge of the outdoors drew my attention elsewhere. The path enters a small rocky passage and rises between two rock faces, a perfect place for an ambush – and the midges were waiting.

There was hardly a breath of wind in this enclosed space so there were clouds of the wee buggers just hanging around looking for passing trade. The only consolation was that with the sweat pouring off me they were struggling to get to grips with any juicy bits.

I was only in there a matter of minutes but it seemed longer. Once I pushed out the other side they stayed put, unwilling to venture out into even the slightest breeze.

Now the emptiness of this landscape hit home, the flat grey of the loch stretching some nine miles off into a remote circuit of Munros whose tops were hidden by a bubbling, boiling broth of dark clouds. The path initially follows the shoreline before one branch heads north into even more remote terrain. I followed this until it started turning east, then took to the open hillside, making good progress over a series of grassy rises. Every crest of every hump produced yet another grassy horizon, a seemingly interminable ocean of green and brown, until the fat, squat cairn of grey slates was reached.

Maoile Lunndaidh was prominent in the west, its flat summit ridge less exciting than the Toll a' Choin corrie embraced in its long arms, but the views in every direction lacked reference points, just a rolling sea of nothingness. If there is such a place as the middle of nowhere, then I was in it. It was time to head back to the middle of somewhere.

Then came the moment that lifted the whole frog-killing, midge-ambushed, green and grey trudge out of the gloom and into a day to remember. As I crested a grassy bump at around 1000ft, I became aware of a huge shape gliding in from the left. It was only around 50ft away but moving directly across my eyeline. It was massive, an avian jumbo jet, wings at full stretch and eyes fixed straight ahead as it continued on its silent traverse, a perfect example of power and grace in action. An occasional couple of lazy flaps of the tips of its wings was the only concession to anything that looked like effort.

There was no chance of taking a picture. One second it was there right in front of me, framed against the flat silver-grey surface of the loch, the next it had disappeared over the horizon. It had been a brief encounter, but the awe it inspired was everlasting. To be so close to such an magnificent creature in its natural habitat was a memory to last a lifetime.

This point was reinforced a few years later when I was watching the BBC Winterwatch programme from the Cairngorms. They had specialist camera equipment set up specifically to catch a golden eagle in flight and, despite the mountain of state of the art gear available for two weeks, they only caught a brief glimpse. Sometimes dumb luck is a better bet, and, if that's the case, I must be a real dimwit. I suppose being out on the hills weekly helps the odds. Being on so many peaks in the early hours doesn't harm them either.

At 4 and 5am, the wildlife is newly wakened and not expecting any visitors. You could be forgiven for seeing something akin to a look of surprise on the faces of deer, for instance, when they come across an interloper at that time of day.

In late June 2007, England was suffering some of the worst floods for years with Sheffield and Hull particularly badly hit. On the west coast of Scotland, the country's designated rain belt, the weather was benign, blue skies and the fluffy white clouds you associate more with the opening credits of The Simpsons. I had been busy for a couple of weeks at work, souvenir football pullouts galore after the climax of the SPL season and then the Scottish Cup final, and I needed the chill-out that only a day in the hills could bring.

I was over in the peninsula of Ardgour, hands tight to the wheel as I negotiated the narrow B-road along the side of Loch Linnhe. It has the feel of a bobsleigh run, an impressive line of broken red granite faces and steep gullies on the right and, on the left, only a stone wall preventing a drop-off into the waters below. It may have been night-time but the light was already rising as I parked near Loch a' Choire, an inlet just off the main loch. The targets were the Corbett siblings of Fuar Bheinn and Creach Bheinn. They are the centrepieces of a horseshoe of peaks which enclose Glen Galmadale in a giant pincer movement and from across the loch they stand out prominently against the skyline.

But to reach them, first you have to traverse Beinn na Cille, so with the early sun lighting the slope ahead I started steeply up a mix of grass and rock, taking care to curve round some crags above the roadside. As I entered a chest-high section of ferns, I saw a reddish streak darting through the vegetation. It was a fox, but it was not the usual dirty brown colour normally seen on hill foxes; this one was bright orange and he stood out starkly against the waving green ferns as he tried to put as much distance between me and him as quickly as possible. It's hard to argue there could be any finer sight to start the day. Unless you are a chicken, of course.

The last time I had seen a fox on the hill it wasn't faring so well. On the walk up Meall Tairneachan in Perthshire early one morning I came across the dull, brown carcass hanging from a fence, a wire noose around the neck, its body put there by the farmer as a warning to other members of its clan to stay away.

I was soon at the summit cairn of Beinn na Cille and drinking in the full sweep of the view down Loch Linnhe. The island of Lismore was rising from the mist while the forest of Appin stood to attention. A relatively gentle drop and then a rise on ever-expanding pavements of granite brought me to the top of the 'cold mountain', Fuar Bheinn.

Curiously enough, its partner, Creach Bheinn, is also thought sometimes to refer to a bare, windswept hill. Seeing that most hills are windswept and cold at many times of the year, these two must have been particularly notorious in the Baltic category. With the winds gusting in unchallenged from the south-west, suffice to say they are not the first choice for a summer package holiday. The hills are linked by a broad, featureless col, Chuil Mhain, which could lead you astray in bad conditions but on a clear day there is no problem and a narrowing ridge takes you on to the rocky summit chaos of Creach Bheinn. The alternative translation for this hill is 'spoil' or 'plunder' and refers to the prevalence of cattle rustling in days gone by.

The map draws attention to a camp on the top of this mountain and there are two huge walls of granite blocks and several circles. Some sources suggest these are the remains of a look-out post from the Napoleonic wars, but the truth is much less romantic. They are the leftovers of a camp from a Ordnance Survey military team who were carrying out triangulation work in the 19th century. Such camps were known as Colby Camps, named after the officer who was commander of the OS teams. The nature of the instruments of that time, the need for precise measurements and the unpredictability of the Scottish climate often meant lengthy stays at high altitude of up to three months to get the work completed. This survey programme laid the backbone of the mapping system that has served until recent advances in satellite and electronic distance measurement.

The walls were likely built as windbreaks while the stone circles were the protection foundations for tents. Three of the tent circles lie close together, the fourth is further away and is likely to have been an officer's billet. There's also a small stone shelter, which was a small roofed building housing the guard and cook-house. Whoever got the posting for this mission certainly drew the short straw. They must have spent some cold nights at these heights.

The walk to the next top, Maol Odhar, follows the contours of plunging dark, wet cliffs and then the terrain opens out for the stroll along the Druim na Maodalaich ridge. While approaching Meall nan Each, I saw a figure standing out on the prow of one of the crags. I was convinced it was another walker. He looked about the same height as myself. Then he turned his head in my direction, stepped off the edge, spread his wings and then effortlessly rose in ever decreasing circles until he was about two miles above me. Once again I had the privilege of watching a golden eagle perform its aerial ballet, a Nureyev of the thermals.

So what could top seeing a eagle demonstrating its sovereignty of the skies? A pair of eagles, of course. A friend and I were served up an unexpected birds of prey feast while we were on the Aonach Eagach ridge in Glen Coe. First we caught sight of what we thought was a merlin diving and swooping alongside the pinnacles at high speed. (In one of those moments that could have been from an early Woody Allen film, we bumped into a friend who is a keen twitcher just a few hours later in the chip shop in Tyndrum. He confirmed it was a merlin.)

About an hour further along the ridge, a buzzard sailed past, the languid beat of its wings matching its overall demeanour. This was one chilled-out bird. But the best was kept for last as we sat having a bite to eat at the summit cairn of Sgorr nam Fiannaidh, the final peak on the ridge. From the edge of the little plateau came a golden eagle, wings fully expanded, undercarriage in full view, rising vertically into the air like a massive spaceship slowly revealing its full size, a la Star Wars.

Hot on its tail came a second, the two playfully performing their aerial ballet for a limited audience. Then they spotted us and made a sharp exit, swirling off in tandem in the thermals, heading for the Mamores. The whole performance had lasted just seconds but we gave it a standing ovation.

Those unexpected moments of wonder just add to the experience of being out on the hills. I have always had a keen interest in the natural world, despite the best efforts of my mum. I remember sitting with my family watching a nature documentary about life on the African plains. My mum wasn't really paying attention but as soon as a rhinoceros appeared on the screen, she looked up.

"Oh I don't like them."

"What, rhinos? Why?"

"Horrible things – give me the creeps."

We waited for more – and then she got to the point.

"You know, during the war they killed more British soldiers than the Japanese."

Even at my tender age, I was lost for words.

This was the first time I had heard of a major rhino effort in World War II, and anyway, you never really question your parents when you are that age. Even if you realise they could be borderline insane. I suddenly had visions of squadrons of rhinos parachuting out of planes, storming the beaches and unleashing murderous ambushes in the jungle.

The history books never mentioned the rhinoceros when discussing the Axis powers but now I knew better. It must have been a conspiracy, some secret push to hush up their involvement. Who would donate to a Save the Rhino fund if they knew they were capable of such atrocities?

And it's probably why I didn't do too well in my history exam that year.

Sometimes these moments of animal magic are just too quick, gone in a flash. Unless you are walking around with your camera permanently pointed – and that's not a good idea on a narrow ridge – you are very lucky to capture these precious wildlife encounters. For instance, I still haven't managed to catch a good shot of an adder. During a heat wave many years ago, I came across lots of them basking in the sunshine on the path up to Ben Lomond but discovered when I got home that the film was ruined and nothing had survived.

Then my reflexes were too slow once again when we encountered an almost pure black adder on a track in the Cairngorms. We were en route for Cnap Chaochain Aitinn when we saw what we thought was a twig moving slightly. As we got closer we could see it was a snake, quite a big one, and that the black zig zags on its back were camouflaged by a darker than usual body pigment.

The increasing vibration of our footsteps had alerted it and it started moving off quicker. By the time the camera was in hand, the adder had disappeared into thick heather at the side of the track. Much as I wanted the picture I was not putting my hand in to rummage around. A black adder, but my cunning plan was more Baldrick, and the chance was lost. I later discovered that black adders are not unusual. There are also pure white ones at the other end of the defective pigment scale.

I also missed a photo opportunity with a burrowing owl which burst out from under our feet and took off as we made our way through the peat bog which links the Munros Carn Bhac and Beinn Iutharn Mhor in the Cairngorms, giving us no time to react.

I have seen pine martens a couple of times but again their speed provides only a split second to take the shot. They are stunningly beautiful animals, long sleek bodies with bushy tails and, best of all, a yellow bib. Apart from that they are all teeth and claws.

When we were staying at a house in Glenelg, one of the guys dropped a box of six eggs on the drive while unloading the shopping. When he came out later to clean up, he found he had been beaten to it by our friendly neighbourhood pine marten and the eggs had been licked clean leaving just the six shells. We saw it a few times more after that in the garden at the back of the house, always scurrying around, hoovering up any scraps from the bird table and sometimes even climbing up on the bird table. They are bold creatures and will face down animals much bigger than themselves. A dog who takes on a pine marten is likely to come out of the skirmish badly.

Sometimes they aren't phased by humans. The owner of a guest house in Cannich told me he had gone out to check on his chickens one morning and came face to face with a marten coming out of the henhouse with one of his birds in its mouth. This Chuck Norris of the forest just stood up on its hind legs and looked at him as if to say: "Well, what are you going to do about it?" After a moment's stand-off, the marten trotted off casually with its dinner. Later, it was discovered the pine marten had a stash of half-eaten chickens up in the rafters of the guy's barn.

When we went away on our group trips, we always adopted an animal of the week. So the pine marten at Glenelg became Martin. It may seem to lack invention, but consider this. We once had an editor called Martin whose behaviour was often not so different from our new furry friend, a Tasmanian Devil on speed. One year we had a baby hare, a leveret, so we called him Kenny.

There were even mythical creatures in the mix. One time when we were listing animals we hoped to see, Neil mentioned that there were supposed to be limas in these parts. It was a conversation stopper and he immediately knew it.

"Have I got that wrong?" he asked.

And then: "What am I thinking about then?"

We really weren't sure.

There is a lemur, but these marsupials tend to hail from warmer climes.

There is a puma, mountain lions exclusive to the Americas.

And then there's a ... bean. Or the capital of Peru, but as far as I am aware it has not yet relocated to the north-west of Scotland.

Maybe it's a strange Scottish amalgam of all the above. Anyway from that moment on, the lima was adopted.

And of course, although they are only seen in the desert plains of southern Africa, the honey badger became a favourite one year after we watched a documentary about the toughest animal on the planet and the rest of the group decided its likeness to yours truly was uncanny.

The nickname has stuck but personally I think it's a bad rap. No doubt, the honey badger does too.

13
Ard Day's Night

Moonwalking in the monsoon season;
mines, minerals and Napoleonic riches; a
misty walk in land of the giants; how I managed
to suffer from sunstroke during a Scottish winter

I KNEW it was going to be a difficult day when I saw a Highland cow repeatedly butting a tree. They're normally quite placid beasts, but they can turn, especially if there's a dog around and they have young ones close. This one just looked mental. It was ramming its head into a tree as if trying to put it down for the count. The others were keeping their distance, avoiding this nutcase like drinkers in a pub edging away when someone kicks off.

I was on the other side of the water but I was keeping an eye on this mad cow. I didn't want it thinking I would be an easier target than the gnarled birch it was assaulting.

For once I felt lucky I had got my directions wrong. I had set off in the black of night from Resipole following a track through the farm and past some wooden lodges before crossing a small concrete aqueduct. Somewhere after this, in the trees and the darkness, I had gone off course.

As my eyes adjusted to the dim light, I realised I was on the right bank of the Allt Mhic Chiarain when I should have been on the left. No real worries, I could cross it quite easily. Then I saw the headcase bullock, and decided it might be safer to stay on this side a bit longer. That bit longer lasted for an hour and a half before I got into the higher reaches of the stream and the glen started closing in on both sides. At last

I felt the day was panning out as I had hoped. Then the rain came.

The peaks of Ardgour, Sunart, Moidart and Morvern may not reach Munro height, but they are rough and tough and every bit as much of a challenge. They are also far less busy. No honeypot car parks here. Wandering the hills of these areas is a lonely pastime, especially on midweek days. Most are accessed from the Mallaig road from the north or by making the short crossing on the Corran Ferry just south of Fort William.

The area has a rich mining history and many fortunes were made here. There is a sand mine at Lochaline, which has been operating since 1939, where pure white sandstone is sourced and used to make optical glass. There are said to be some 30 miles of tunnels at this mine. The super-quarry at Glensanda, which sits under Beinn Mheadhoin, is a rich source of granite which is shipped out in huge container ships down Loch Linnhe. Materials from here were used to line the Channel Tunnel.

The history of the mines east of Beinn Resipol dates back to the early 1700s. One of the first shareholders was General Wade, whose roads can still be seen snaking across hillsides all over the country. During the Napoleonic Wars, French prisoners were used to extract lead to be made into bullets. It was also used to re-roof Inveraray Castle. In 1764 there was a new mineral discovery. Strontianite, named after the nearby village of Strontian, produces the element strontium, a yellow metal which is used for fireworks. Production stopped in 1904, but the largest mine was re-opened nearly 60 years later and then again in 1983 for barytes for the oil industry.

If you ascend Beinn Resipol from Ariundle just north of Strontian by the old miners' track, it will take you past some of the abandoned mines. For reasons that now elude me I had decided to approach this standalone hill from the west, and the farm at Resipole. The mountain's name is believed to originate from the

Norse word for farmstead but a Gaelic translation suggests it could be 'cairn above the pool'. If you have the time and can get round the transport enigma, a full traverse on a fine day would be the best option.

I had to wait for the first ferry before I could get over there but I didn't trust myself to go home after work, have a few hours' sleep and then rise refreshed ready for the climb. After all, I just had finished a busy night with Rangers in Euro action against Stuttgart and the next evening would be another late one with Celtic taking on Shakhtar Donetsk at Celtic Park. I went for the less disagreeable option. I left the office and my homeward bound colleagues at the usual witching hour with the idea of grabbing a few hours' rest in the car in Glen Coe.

I pulled into the car park under Buachaille Etive Beag and settled down for a rest. The first thing I noticed was the wind. The car was being buffeted by some vicious gusts. Then it was joined by heavy pulses of rain, sweeping in from the west and striking the windows and body of the car like bullets. This had not been in the forecast. All I had seen was a calm, dull November day.

The noise must have increased during a fitful few hours' nodding off and on because I leapt awake thinking I had been hit by an avalanche. Another one chalked down to the experience of trying to sleep in a rocking car beneath the mountains in winter. I dug my way out of the imaginary pile of snow in the car and set off down to the ferry terminal. The place was a hive of activity in a sea of blackness. Arc lights lit up this little kingdom as the crew prepared for the first sailing and the metallic bangs of the trucks and vans loading on to the boat echoed into the night air.

Duelling currents and washes were picked out from the blackness by the occasional appearance of a moon fighting to be seen, and the sound of the mostly invisible water pushing against the ferry as we made the half-kilometre trip over the Corran Narrows was eerie. A few minutes later and I was disembarking in Ardgour. The road journey round would have taken around an hour. This was money – and time – well spent.

It was still pitch dark when I set off from the farm. Now I was making the final push to the summit in a constant drizzle. It was turning out to be one of these days when it simply refused to get light, and the rain was just adding to the misery. When I hit the cairn at the top, my optimistic half was telling me that it would clear up soon and I would get a view; my pessimistic half was pitching its case for another few hours of gloom. Both turned out to be wrong. It got worse.

After 10 minutes hanging about, I started down, on the right side of the water this time. The rain just kept getting heavier and heavier. The path was overflowing, the water was running over my boots and it was getting in everywhere. I saw a few deer watching me from a stand of trees close by. They looked almost as miserable as I felt. I gave up any pretence of trying to stay dry and surrendered to the elements. It surely wasn't possible to get any wetter.

Of course, I was on collision course with the mad cow but I was now ready to take it on. It may be able to header trees but I had once demolished a coffee table and various other items of furniture with my head, and in my current, drenched, miserable state I was ready for anything. There was no sign of the cows now, though. Maybe they had spotted this angry nutcase rampaging down the path and had done a runner, a role reversal from earlier.

Now there was just the small matter of trying to get changed out of these soaking clothes. But no matter which part of the car I tried to shelter behind, I couldn't get out of the wind and rain. In the end I just jumped in wearing the full wetsuit and drove off to find a more sheltered spot, but the rain kept coming and in places was turning to snow, and I ended up shivering all the way back to Glasgow. I arrived at work in time but with a severe chill and a bad attitude. Five hours' walking in constant rain in the middle of the night will do that.

The irony was that two weeks' earlier I had been in Ardgour on a day that had promised rain but which ended up staying dry despite the constant menace in the air. It had been a year of sequels in the cinema – *Spider-Man 3*, *Pirates of the Caribbean 3*, *Shrek 3*, *Rush Hour 3*, *Fantastic 4* (okay, that's not really a sequel) and the continuing saga of Harry Potter – so I knew I was probably buying a ticket for *Rain 4*.

It had been chucking it for three days and there was to be no let up. It had rained overnight and was forecast to continue not only for the rest of the days but for the two as well. Sections of the drive up had been on part road, part river. So why was I heading out if the weather was this foul? Part of it was down to cabin fever. When the rain is constantly battering the windows and the light outside never seems to change at all, there's only so much a person can take.

I figured that if you can't beat it, join it, so a short hill day was the answer. There was also the thought that if I was going to get wet, I may as well go somewhere nice to be soaked. Just get the full waterproofs on and get going. But as often happens when you throw caution to the wind, or rather, rain, I got lucky. Stob Coire a' Chearcaill was the target but as I prepared to board the ferry to Ardgour, I could hardly make out the hill through the sheets of rain sweeping down on the horizon over the waters of Loch Linnhe.

The short drive north-east to the start of the route at Stronchreggan was accompanied by the patter of rain on the roof and the metronomic sweep of the wipers on the windscreen. I parked up and paused for a minute before taking the plunge. The solitary raindrop that landed on my head as an introduction to the great outdoors turned out to be the last, however. I thought I had caught a break and that this would at least be a little respite. I didn't realise that respite would last for five hours.

I set off into the dripping undergrowth with a purpose. No point in hanging around. If you keep moving it won't find you. I stuck with the path by the raging waters of the Abhainn Sron a' Chreagainn but instead of the perceived wisdom of taking a direct line from the end of the path straight on to the ridge on the right arm of the corrie, I decided to stay low out of the strengthening wind as long as possible. When the walls of the gorge started closing in around me further up I made a short, sharp ascent to the ridge.

I couldn't believe my luck. Not only had the rain stayed away, but the wind had blown the cloud clear and the sun was making a late appearance. It was a short distance to the open summit and although the wind was doing its best to knock me off my feet I was rewarded with open views all the way out west over the Ardgour peaks and east over Fort William where the Ben and its acolytes had made a fleeting appearance. I stuck high to the ridge heading north-west over Braigh Bhlaich before dropping down slopes of thick heather and scattered legions of twisted, bare birch trees, now dried out completely by the wind and sun. I made the next ferry by minutes and was back in Tyndrum before the rain took control again. I had lucked out big-time. I only wished I had put a lottery ticket on for that night.

After the flood, the weather relented and started a major mopping up operation. It was dry and clear, the mornings frosty and calm, a lull before winter got its act together. First light was piercing the horizon as I drove down Glen Torridon at the end of a long journey. It had been another long day of dealing with words and pictures, but there were few words that capture the beauty of my surroundings and few pictures that could do it true justice.

First there was the classic view down into Kinlochewe, lines of mighty mountains framing Loch Maree. Then came Beinn Eighe and the natural blonde screes of its eastern ridges sparkling as the infant rays of sunlight vied with the swirling mists on its flanks. And finally there was Liathach, the leviathan of Torridon, soaring out of the low cloud layer like a mighty sea beast breaking the waves, its air of impregnability looming large.

I left the NTS car park and took the path south past the white walls of the lonely Ling Hut until it ran out and then headed directly up slopes of broken rock to the summit of Sgurr nan Lochan Uaine, the 'peak of the green lochs'. Unfortunately, the mist which had contributed to the atmospheric light show on the drive in had since called in reinforcements and followed me up the mountain, so I only had rare glimpses of the little bodies of water which are strung out like pearls dropped amongst the bare Torridonian rock.

It stayed with me for the 2.5 kilometre walk over complex mix of water, rock and crag which lead to the second Corbett, Sgurr Dubh. The silent gloom was broken only by the echoing of moving stones under my feet. At one point I came face to face with a small female deer drinking from a pool just metres away, neither of us aware of the other's presence until the last minute.

The pull up to Sgurr Dubh was less a path, more a high-stepping rise over rubble, but it was short and fast. I didn't hang about – the mist wasn't going anywhere – so I retraced my steps for a bit and then picked up the stalker's path leading down to Coulin Lodge where there were few signs of life. I crossed the bridge and took the track north along the shores of Loch Clair to the main road, the waters lying still and untroubled, a November day in repose.

December arrived and the first real snow had given the hills an undercoat, priming them for the fuller paint job to follow. I had a brief day out on home territory in Glen Doll but retreated from the slopes of Crow Craigies above Jock's Road, after becoming tired of the constant battle against the icy wind and deep snow.

A week later I was heading west into the blackness for the Corran Ferry once again, this time with the promise of a sensational day. We were locked in a high pressure system and even the bitter cold of night and icy roads couldn't dent my confidence as I drove to Strontian. Sgurr Dhomhnuill is the highest peak in Ardgour and is the centrepiece of a vast swathe of land that was ruled by the Clan Donald. The naming of the peak in this manner suggests confidence in their power and influence, a defiance that even the might of the king couldn't challenge.

The initial cold on the approach walk was quickly dispersed by the brilliance of the sun in a clear blue sky. I followed the nature trail from Ariundle through mixed oak and birch woodland, coming out of the trees beside a cluster of disused mine shafts. Sgurr Dhomhnuill sits at the junction of two long rocky arms and my plan was to ascend by the right hand ridge of Dreac Leac a' Sgiathan and then drop down the left-hand one, the Druim Garbh. The snow was still lying thick on the tops and the run-off from the lower slopes made the river crossing a problem which took me some 15 minutes to overcome.

I dodged round the rock faces which formed the prow of the ridge by a steep, grassy gully and then cut back left on to the true line. There were a lot of ups and downs on the way to the subsidiary peak of Sgurr na h-Ighinn but no problems. The descent from here provided a bit of sport though, a tricky route down a steep rake in deep snow, before I emerged at the col and made the final push to the main summit.

The walk had an Alpine feel to it; clear air and snow-capped peaks, a view that seemed to stretch forever and the sun beating down relentlessly on slopes of pure white snow. Beautiful, certainly, but I wasn't too confident about the snowy descent on to the next ridge. I decided to quit while the going was good and head back the same way. With weather like this I planned to go out again the following night but as often is the case, you pay the price for being greedy.

I endured the office ribaldry about my amazing overnight suntan but instead of being able to head out again when I finished work, I spent the night alternating between shivering uncontrollably in my bed and bending over the toilet bowl being violently ill.

I had managed to get sunstroke in Scotland in December.

The month counted down the days benignly providing more opportunity to rack up ticks. A bright but freezing morning saw me deep in Strathconon, a cautious drive on a tarmac ice rink, watching for the patches of road hidden in shadow which could provide a sudden and violent parting of the ways. The low sun had turned the high tops on each side of the glen orange but far down below the path heading from the bridge at Inverchoran was trapped in cold storage. Trees took on the role of icicles with glistening pure white crystals set solid, the grass crunched and snapped with every step and passage over the little side stream meant teetering on any piece of rock or vegetation which sat partly free of the thick ice.

Staying out of the shadows was essential for any fast progress and from the summit ridge of Bac an Eich I could relax and peer down on the frozen glens which remained smothered by a thick white blanket of icy mist.

For once the Gaels and the Norsemen found themselves in some sort of agreement here as the name 'bank of the horse' appears to derive from both languages. The grass here would have proved an attractive proposition to the free-running herds. The horseshoe ridge of the mountain was bathed in yellow and orange but the loch pinned in between showed a pale snake slithering up the centre of the water where the ice was beginning to settle in for the next few months.

It was late morning when I arrived back at the car but the conditions hadn't shifted an inch. The sun wouldn't reach these lower spots until spring made a reappearance.

A day before we had said goodbye to the old year and I was even further afield in the freezing conditions, a long journey of more than four hours beyond Inverness on the A9 then a convoluted series of switches west from Bonar Bridge into the mountain country at the heart of Easter Ross. Glen Calvie provided a good track for a rime-coated walk beside the river and Carn Chuinneag sat dead ahead drawing me onwards, its twin peaks dominating the horizon. For such a remote and unheralded mountain though, it was remarkably busy, as if suffering from some kind of post-Christmas rush.

As I reached the house at Diebidale where the track changes course, I noticed a party probably using the house for a festive holiday. There was something bizarre in seeing groups sitting round picnic tables with food and drink in the middle of nowhere on December 30.

A good stalker's path skirts along the western side of the hill then cuts back sharply on to the ridge just below the lower of the two summits. The trig point and surrounding cairn held a fair depth of snow and even the nearest mountains seemed far distant from this lonely summit. I met one walker coming down this path near the start and then later on my way down from the main summit, two or three parties, including three people who had somehow ended up on the wrong mountain. Considering its distance from any other hill of note, that was a fair achievement.

14
Winter Wanderland

*Shimmering peaks, timid birds and tragic
damsels; stepping into the world of Ansel
Adams; how one metre makes a world of
difference; chirpy, chanting sheep sheep*

I EMERGED from the freezing February mist looking like I'd been locked in a meat storage locker for 12 hours. I suppose in some ways I had – sleeping in a car for a few hours at this time of year can be similar.

I had arrived at the car park near the Cluanie Inn around 4am and tried to settle down for a few hours' rest before heading off up Beinn Loinne, the long hill which resides between Loch Cluanie to the north and Loch Loyne to the south. There were a few hours of darkness left and the thick, icy mist had settled all the way down to road level. Nothing stirred, nothing could be seen, just a wall of grey that had swallowed the land.

Two hours of attempted sleep had been in vain, the cold was simply too much. I was trying to hypnotise myself into thinking I was back in my warm bed. It didn't work, no trance of success. Now I was just miserable. It was time to get going, mist or no mist.

It may seem unlikely but I failed to see the track leading from the main road. In normal conditions it is obvious, but these weren't normal conditions. This was a real pea-souper, only it was in deep freeze mode. I had to turn back and on my return I found the track. Ten minutes wasted walking down the road in zero visibility, not another soul around.

I could feel the icy particles settling on me, crackling, turning me pure white like the Terminator when he is engulfed in liquid nitrogen. But as I gained height on the track, the mist was left behind and the light was beginning to make its presence felt. The higher I rose the warmer it got. I came to a lone tree, its skeletal branches rising up from the dark into the light. Streaks of orange, red and pink lit the sky as a backdrop, a sea of icy grey beneath. Suddenly this dead tree looked alive, burning in the warm colours emerging on the horizon. Another 10 minutes, another tree. This one looked like a more robust version of the first, as though it had wakened and decided to get dressed, donning foliage recently lost for the season. The peaks on the north side of Glen Shiel were now poking their heads above the sea of cloud as if testing whether it was time to come out. Meanwhile, I had regained my colour, the rime evaporating in the early sunshine.

By the time I reached the high point of the track it was hard to believe it was February. It was 7.30am and the mist had retreated to cover the surfaces of the lochs, leaving the mountains to rise and shine. I now faced a trek across boggy ground to reach the ridge but my task was helped by the freeze. The terrain was solid and I crunched my way over confidently, until I reached the final rise. The trig point which marks the highest point stood out starkly on the skyline, a pencil of concrete amid a jumble of low rocks and stones.

Beinn Loinne is more a ridge than a hill, and its correct name, Druim nan Cnamh, reflects that. It means 'ridge of the bone or spine', a reference to the exposed rocks along its length which give resemble the vertebrae of the spine. Beinn Loinne is the name given to highest point. It comes from the word 'loinn' which means to shimmer, from the same origins as Loch Loyne, and suggests the rock shining along its flanks after the rain.

It was certainly shining and shimmering in every direction from the summit. Most of Scotland seemed to be visible over an ocean of fluffy cloud. It had changed from the depths of winter to full suntan weather in a matter of hours. A deck chair wouldn't have been out of place here, the light of the sun being made even more brilliant by the reflection from the cloud.

Off to the south Ben Nevis stood tallest, a light dusting of snow, lording it over the whole range. To the north the mountain chains seemed to run on forever. It seemed a shame when I had to head back down. The icy fog was still holding its ground but the intensity had diminished – it would gradually fade to nothing over the next couple of hours leaving behind a lovely day. As I descended I heard a loud buzzing sound. Out of the mist came a mini-copter, the local stalker's way of getting around. Also coming out of the mist was another walker. For once, he didn't appear startled or draw conclusions as to my possible mental state. He seemed genuinely impressed by my early start.

I thought I had just got lucky with the weather. Little did I know that we were in for a whole series of inversions over the next few weeks.

Once again the Scottish winter had kicked summer's ass, and the next week it gave me the opportunity to go for it again. I did a 3am run to Braemore junction on the road to Ullapool. It was a cautious drive; the roads were icy and I felt the car sliding at one or two points. There were a couple of stops on the way – the constant pressure of clutching the wheel tightly was taking its toll.

It should still have been dark when I started walking but the clear sky and early sun gave enough light to hoodwink the eyes. The muddy path which runs round to Home Loch was icily solid, crunching with every step. I got a reminder of the true time of year, a cold chill suddenly biting as I vanished into the shadows behind Meall Doire Faid, but I was soon back into sunshine and got up a good sweat on a direct line north up the slopes of Beinn Enaiglair.

As I rose, I noticed out of the corner of my eye a split-second movement to my right. A deer. I looked closer. There was another, then another. By the time the heads had all risen on alert I had counted around 50. They were all perfectly blended with the brown vegetation. A few seconds earlier I hadn't noticed any. If that one hadn't raised its head I would probably have walked on past oblivious to their presence.

The summit area was bathed in gold. This was the sort of brilliant light which would have the sun reaching for a pair of shades. Loch Broom was a shining blue patch in the terrain, the whites of the houses in Ullapool glowing specks. I had the Beinn Deargs, the Fannaichs and mighty An Teallach as companions but the view spread much further.

Beinn Enaiglair is the 'hill of timid birds' but the reasons why these creatures should be so particularly fearful on this hill is steeped in mystery. There was a distinct lack of any kind of birdlife here today, so no chance of asking any why they had been geographically called a bunch of chickens.

This stunning weather pattern was about to wave goodbye but there was one last chance to get out before the normal winter patterns resurfaced. Five days after my Ullapool run, I was heading even further afield. Fisher-afield to be precise. Any venture in here is going to be a long one. The distances needing to be covered mean it's not ideal for fast raids but it's the perfect area for night walking, long approaches to remote peaks on good paths and the sunrises always seem to throw up something different. A full circuit of the peaks here can take you from the dead of night through the wakening and fast-changing moods of the morning; from the heat of midday to the shadows of late afternoon; from the gradual dying of the light at sunset and back into darkness.

Millions of pinpricks of light sparkled like glitter in the sky and the moon dipped its wide beam into Loch Maree, casting a spreading white searchlight on the water. On the other shore of the loch, the fortress of Slioch stood tall, a dark citadel to rival any from Lord of the Rings, its satellite peaks just shadow shapes bowed in the presence of a greater force.

I set off from the car park at the hamlet of Poolewe, picking up a good pace on the tarred road which breaks you in for the first few miles. Once it turns past Inveran, the track becomes rougher, stonier, and the trick is to watch out for a cairn which marks a shortcut over open ground to save a huge loop in the track. I was now high above the shoreline, captivated by the rising sun spreading over the landscape, rendering the Torridon peaks so many contrasting depths of blue and defining the myriad of tree-covered islands in the foreground as mere blemishes on the water. The effect was so hypnotic that I missed another cairn marking the turn-off to Beinn Airigh Charr, my objective for the day. The loss of 20 minutes was a small price to pay for such a view.

A quick change into reverse gear and I was following the excellent path east and to the gateway to the mountain between the guardian twins of Meall Chnaimhean and Spidean nan Clach. Like all the best engineered stalkers' paths, this seemed to be leading me away from my target but then, keeping to the best line for ease of ascent, cleverly swung back between these two rocky bastions. I was now in a hollow of boulder chaos but the quiet on entering this arena is reminiscent of walking into a cathedral. It would make a great camping spot. The main summit is now just a short push away. This sharp rocky peak is another wonderful wilderness breakfast perch; Loch Maree and Torridon to the south-west, the Fisherfield Munros to the north-east and Beinn Lair and Slioch in a direct line to the south-east. But the most breathtaking view is north, a vast expanse of empty land, studded with lochans and bare rock, stretching, it feels, into infinity.

Beinn Airigh Charr is the 'hill of the rough shieling' and is associated with cattle herding in summers gone by. On the north face of the mountain is Martha's Peak, a rock tower so-named for the young woman who is said to have fallen to her death while tending her cattle.

I must have sat there for over an hour.

Winter was proving to be the perfect hunting season for Corbetts. Their slightly lower elevation often made the difference between reaching a summit or having to turn back. I had never had to bail out on a Corbett, but it had happened on a few Munro days. By chasing both at the same time, I had decided to go big for them in the winter and leave the long summer days for the Munros reprise.

By the time I had ticked off all the Corbetts, my list was almost an opposing variation of my first Munros round. Whereas May, June, August and September had seen me rack up the majority of the 3,000-footers, the winter months were where my Corbetts tally really took off. For instance, I had climbed 24 in January, compared to just four Munros. February provided an even starker contrast, 26 compared to just one. But September was a mere ten compared with 45 Munros, and June saw less than half my Munro tally, 36 compared to 75.

Doing the lists in tandem was allowing more flexibility, a method I have employed since, but now it's the lower Grahams and Donalds which have a big role in my winter adventures.

Beinn Airigh Charr had given me a grand day out which I probably would not have managed on one of the bigger Fisherfield peaks. It seemed strange to be enjoying the novelty of sunbathing at this height in February while the norovirus was rampaging round the country. There was also the realisation that tomorrow would bring a return to cold, wet conditions and that was helping keep me sitting tight until I really had to move.

By the time I was heading home from the office that night, the sleety rain was driving in from the west on a strong wind. The winter summer was over it seemed.

About a week later I was out on two Perthshire Munros in icy weather, treacherous ground that had held the water, a minefield of frozen booby traps. It was hard work with the crampons, one minute they were biting into the terrain, the next they were sinking in churned-up grass and mud which needed cleaned off before you hit the next hard spot. The soles of my feet were tender that night.

Then the snows arrived, back from their summer holiday with much work to do. Closed roads and avalanche danger meant chances to get out were few and far between, the price we had to pay for such a glorious spell. Once it settled down, there was a fabulous long day in the Fannaichs in deep snow with soaring, ice-crystallised crests throwing off a blinding light from the low sun, creating a surprise heat in landscapes that would have made the American landscape photographer Ansel Adams green with envy.

By the time April arrived, the elements were in a constant battle for supremacy, shifting daily if not hourly. Then came the big melt and I saw a chance to get back on the Corbetts trail. However, I was keen to hedge my bets. Instead of a midnight start, I went for the harder option and went back to my flat to grab a few hours' sleep.

More often than not, this tactic ended in abject failure. The prospect of getting out a warm bed after a few hours' nap to head off into the dark night was always on a knife-edge. This time I made it, probably because the torrential downpour pounding on my window had kept me awake.

I set off towards Corran at 4.30am with the monsoon still at its height. Have faith, the weather forecasters will come through. The forecast for next morning was good. And it did change. By Tyndrum the rain had disappeared and I was driving in a white-out, the wipers struggling to cope with the onslaught of snow, the road somewhere ahead. But just as predicted, by the time I hit Glen Coe the snow had gone off and the night was turning. The only problem was that the snow had held me up and it was now a race against time to get the ferry at 6.30am. I made it with a minute to spare.

Fifteen minutes later I was heading along a rough farm track from Sallachan. Well, the track was merely a rough guide to my direction of travel. It was mostly under water and I spent most of my approach in the soaking grass and mud at the sides. Ahead on my right was Beinn na h-Uamha. I could only make out its lower slopes, the higher parts still covered in snow and wrapped in a blanket of cloud rendering it invisible in the merging of two white horizons. The contrast made it look as though a giant had lopped off everything in the landscape above 1500 feet.

I managed across the river comfortably thanks to my waders and then it was initially a slip-slide ascent on mud and grass with the water running everywhere. The terrain changed and I found myself going up a series of rocky gullies, picking a careful route ahead. It seemed to take an eternity. Once I felt I was heading off the side of the mountain.

The cloud had risen with me most of the way but then set up camp just at the summit cairn so any vista remained hidden. The plethora of caves that give the mountain its name are on the rocky north face but there was no chance of seeing them anyway. Had the visibility been better I may have been tempted to continue along the ridge to the twin peak of Sgurr a' Chaorainn. It sits at 761 metres compared to Beinn na h-Uamha's 762 metres but that throws it into a different mountain category, a Graham instead of a Corbett, failing to reach a dizzier height by virtue of one metre. That metre doesn't make much of a difference in the effort needed to reach it but those are the vagaries of mountain lists.

It would also have pulled me a long way from my starting point and, combined with complicated rocky slopes, possibly cost me a lot of time and anxiety. I had to stick to my original timescale – work was calling.

A mere two days later the now settled conditions tempted me out again, back up the same road but this time carrying on further to Glen Roy, near Spean Bridge. I left at 1am, had an hour's rest in Glen Coe and then another hour at the viewpoint car park in Glen Roy. I was wakened by the sound of what I thought was a football crowd chanting: "Who are ya, who are ya?" A quick check confirmed I wasn't in the Bernabeu and then I was out of the car to find the source of this baffling sound. It turned out to be a flock of sheep, bleating as one, the noise carrying across the glen at this early hour.

The sun was washing over the Parallel Roads, the two glaciated scars which cut in straight lines across the mountainsides. They are terraces formed by ice-dammed lakes thousands of years ago but from afar they resemble man-made roads. Carn Dearg was the first objective, and I had to make sure I got the right one. After all, there are three peaks up this glen with that name. There are also two called Leana Mhor. It seems that whoever was in charge of naming duties was having a lazy day. Thank goodness the other hill was called Beinn Iaruinn. I was often confused enough with these early starts. It was an easy double, enlivened by the massive cornices wrapped around the ridgelines, and I was back, showered and at my desk for 3pm, ready for all the nonsense the world of sport could throw at me for the next ten hours.

The Deargs thing was obviously still floating around in my subconscious because just four days later I was on another one, this time the Munro Beinn Dearg. That wasn't the main target though. I needed to get to Beinn Bhreac, a remote Corbett a long way in from Blair Atholl. It's 18 kilometres to the summit over a swathe of featureless ground and there's no real time to be saved on the return journey. It's a big, committing day whichever way you look at it.

But including Beinn Dearg in the expedition doesn't add any more time to the day and it saves a return to climb this on its own. The addition of Dearg meant I was able to persuade a Munro-bagging friend to join me. It took us more than five hours to reach Beinn Bhreac but that included a lunch break at the Allt Sheicheachan bothy. The route descended into an exercise in dodging booby traps hidden by snow and bog on the featureless terrain from the end of the Allt Beinn Losgarnaich but despite the snow melt, the crossing of the Tarf Water proved no problem.

The summit came as a bit of disappointment. I always feel that when you have expended so much time and effort to climb a mountain there should be more of a reward, but this distant lump didn't even put out the bunting.

We ascended the deeply covered snow slopes on the northern side of Beinn Dearg and our pace slowed dramatically, the blazing sun, the deep snow and the effects of the strength-sapping terrain covered so far now taking its toll. It was two weary walkers who arrived back at the car 11 hours after starting out.

The prospect of climbing all the Skye Munros in five days seemed like a picnic after that. If I had struck it lucky with the February heat wave, this was the jackpot. A full week in Skye, Mediterranean-style sunshine all the way. And I had managed to fit in one more Corbett, Meall Dubh, en route. Even the vandalism perpetrated on the northern side of this hill by the construction of a monstrosity of a wind farm couldn't spoil the moment. Well, almost.

15
Wizards and Lost Soles

Solitude under multi-coloured skies; into
the heart of a forest with no trees; why
water filter proved a hard sell; agony
as my feet were turned to sausage meat

WHEN it comes to being laid up by injuries, I count myself relatively fortunate. The fall in Wales kept me out of action for three months, but that was mainly a reluctance to put myself back out in the hills too quickly for fear of a relapse. In truth, it was only a two-week lay-off.

I've had a couple of close things – once on Buachaille Etive Mor when an earth shelf collapsed under my feet and another on an icy circuit on Arran – and niggling knee and Achilles problems which have never amounted to any long-term gaps in my mountain plans.

Once while chasing down the last few remaining peaks of my second Munro round, I managed to do a long day in Glen Affric with a heavily strapped knee and ankle and a liberal dose of painkillers. They must have been good – I was sitting at the summit of An Socach watching little bunnies dancing in a circle while holding hands as clouds of pink candy floss drifted lazily across the sky.

The nearest I came to a long absence was caused by a clash with a coffee table in my flat. I had got up in the middle of the night to head for the kitchen for a drink of water. My flatmate Jim couldn't sleep well if there was any light showing through so had blackout curtains in the living room. As I went from my light bedroom to the pitch-dark of next door, I collided painfully with the table, and, as strong drink had been taken, a fight ensued. I got my drink, went back to bed and thought no more of it until I woke up next morning.

My leg was throbbing and there was blood all over the bed sheets. The coffee table hadn't fared well either, it was in bits. I had to visit the company doctor next day as the pain got worse and she said I was lucky my leg wasn't broken. I had cut it to the bone. But nothing prepared me for the excruciating pain of losing the skin off the soles of my feet. After that experience, I've decided I can never again watch the scene in *Midnight Express* where Brad Davis gets his soles paddled by a prison guard.

It all came as a bolt from the blue. We had just come off the back of an unlikely Mediterranean week in Skye doing the island's 12 Munros and with the sun continuing to shine I was running round ticking off peaks right, left and centre. My fitness was good, the weather exemplary and I was seeing the best of Scotland. A laidback midnight drive along the Mallaig road with me joining Eric Burdon and War for a rendition of 'Low Rider' seemed appropriate. I was so chilled out that I managed a couple of hours' nap in the car park before setting off up the track at Callop by the whispering waters of the Allt na Cruaiche.

Work on a new hydro scheme meant I had to take to rougher ground but I was treated to a blazing pink, red and purple sky on the horizon, which stretched over the deep V of the mountain silhouettes ahead. My target was Stob a' Bhealach an Sgriodain and to reach it I had to climb over one bealach then drop into lonely Cona Glen.

The river crossing here can be a problem but dry conditions meant dry feet and I was soon climbing back up steep grassy slopes alongside a deep rent, filled with a shambles of dark rocks and trees clinging on to their precarious footholds for dear life on the weeping walls.

The tiny cairn on the summit of the 'peak of the pass of screes' is perhaps a fitting representation of the few visitors who make their way here. Solitude is the watchword, a light breeze my only companion, and a walk out to the end of the Druim Tarsuinn ridge gives a splendid view over the long, narrow confines of Loch Shiel to the innards of Moidart, while the long track of the Cona Glen snakes off to the horizon in the east.

The return journey took on the feel of a new expedition with the sun casting long shadows and picking out golden highlights in the grass and heathers.

A few days later and I was off to Torridon, straight after work. By the time I was heading up the side of Loch Maree, the light was rising and the mountains taking shape either side of the water. The fortress of Slioch is best seen from this road, its seemingly impregnable ramparts offering no comfort to those looking for a way up while the sprawling Beinn Eighe and its white caps dominated the landscape on the left. The road leaves the shores of the loch behind just after the cluster of islands are reached and swings round towards Gairloch.

I found the Red Barn, despite it being cunningly painted green, and set off on a good path south-east straight into the heart of the Flowerdale Forest. You may reckon you have a case under the Trades Descriptions Act here and in the adjoining Shieldaig Forest because there is a distinct lack of trees. In fact, a game of Spot the Tree could prove a frustrating pastime such is the absence of greenery. Robin Hood would not have been impressed.

Instead, the walker is faced with a succession of granite walkways, pale red and split like crumbling cheese, which provide easy progress on the pull up to Beinn an Eoin. The western slopes of the 'mountain of the bird' are ferociously steep and the view down into the glacial pool of Loch na h-Oidhche feels almost vertical. Its lofty stance makes it easy to see how this hill could be associated with eagles or other birdlife.

Across the trench sits the second Corbett of the day, the wonderfully alluring Baosbheinn. Local knowledge suggests it means 'hill of the face' due to its resemblance to a human head when the morning light catches the craggy end of the ridge to the north-east. But the more romantic among us prefer 'wizard's hill' and all the connotations that throws up. This can also be taken to refer to a soothsayer, a witch, a fairy or a wicked person. Nothing like covering all the bases.

I dropped down steeply from Beinn an Eoin on loose slopes, one of the most vertiginous scree runs I've ever done, but it was always controlled and if I ever felt the momentum was building too much I could run to the side and put the brakes on. Within minutes I was at the locked, private bothy of Poca Buidhe and the head of the loch. The route over to Baosbheinn took me through a series of channels between small lochans and then a gradual rise north-east, bouncing upwards on granite spreads.

The ridge is a typically Torridon rollercoaster; pancake stacks of rocks sitting at chaotic angles, dark hollows plunging into deep shadow and stony paths leading over a series of peaks, narrow at times, big drops off to one side or the other at regular intervals. The summit is a curious affair, a cairn sitting in a cleared circle of yellow grass, like someone had erected this pile of stones in the aftermath of a meteor strike or a mini nuclear explosion. The flatness of the summit area also draws a line over the view into the back corries of Liathach and Beinn Eighe, cutting off any feeling of depth. There's still a way to go along this ridge though, more up and down with sparkling waters all around, and coming off the end of the ridge needs a bit of care.

After a good night's rest and recreation at the Old Inn at Gairloch, I was off early to scale Beinn Damh and, in common with its neighbours, there's a superb path all the way from start to finish. It leaves the lodges at the Torridon Hotel, pushes through a stand of rhododendron and mixed woodland before topping out on open ground above a waterfall which roars down to the roadside. It has cuteness in abundance.

The sun was still shining but the wind had picked up, pushing me along at times, trying to push me over at others, and there was also a distinct nip in the air. The 'stag mountain' puts many a higher hill to shame, its long rocky spine is surrounded by deep trenches of sparkling water and some of Scotland's most majestic peaks. The view north over Upper Loch Torridon to Beinn Alligin is particularly fine. Even the large cairn which marks the summit aims for the dramatic, sitting right at the edge of a very deep hollow. The mountain can be approached from this direction as well, a steep scramble up Stuc Toll nam Biast, which allows a good circuit combining both routes. Immediately below the summit is the 'stirrup mark', a band of light rock which breaks the continuity of the sheet of grey screes pouring down the face.

A few days later and I was back in the north-west trying to mop some more of the lone peaks before meeting up with a group of friends for a weekend near Ullapool.

We were bang in the middle of Euro 2008 but as neither Scotland nor England were involved it was all pretty low-key at work. Wayne Rooney was also taking advantage of the break and was getting married in Italy that weekend. For some reason my invitation had not yet arrived so I decided I would just head for the hills instead. His loss. Just think what he could have bought with that £20 Argos voucher.

Glas Bheinn, just north of Inchnadamph off the tourists' favourite A984 to Kylesku, is one of those hills that no one pays much attention. Even the name 'grey hill' suggests it would be left sitting unattended in the corner at parties, but it has a few surprises up its sleeve. Tucked away at the back of this neglected hill, amidst a riot of little lochs and a jumble of rock and bog, is Britain's highest waterfall, the Eas a' Chual Aluinn, which tumbles down over precipitous cliffs to feed into Loch Glencoul. And standing proudly beyond that is the Stack of Glencoul, a stripped-back wedge of rock which struts its stuff like a Chippendale.

The day hadn't properly wakened, the grey still languishing at a low level, but it seemed to suit the landscape perfectly. By the time I was at the upper reaches of the back corrie, I was glad to see it had stayed that way. The stepped lochans which resided on every contour stood out grimly against the bare rock, the lustre of the grass had been toned down to match the water, and the road disappeared like an old snail trail off into the distance. Sunshine would only have ruined the mood.

Glas Bheinn is an afterthought on the long-reaching arms of the Conival and Ben More Assynt massif. Their vast bulk filled the sky to the south-east, while west the triple-headed Quinag lay dulled by the low cloud which sat just above its roof.

Mission accomplished, I charged back down to the car, passing a couple heading out to the waterfall. This is an area which demands further exploration but it would have to wait for another day. I had part two of my mountain menu to devour. A short drive back down the A837, a spot of lunch in the car and I was ready to take on Canisp.

This is another hill where Gaelic and Norse clash. Can is an old Gaelic word for white, a possible reference to the white quartzite seen on its north face. But it could also come from the Norse 'kenna ups' which refers to the shape of a house roof. The verdict seems to come down in favour of the Gaelic, so take that, Ole Gunnar Solksjaer et al.

Unfortunately, the sky had slowly changed from nice grey to not so nice grey, and I was accompanied by a steady drizzle on the long rising ascent to the summit. Still, two separate hills in one day and I was going well. Just as well – next up was the remote Carn Ban, deep in the Freevater Forest.

This is the biggest trek for any one Corbett, some 27 miles round trip on the southern approach. It takes a lot of stamina and

a lot of fluid. I was carrying eight litres of juice and water, a lot
of extra weight. I also carried tablets to purify my water bottles so
that I could fill up from streams. They did the job but the chemical
taste they left in the mouth was foul. These days I use a water filter
which means you can reduce the amount to carry to virtually zero.

I could have been using one years ago. A friend who ran a shop
selling hill gear once tried to persuade me to buy one.

"They're brilliant, they filter out everything. You won't need
these awful tablets."

Maybe so, but the price seemed a bit excessive at the time. I
expressed my reservations.

Then he brought out the sales pitch which clinched the deal. At
least it clinched the fact that there was to be no deal. He held up a
bottle of water with a filter attached. There was something floating
in the water. Something unpleasant.

"Is that . . ?"

"Sheep shit," he finished for me. "See, I can drink straight from
the bottle and it will be perfectly safe."

It's a hard sell. Besides, who has sheep shit at hand to try to sell
water filters. I began to think that it wasn't perfectly safe, that it had
affected his judgement over the years. Or maybe he just liked to
that flavour of water. Either way, I passed.

You can also come at Carn Ban from Strath Mulzie in the north
but that's also a long way. I set off from Black Bridge in the dark.
I was feeling confident. The first couple of miles are on a tarmac
road, then the track dissolves into grass and mud for a mile or so
before it emerges just above Strathvaich Lodge changing to a long,
straight stretch of rubble running alongside Loch Vaich for the
next seven or eight miles. Then it swings round into Gleann Beag
where you follow it for another three miles – and that's just to get
to the start of the climb.

The weather forecast was favourable so I decided to go with a
pair of lighter boots. That was my big mistake. I suppose if I was

looking for omens that all was destined to end badly then the sight of a stag lying on its back with all four legs stiffly rising straight up in the air would have sufficed. It had certainly ended badly for this monarch of the glen. He looked like a museum exhibit that had fallen out of a plane.

I took the path which climbed steeply up from the main track in Gleann Beag to Loch Sruban Mora. I had come 12 miles and I still hadn't seen another soul, but so far it hadn't seemed like I was in the middle of nowhere. The Land Rover tracks suggested civilisation, a vehicle likely to come round the corner at any moment. Now, on the rough shores of the little loch, with the skies turning darker and the wind picking up, I had that feeling of being miles from any help.

The angle of the vegetated slopes ahead was easy but the walking felt interminable. Every rise brought another horizon, a giant grassy stairway with no end, every step felt laboured, the lack of any path dragging me down. Eventually, the terrain levelled out to moss, earth and stones and I reached the summit cairn. My hopes of the consolation of seeing Seana Bhraigh were dashed. There were no views in any direction, just a grey line above a green line, no undulations, no contours. Members of the Flat Earth Society would have loved it. I had taken just over five hours, walked 13.5 miles, to stand at a pile of stones in a level field. Now I had that same distance to get back.

Well, at least it was dry. Emphasis on the word 'was'. Just as I hit the track in Gleann Beag the heavens opened, a rainstorm of biblical proportions, sheets of water wiping out my vision. I was out in the open, not even a tree or a big rock I could use to deflect some of the watery fury. It went off for a bit – and then it came on again. This pattern repeated for the next three hours. I was soaked, every bit of gear had been penetrated. Worst of all were my boots. My feet were swimming around trying to keep afloat but every step was a squelch. I stopped at one point and wrung out my socks. I wish I had been able to wring out my boots.

I was only about an hour from the car when the most excruciating pain shot up through the sole of my left foot. I thought at first something sharp had burst through my boot and pierced my foot. I couldn't put any weight on it. This was going to be a slow hobble back. Then a similar pain shot through from the bottom of my other foot. Now I couldn't put either down without being in agony. I sat down and examined my boots. They seemed fine, soaking wet, but otherwise unbroken. I didn't want to take them off in case I couldn't get them on again.

I was still three miles from the car. That walk was the most painful three miles of my life. Every step felt like someone was shoving red-hot blades into my soles. The relief when I reached the car and was able to sit down was immense. The problem would be pressing the pedals. It was only a couple of miles to the hotel, but it felt like forever. I hobbled in, eased off my boots and gingerly peeled off my socks. The outer layer of skin covering the soles of both feet had separated entirely from the next layer. It looked like I had sausage skins on my feet – and the colour underneath was the colour of raw sausage meat.

My next mistake was reckoning a soothing bath would help matters. As soon the water touched the raw skin I was on fire. I was out of the bath in seconds. I put on antiseptic cream and bound both feet as firmly as I could. I now looked and walked like a geisha but at least the pain was subsiding and I could move around. So I moved around to the bar to enjoy a few painkillers.

The rest of the group turned up about an hour or so later ready for a weekend in the hills. I had to break the news that due to a serious lack of feet I wouldn't be joining them.

The skin welded itself back within a couple of days but it would have been foolish to have ventured out too soon. Ten days later, though, I was back on the horse (had I really had a horse I don't suppose this would have happened in the first place). The hill I chose for my return? Beinn a' Chaisteil, a Corbett above

Loch Vaich which I had passed on my ill-fated trip to Carn Ban. That meant walking five miles along the same track that had contributed to the destruction of my feet, but I was determined to show it who was boss. You could only assume I wanted to punish myself further for my stupidity.

I finished work before midnight having just watched Spain's fancy footwork ensure they become Euro champions with victory over Germany. I would need some fancy footwork of my own on this first walk since my soles had reattached themselves. But this time out I wore double socks and heavy boots, and I started at 3am in darkness.

I may have had to walk the same road but that didn't mean I wanted to see it again.

16
The Place You Are Calling From Does Not Exist

Shredded tyres, wild pigs and a rescue
gone bad; mountain with an identity crisis;
wolves, bears and the MFI connection;
wet smelly gear, wet smelly people

THERE'S many a time during my years of night mountains I have felt I have been in the middle of some great illusion but only once have I been told I was totally delusional.

Sometimes I have wondered if that was the case; being on the side of a mountain at 4am with a man wearing red rubber trousers for instance. Or talking to trees on the way out of a particularly long circuit in Knoydart. But it wasn't until I needed help from the RAC that the confusion factor was upped by the power of one thousand.

My daughter Lucy was due back from holiday and needed a pick-up from Glasgow Airport so that meant I could head out on the Monday night and have the whole of Tuesday on the hills before a relaxed drive back down the road in time for her flight getting in. What could possibly go wrong?

Well, for a start I was planning to tackle the worst road in the country, the 22-mile rollercoaster along the side of Loch Arkaig, a throroughfare that had given me problems before. Then I was going to climb Bidein a' Chabhair. Or was it Sgurr na h-Aide? You see, this twin-peaked mountain has gone through a bit of an identity crisis over the years.

Sgurr na h-Aide, the 'peak of the hat', was originally listed as the Corbett summit, but that was the name which referred to the whole mountain at one time as the view seen by residents at Kinlochmorar was thought to resemble a bashed-in hat. Bidein a' Chabhair is the higher point, but the name was largely ignored. Now the 'pinnacle of the hawk' is rightly recognised as the prime peak. Just to add to the mix, the mountain is often confused for the higher nearby Munro peak of Sgurr na Ciche when viewed along the loch.

I had all this figured out by the time I left the office before midnight in my Peugeot 206Gti. The heat outside was oppressive – it was shaping up to be a tee-shirt and shorts day. The usual drive via Fort William was uneventful, mood music keeping me chilled along with the air conditioning. Even the Mile Dorcha – the section of road known as the Dark Mile – wasn't looking so dark tonight. All I had to do was survive the next 20 or so miles on the Wacky Races circuit and I was ready to rock. It was all going so well until just about three miles from the end of the road.

It was then I heard the dreaded slapping sound. First thought, a flat tyre. I stopped, got out to take a look. Not so much flat as shredded. The guilty wheel must have nicked a pothole or the little ditch at the side of the road a while back, which nudged the tyre off the rim and it had been tearing up as I was driving along. Now I was in the middle of nowhere, with one tyre missing. There's no mobile phone reception, no houses for miles, so no chance of calling for help. The road is never that busy at the best of times so there's little likelihood of anyone else coming along soon.

I decided the best, maybe only, option was to drive on the three tyres and one rim – the tyre was beyond help anyway – to the parking area at the end of the road. At least there may be someone else there. No such luck.

I got out the jack and the spare runner wheel. Next problem. I tried to loosen the wheel nuts but they wouldn't budge. It's 2.30am, I have on my heavy mountain boots and I am jumping up and down on the cross spanner trying to gain even a semblance of movement. The best thing at this moment for myself and the car would have been to give it a damn good thrashing but even this idea was thwarted by a lack of trees. I was faced with a dilemma. I could spend the rest of the night waiting it out in the hope someone would come along or – and this is where the mountain fanaticism kicks in – I could abandon the car and climb the mountain. That way I could call the RAC from the summit where there was a better chance of a signal or, worse case scenario, be back down at a time when there would likely be someone else here to help. Genius.

Now all I had on the lens of my sunglasses were the twin peaks I had come here to scale. It was the Scarlett O'Hara solution: Tomorrow is another day. Or, more precisely, later today is another day.

It's not the first time I have had run into trouble at the end of Loch Arkaig. During an earlier foray, I discovered that my petrol tank had been leaking so all the time I had been climbing my fuel was ebbing away. I had barely enough to make the run out to civilisation. I have also had one of the politest run-ins ever with a pompous land manager in which we danced round the event both fully aware we were at it. We parted on good terms but it's safe to say we shared a mutual disrespect. It's good when you can come to an agreement.

On a more recent visit, I found the road in the worst state it's ever been. No surprise when you realise huge logging lorries were now using it. I was almost wiped out by one juggernaut stacked with cut trees coming round a corner. There's not a lot of places to hide. This constant rumble of giant trucks has seen the already narrow driving space narrowed further, verges crumbling under the thunder of oversized wheels. The usual rollercoaster ride was now aligned with the dodgems, a continuous struggle to avoid massive potholes and sections of collapsed road edging. One centimetre too far either way and you could be off the road.

There have since been repairs to the surface but I suspect that with these huge lorries still barrelling up and down it won't be long until it needs further treatment. And if the road or the giant trucks don't get ya, there's also the pigs to watch out for. Yes, wild boar roam free on the Glendessary estate, but it has become a controversial issue.

The animals have thrived since escaping from breeding farms and there are thought to be now be around 70 roaming free. Initially, they were to be hunted down but then it was decided to manage the problem in a different way. Now hunters pay up to £4,000 per week to stay in the estate lodge, but the way in which the boar are stalked and killed has been condemned by animal welfare groups.

The animals are lured into the rifle sights by regular feeding in areas close to their woodland hideouts and picked out by spotlights triggered by sensors. Young males are the most regular target, while the patriarch and matriarch and youngest ones are left. The estate argues that concentrating on the young males prevents further splintering of the group and their spread into other areas. One ghillie told me that apart from this feeding lure, the animals stay well hidden and it is unlikely you would bump into one during a walk. Just as well. An encounter with an angry boar would not end well.

Ten minutes after this conversation, I was chatting to another walker at the road end. He told me that on his drive in a pig had come charging out of the ferns and ran straight across the road in front of his car forcing him to brake sharply. It then disappeared just as fast, so quickly he began to doubt he had seen it. I was happy to inform him that his eyes had not deceived him.

The rise of the boar at Arkaig brings the whole debate of the rewilding of Scotland back into focus. We already have the return of sea eagles and beavers, and there are many who would love to see wolves, lynx and even bears back as well. The romantic in me loves the idea of seeing animals that were hunted to extinction reclaiming their place. The realist in me suspects that's not going to happen.

Paul Lister, the multi-millionaire heir to the MFI furniture fortune, bought the Alladale Estate in Easter Ross in 2003 with the intention of 'rewilding' it. He was given permission to bring in elk and wild boar with the proviso that they were kept in enclosures, and there is also a small herd of bison. Wolves and bears were a no-no, as they required a zoo licence.

The experiment with the wild boar was not exactly a success, the animals' rooting habits causing huge damage to native trees, but Lister has not given up on his dream. He wants to create a massive wilderness reserve but to do so would mean building a 10ft high electric fence which would cut off access to around 50,000 acres to the public. The remote Corbett, Carn Ban, would be off limits and some routes to that wonderful Munro Seana Bhraigh could also be compromised.

Apart from being contrary to Scotland's access laws, Lister's plan would need the co-operation of other landowners in the area as his estate covers just 23,000 acres. Anyway, that's not re-introducing animals to the wild, it's just creating another artificial wilderness. He rightly says the deer population is out of control, and so is the damage they cause. But putting them into an enclosed space with bears and wolves would surely have alarm bells ringing over animal welfare.

We have a safari park near Stirling and there's the Highland Wildlife Park near Aviemore, but the Alladale park wouldn't be for ordinary mums and dads to take the kids along. This would be a wildlife park for the rich, with guests paying anything up to £20,000 for a week at the lodge.

It all sounds very noble when you say you're putting the animals and the landscape ahead of human needs. What it really means is that the plebs have to be kept off the land.

Lister's plans didn't go down too well with his neighbours last time, and it's likely he would get short shrift again. Anyway, I would be nervous about trusting anyone with links to any furniture flatpack company building a fence that would keep large, scary predators secure.

There have been access problems at Alladale before. Many people remember a huge sign saying there was no unauthorised access for hill walking, camping or cycling during the hunting season, which, according to the estate, lasted for nearly eight months. At all other times, you were expected to call ahead for permission to walk there, the probability being that they would have managed to come up with another excuse to try to keep you out.

The fear among many is that any attempt to introduce a massive fenced-off area would be the ultimate Beware of the Dog sign.

Blissfully unaware of being under the watchful eyes of any wild pigs, I put my car problem to one side for a few hours and set off into the massive shadow shapes that surround this area, the Corryhully summits and Streap on my left, the start of the long column of peaks that stretch all the way into Knoydart on the right and, dead centre, Bidein a' Chabhair.

The track took me past the big house at Glendessary, then on to the cottage of Upper Glendessary, both devoid of any sign of life, before curving off to the right and picking up the muddy path round the top of a pine plantation. I ignored the cut-off path to Sgurr nan Coireachan, and kept going under the walls of Garbh Chioch Mhor before turning south to pick the best line up broken rocks on to the first obstacle of Meall na Stroine.

This area is known as the Round Bounds of Knoydart and soft walking is not an option here. Greenery is in short supply, the slopes smothered in broken rock slabs and boulders with patches of water looking more like snow in the bright sun, but in dry weather it speeds the progress – good, solid ground to push off quickly.

The Druim Coire nan Laogh ridge stretched ahead, another shattered stone monument rising, falling and rising again to a cone sitting slightly skewed at the end of the highway as if it had slid away from its fixed position. At times, the route onwards looked impregnable but there was always a ramp or a feint to take me onwards and upwards. When you finally come face to face with the final tower it also appears intimidating but skirt round to the left and there's an easy passage to the top.

The view down to Loch Nevis and Loch Morar is good, but an even better one awaits the walker who makes the short trip across to the other peak, Sgurr na h-Aide. But first, I had a phone call to make. I had four bars on my mobile now and got through at the first try to a young lady at the RAC centre in Birmingham. After the initial pleasantries, we got down to the nitty-gritty.

"And where is your car just now, sir?"

"It's at the end of the minor road along Loch Arkaig. That's near Fort William."

"Did you say Arcade?"

"No, Arkaig."

"I can't seem to find any Loch Arcade."

"No, it's Arkaig. A-R-K-A-I-G."

"Are you with your car at the moment, sir?"

"No. I am at the top of a mountain, but by the time someone comes out I will be back at the car."

"Which road did you say it was on?"

"It's an unclassified road, but it's the western extension of the B8004 and B8005 near Fort William."

"I've found Fort William."

If she was expecting a round of applause, she was left disappointed.

"I can't seem to find any road beside Loch Arcade. I just can't find it anywhere on our maps. It doesn't seem to exist."

Ah, that explains it. Maybe my whole life so far has just been one big dream. But if that were the case, this phone call is also part of that dream, so I still needed the car sorted.

"I can assure you it does exist. I have just driven along it for an hour."

"Oh dear, I'm sorry, I can't find it. Where did you say it was again?"

This geographical ping-pong was going downhill fast – but not as fast as the phone battery. I had to ring off now or the phone would soon be dead.

"Look, forget it. I will try again later."

"Okay, and maybe you could get a more precise description of your whereabouts by that time."

Listen lady, I'm the one with the grid references; you're the one who can't even recognise a word when it's spelled out. Maybe I should have tried the AA – and I don't mean the motoring organisation.

Just as well I hadn't had my car totalled by a wild boar. That would have been beyond the pale for my RAC phone friend. "Yes, that's what I said. My car has been badly damaged in a collision with a giant pig on a road that doesn't exist. It's near Fort Will.i.am."

"Will all due respect, sir, I think you should be phoning a psychiatric hospital."

I thought it prudent not to walk to the other peak. It was now 6.45am and getting down to the car and looking for help had become the priority. I reached the car park at 10 and, by this time, there were a couple of other people around. I tried to loosen the wheel nuts again and one guy came over to lend a hand. Still nothing. No mobile phone signal either. It wasn't looking good. Then came a most unlikely saviour. A car coming along the road turned out to be a taxi bringing in a couple of walkers. His fare dispersed, he came over to evaluate the problem.

"Hmmm, no chance of that budging mate. That's the trouble with putting nuts on with pneumatic hoses. They're stuck fast. Best bet, I could give you a lift to Spean Bridge and you could call for help from there."

That would work. After all, the RAC woman had heard of Spean Bridge. Even if she had pronounced it 'Speeing'.

An hour later and I was in Spean Bridge. The taxi driver refused to take any money for his unlikely passenger – he said he had already factored in the return journey from the two guys he had brought in as he could never had hoped to find an incoming fare. Highland generosity at its finest.

I made my call and was told someone would be with me within two hours. That would take me to 1.30pm. Factor in another three hours for the journey back in, the repair and then the journey out and my time window was shrinking fast.

There's not much to do when you need to kill time in Spean Bridge, and every minute seemed like ten. By the time the RAC rescue van picked me up, I had all the qualifications to become the village idiot. I was even sitting on the wall watching the world go by. All I needed was a bit a straw in my mouth.

My rescuer informed me I could have been sorted out much earlier. The RAC had a contractor who lived at the foot of the glen where I was stranded but because they had a staff man on duty, even though he was an hour and a half away in Inverness, bureaucracy decided to pass on the quicker option and send their man on a four or five-hour round trip.

My driver wasn't too chuffed with the madness of the decision either but he turned out to be the father of an Inverness Caley Thistle footballer and we passed the time chatting about football. Even with all the specialist gear, he struggled with the wheel nuts. Not only had they been put on solidly, they had also rusted up. In the end he had to use a blowtorch to ease them off. I now had the runner wheel on, but there was no way I could keep it on all the way to Glasgow for my airport pick-up and then a journey home. I needed to get my damaged tyre replaced as soon as possible.

I had just under an hour and a half to reach Fort William – it would be tight. A leisurely day on the hills was turning into a race against time. It was often this way during these nocturnal flights to the mountains.

Journeys in cars driven by my old hill walking buddy Malcolm were always unpredictable, from £50 bangers bought from guys called Tonto or Geronimo to one car that started to split while travelling through Glasgow on the M8.

Not that my record was much better. I have always viewed cars as a means to get from A to B rather than as some status symbol. They have always been functional rather than pretty, and even when I did have a decent one, it tended to be reduced to the level of a moving farmyard fairly quickly. I just didn't see the point of having a nice car when it would be getting thrashed up dodgy B-roads and, in some cases, roads that didn't even exist.

My cars were always filled with wet, smelly gear, empty bottles, apple cores and banana skins, dogs and wet, smelly people There was always the attitude that I would like to be able to cut the car loose at any moment and not have any regrets. If I regarded it as just a lump of tin that took me places then I was happy.

I had been prepared to sacrifice a car a few years earlier on an icy road in the Borders and I also drove my beloved Peugeot Gti into the ground during a trip to Jura, the same way Pony Express riders used to spur their horses past the point of exhaustion.

I got to Fort William with minutes to spare, the tyre was changed and I then made it down to Glasgow in time for my daughter's incoming flight. She had come home from a holiday and I was looking like I was desperately in need of one.

17
Lights Out

A desperate run to reach dry land; the
taxi driver we turned into a nervous wreck;
the tearoom at the end of the world;
the man who walked with an umbrella

THE rain had been falling so relentlessly no one could remember the last dry day. Glasgow was buried under a sea of umbrellas. The water poured down buildings, fired out of broken guttering and pipes with the same pressure as a fire hose and ran like rivers down the roads. It seemed like the end of days. Dry ones, at least. After all, when they had rain like this in times gone by, some guy went and built an ark. In the west of Scotland, though, 40 days and 40 nights of rain were met with shrugs and wry smiles.

The Beijing Olympics were about to get under way so I suppose our swimmers should be feeling confident of a few medals, even if it would seem drier in the pool than walking the streets back home.

I suppose it was the price to be paid for a half-decent summer. It may seem surprising that I decided to head for the wettest part of the country. The peninsula of Knoydart regularly wins the title for highest rainfall. Bridges are washed away and rivers become roaring torrents in a matter of minutes. But the need to get back on the Corbett trail was over-riding these concerns so I packed all the wet weather gear I could find and headed for the ultimate ride on Splash Mountain.

I left the monsoon conditions of Glasgow before the rush-hour traffic got into full swing and spent the next three hours listening to a back catalogue of music while floating up Loch Lomondside, through Glen Coe and past Fort William until I reached dry land at Invergarry.

I was heading along the 22-mile stretch of single-track road which terminates at Kinloch Hourn, the start of the historic Barrisdale Path into Knoydart. I had booked an overnight stay at Kinlochhourn Farm, a good base for an early start the following day, but first I had the small matter of climbing Sgurr nan Eugallt, a knobbly, rocky ridge with multiple peaks which fills in the scenery between Loch Quoich and Loch Beag.

Despite the bumps and grinds, the twists and turns, it's a road I've grown to love, possibly because it's the introduction to so many wonderful hill days. It's also a thing of a beauty, a continuous box of delights which can throw up surprises no matter how many times you have travelled its length. It changes from ranks of forestry to deep ferns and vast views, from a run along the loch side to steep slopes of boulders and heather and finally to a tight descent by cascading waters to journey's end.

Be warned – you won't share my joyous description if it is your maiden voyage. It can feel intimidating, agoraphobic and claustrophobic in quick succession, and downright dangerous. In winter reaching the end of the road is no guarantee you will make it back out again. If you have avoided going off the road on the final downhill twists, chances are the snow and ice won't allow an escape. Even experienced drivers can have a bad case of the shakes here.

A couple of years' earlier, I took a party into Knoydart for a few days. We had driven to Fort William where we left the cars and hired a taxi to take the five of us to Kinloch Hourn. We would spend three days in Knoydart then take the ferry back to Mallaig and catch the train back to Fort William.

When we arrived at the pick-up point, we saw two taxi drivers having what looked like an argument. Then our man came over, grinning widely. He and the other driver had been wrestling over who would take us and who would take a fare to Liverpool airport.

"I won the toss," he told us. "Who wants to have to drive to Liverpool?"

Our journey was 52 miles, about an hour and a half, but it soon became apparent he had no idea what he had taken on. He had just looked at the distance and thought it was an easier fare. His mate was probably laughing to himself as he headed for the Mersey.

As we turned off on to the single-track road, he remarked on how beautiful it was.

As we got deeper and deeper into the rougher terrain, he started making jokes about the grass growing in the middle of the road.

As we bumped across the first of the bridges patched up with chipboard and roofing felt, he started asking if we sure this was the right road.

As we twisted round corners with water on one side and crags on the other you could see he thought he possibly the butt of a practical joke or, worse still, some kind of ambush.

And as we descended into the steep, tight curves hemmed in by an old wall and rushing waters dropping down to the right he was looking for reassurance in a pleading voice.

By the time he had reached the flat and dropped us off, we were having to give him counselling for the journey back. We reckoned he would spend the journey home thinking fondly of John Lennon Airport.

Experience had taught me to expect surprises but the last thing I expected to see as the rain started falling again was a man walking along the road under an umbrella. He was wearing walking boots and good waterproofs but it didn't look as if he was going near a hill. Not with an umbrella. It's not an uncommon sight in the Himalayas, but the most likely result of venturing into the high places of Scotland with an umbrella would be a Mary Poppins impersonation as the winds sent you scudding across the sky, and no amount of sugary songs would save you. He waved as I passed, no effort to hitch a lift. He seemed happy with his lot.

I reached the ruined cottage of Coireshubh, where a stalkers' path begins that will rise about 2,000ft on to the ridge. The rain had eased to occasional light showers and all the way up I was treated to rainbows dashing in and out of the sunlight.

This welcoming approach to Sgurr nan Eugallt is in direct contrast to its name, which translates as 'peak of the death streams'. This is likely a reference to precipices but not to worry – these are to be found on the slopes falling off the other side of the mountain into Glen Barrisdale where any type of passage would be perilous in wet weather. Not that any part of this hill should be treated lightly. Like most of the peaks that make up the area known as the Rough Bounds, it is brutally tough, complicated ground, a constantly twisting line of aggravation, where you can easily go astray. This is one of the many hills where Bonnie Prince Charlie was said to have almost come to grief as he and his companions made their escape across the country from Hanoverian troops.

There seems to be about four or five possible contenders for the summit, with opinion shifting regularly on which is the true top. In cases like this, it is always better to visit them all. There are also two other peaks on the ridgeline worthy of a mention, Sgurr Sgiath Airigh just to the north-west, and Sgurr a' Chlaidheimh to the south-east.

I was accompanied for most of the ascent by mist rising in the heat from the wet grass, following me like a faithful mutt clinging to his master's tail, afraid he might miss whatever treats may lie in store further on. The cloud bobbed and weaved playfully, evanescent at times, threatening at others, continually shifting the focus from peak to peak, dancing up the slopes and swirling round my feet, a moisture-laden equivalent of a dust devil.

Loch Hourn came and went, as did the Ladhar Bheinn and the rest of its pals, all the more special in this nebulous game of hide and seek. Once I was treated to the landscape being split vertically by a curtain of cloud being led from the front by a rainbow.

On a clear, warm day it would worth spending a few more hours on this skyline, a bird's eye view of Knoydart's mountains laid out in the foreground, but with a few soakings under my belt I was just looking forward to getting down to the farm and a hot shower, hot meal and comfy bed.

The old stone buildings are more than 100 years old and have a variety of accommodation, from bed and breakfast to self catering. They are open from April to October. Being so remote, there is no mains water and no electricity. The farm relies on water from the hills – no problem with that over the past few days – and it has a generator. When I arrived, mine host Joe gave me a warm welcome and a torch. The electricity went off at 9pm and didn't come back on until breakfast time. Although there are a couple of other residences scattered around, it's not difficult to see why the farm is sometimes referred to as the tea shop at the end of the world.

A couple of years earlier my Corbett quest had seen me venturing in here in late November. I had driven in tentatively in the dark, light snow showers dusting the road, a dreamy white gauze picked up in the car headlights. The end of the road was devoid of life, a snowy and windswept landscape with only the sounds of running water cutting its way mostly unseen through channels somewhere close by. The farm was shut up for the season, a refuge now off limits.

I wanted to climb Buidhe Bheinn and Sgurr a' Bhac Chaolais which lay to the north of Loch Beag at either end of a scimitar-shaped ridge. This was a list anomaly, two distinct peaks of exactly the same height which couldn't be separated and therefore had to both be climbed to claim one tick. They straddled the ground between Glen Shiel to the north and Kinloch Hourn to the south. Either starting point would have sufficed as distance, ascent and times were almost identical. They were the Siamese twins of Scottish hills.

I chose the southern approach because it seemed the more aesthetic, and the thought of going into the heart of this wilderness in winter also appealed to my spirit of adventure. Had it been a hard winter I would never have attempted it. Being stuck 22 miles from the main road in temperatures of minus 10 or worse didn't seem sensible.

I followed the right of way to Arnisdale above the treeline, a steep push whose wilderness credentials are slightly diminished by the line of pylons shadowing its progress. But as soon as I turned off on a side path and headed into the snow the feeling of solitude returned. Loch Hourn lay grey and calm, a sheet of glass reflecting dark leviathans while Ladhar Bheinn loomed menacingly under black skies.

Once on the ridge, the walking is easy. The first top was reached and soon after I was on Buidhe Bheinn's main summit. The walk onwards to Sgurr a' Bhac Chaolais involves crossing another couple of summits as the ridge curves round to the left. Next along the skyline is the Munro, Sgurr na Sgine. I had still to tick this peak as part of my second Munro round but a combination of factors came down against it – the snow would slow me down, I was expected to check in by a certain time for safety reasons and there was always the possibility I may have trouble on the drive out.

The more you climb, the more you realise the wisdom of combining peaks of different categories. On an ascent of Ben Wyvis earlier in the year, I had managed to take in four tops and the adjoining Corbett of Little Wyvis. One of the tops, Glas Leathad Beag, had been touted as being given separate Munro status so it made sense to take the long detour out the back of the massif to reach it. A couple of hours and a few hundred feet more had given me a lot of satisfaction that in my early days I would have passed up.

It's easy to talk your way out of things sometimes and I look back now and see I should have gone on to Sgurr na Sgine, but I was also satisfied with having bagged both these peaks trouble-free so I cut my losses and headed out.

Not long later, the powers-that-be decided Buidhe Bheinn was the superior peak and Sgurr a' Bhac Chaolais no longer had to be climbed, but I was glad I felt I had to do it. Had it been removed earlier I may have been tempted to do a quick smash n' grab and I would have missed out on a great day. I have since climbed Chaolais on a round in Glen Shiel and it is still worth the effort.

I made my escape up the road without any descent into a white hell, possibly secretly disappointed I hadn't had to battle my way out. What's the point of being in wild country if it's just going to behave itself?

It was certainly behaving itself this time. Newly showered I came through to the dining table where the only other guest was already seated. It was the umbrella man. His name was Nick and he was an artist and writer. He lived in Invergarry, about 27 miles back down the road, and was walking to Skye to take part in a book fair. This was the first stage of his four-day journey, which would take him over to the Misty Isle via Kinloch Hourn, then over by the Bealach Aoidhdailean and past the brochs in Gleann Beag to Glenelg, round to the small ferry at Kylerhea and then the walk through Glen Arroch and out to Broadford. If there was a better way to find inspiration for the festival, I couldn't think of one.

The food was comfort fare, just what was needed after a bracing day on the hills, a bowl of thick soup followed by chicken pie, potatoes, carrots, cabbage and peas. Then it was off to bed, clutching my torch. The room was comfortable but the chill was noticeable soon after the electricity went off. I was up at first light – no cockerel required. When the darkness of the night is so absolute, the smallest pinprick of light is as good as any alarm clock or over-enthusiastic rooster.

The mist was sitting on the loch and halfway up the trees, and there was a wash of dampness all around, every leaf, rock and blade of grass coated in fresh pearls of moisture, the only sound the hum of the generator and the putt-putting of a small boat somewhere out on the water. Nick had already left, brolly at the ready no doubt for whatever deluge may be lying in wait.

I was taking to the historic Barrisdale Path and, although it wasn't raining, previous experience of this route told me it was wise to start in full waterproofs. The water-laden vegetation along the five-mile stretch of shoreline can give you a regular shower so I was taking no chances in getting my gear unnecessarily wet. But when it's wet, you will get wet no matter how good your gear is. Water will always find a way in, the line of least resistance, whether it's leaking in through a gap in your boots, running off your jacket and trousers and down the top of your boots or down your neck from a wet buff.

Even the deer were suffering in this weather. A couple of estate stalkers had told me the mortality rate had soared. They can survive deep snows and freezing conditions but the constant soakings take their toll, their inability to dry out sufficiently and for any length of time eventually wearing them down. Normally, a young deer has around a one in four chance of survival; the stalkers told me that during a spell of weather as wet as this it was now around one in eight.

I left the farm, passed the small car park with its honesty bucket for car park fees, and headed along the broken shore wall. Soon I was among the birch trees, leaving even the smallest semblance of human company behind. With the mist rising lazily upwards in the building heat it felt as if I was entering a lost world.

There's always that moment when you catch the first glimpse of Barrisdale Bay, the signal that the ups and downs of the path are at an end, and then Ladhar Bheinn appears, its spires dominating the skyline, a Tolkien treat. The path turns back to track alongside the tidal basin, gulls screeching and swooping as they hunt for breakfast in the veins of water running through the wet sand. There was no sign of life at the Barrisdale bothy or the more upmarket version, the White House.

The path splits here and I took the left-hand branch which passes between stands of birch and rowan before swinging into Gleann Unndalain, the gateway to my target for the day, Sgurr a' Choire-bheithe. This is the 'peak of the birch corrie' and it is one of the highest Corbetts, just five feet preventing it from being promoted to the bigger league. It's a long, bulky beast, its ridge a high-level series of rocky knolls running for around five miles right out to the waters of Loch Quoich. It was on the peak at the far end, Meall nam Spardain, that Bonnie Prince Charlie was said to have his closest brush with death during his flight west, only a small bush preventing him plummeting down the slope.

The full traverse of this hill is a wonderful expedition but it is extremely strenuous and involves the crossing of the notorious Abhainn Chosaidh, a dangerous, if not impossible, task during any time of heavy rain or snowmelt. With the couple of weeks' downpours we had been having, it wasn't even worth contemplating.

The cloud was now boiling up, filling in all the gaps along every bite of the ridgeline. On days like this it's easy why the word corrie derives from the old Scots for cauldron, the steam of white and grey like a witches' brew bubbling up from below. Meall Buidhe and Luinne Bheinn were playing peek-a-boo and Ladhar Bheinn would occasionally pop in to see what was going on. It was certainly bewitching and I was caught in its spell. A combination of being the only human for miles in this kingdom of theatrical atmospherics and the thought of the long, long march back kept me sitting at the summit cairn drinking in as much of this dreamscape as I could.

If I had lain down and taken my last breath at this moment in time I would have died a happy man. But we are not on this earth to be happy – at least that's what my wife tells me – so I left the summit with a heavy sigh.

It's a hard place to say farewell to, so you won't be surprised to hear that I would be back in this area just two weeks later, this time leading a group of friends round the Munro circuit of Gleouraich and Spidean Mialach above the shores of Loch Quoich in almost identical conditions. I may have had to go home but it seemed the weather had no intention of getting out just yet.

There was life at the bothies on my return journey, the few hardy occupants spilling out to grab whatever sunshine was left in the day, and then disappearing back inside as the midge hordes descended for a feast. Keeping on the move was the best plan and I managed to escape relatively unscathed. Until, that is, I stopped on the path back to change my soaking socks and they emerged from the ferns like microscopic Apaches, surrounding me then striking with no mercy. My desperate attempts to spray enough repellent to keep them at bay failed miserably when I managed to fire it into my eyes during the uneven battle. Now sockless and blinded I had to beat a hasty retreat, a bit of judicious hopping getting me going again.

I arrived back at the farmhouse, swollen eyes the proof that I had just lost a flyweight contest to a superior opponent.

18
The Supermodel

Venomous snakes and giant chickens;
a vision of loveliness in the morning mist;
how to win a staring contest with a goat;
never trust a mouse when choosing cheese

I HAVE had occasion to disbelieve my eyes quite a few times during my years of nocturnal rambling; talking trees, otters wearing Celtic and Rangers football tops and ghostly Victorians to name but a few. The morning I met the supermodel postie in a land of venomous snakes and giant chickens really took the Custard Cream.

I am well aware that a lot of this walking in the half-light while the mind is sound asleep can have a weird effect. After a particularly hard shift in the office, there was a tendency for systems to switch to cruise control and induce sleepwalking. All I wanted was peace and happiness, to take in the sights, sounds and smells of nature without having to expend too much mental effort. When my brain was full, it was time for the legs to run the show.

Maybe it was just the time of year. As soon I reach November, strange changes start taking place. All the energy I've had since March seems to evaporate, I sleep longer and longer and the get up and go just gets up and goes. December and January are a battle but then it all starts to swing back again in February. Malcolm used to suffer badly from Seasonal Affected Disorder, the lack of sunlight affecting his performance. Mine isn't quite so extreme, but I think I would quite happily embrace hibernation. I'm convinced I was a bear in a previous life.

Carn na Nathrach was the last of the Ardgour peaks I had to climb but it was proving to be more of a problem than I had anticipated. For one reason or another, it had been the hill in this region that was continually put on the back burner. The ones to the north were easier to reach, the ones to the south more attractive. Carn an Nathrach was the ugly sister, the one left sitting on the shelf until there was no other option.

To be fair, it was more difficult to access than most. Its name, 'cairn of the adder', could also be a bit off-putting. They must have been here in some number at one time to have the hill name checked. This is definitely not a hill of anyone with a fear of snakes, although at this time of year it's likely they were all curled up fast asleep deep beneath the ground. They had the right idea.

This ascent depended on either catching the Corran Ferry or driving all the way round the top of Loch Eil and then a tortuous, never-ending run down the other shore. Having done this once I had learned my lesson – it was the ferry for me. With the earliest sailing at 5.30am, it meant deviating from my normal midnight runs and instead leaving around 3am or catching a nap at one of my usual spots in Glen Coe. It was too cold for the latter so I made my way back to the flat after work to gather my gear and my thoughts.

I felt like a totally different species from the human flotsam spilling out of the clubs on to the streets as I headed out of Glasgow with light snow falling. It hardly felt less strange than arriving at the ferry slipway where the lights and shouts of the crew punctured the darkness as the snow fell heavier. It reminded me of those scenes of emergency rescues at sea.

Five minutes later I was in Ardgour, and by the time I reached Strontian the sky had switched from dark to light. The snow had gone off and the light covering on the roads had vanished, turning the surface back to black.

The start of the walk was Kinlochan at Loch Doilet, five miles up the B-road over a high pass. The melt hadn't kicked in up here and with every turn of the wheels the lying snow was getting deeper and the grip on the road more precarious. It began to occur to me that even if I did make it to the highest point, the drop down the other side could be hazardous. I would struggle to get back. At first I thought I could just leave the car here and walk the remaining couple of miles. But that would add a couple of hours to an already tight schedule. Reluctantly, the only sensible choice was to abandon the attempt and try another day.

The cost of a double ferry trip and six hours of driving, coupled with missing a night's sleep for what had turned out to be no good reason, had put me in a foul mood. It also bit into my obsessive nature. I couldn't just let this mountain go. The snakes had got inside my head.

So, the following week, I went through the experience again, almost to the very second. It was now November but the snow of the last few weeks had melted away completely and the road up over the pass was clear. It also showed me, however, that had I attempted it last time out the car would most likely have ended up in among the trees and possibly not in an upright position. My thoughts about walking it were also put into perspective. I had made the right decision even if it had pained me at the time.

That righteous feeling lasted all of 30 seconds, the time it took me to walk down the farm track to the cottage. There I was greeted by a traffic warning sign luminating out of the early gloom, a red triangle with a giant, black image of a chicken inside.

Underneath it read: Caution, free range poultry.

They must have been fearsome beasts to necessitate warning signs.

With the amount of tree cover around, it would be hard to spot one of these giant black cluckers until they were almost on top of you. I proceeded with caution as requested.

Then she appeared from the end of the track, a vision of loveliness, like Ursula Andress emerging from the sea in Dr No, or Bo Derek running along the beach in 10, a siren in a blue uniform, the Cara Delevingne of Ardgour, a beaming smile, a welcome face in this chicken and snake-infested hellhole.

This was the local postie, walking her dog before setting off on her rounds. Good mornings were exchanged, goodbyes were said, my tongue was repositioned, and we walked on.

The more I think of this encounter, the more I realise that I may have been wearing the somnambulistic equivalent of beer goggles. It's even possible I may have even still been in bed in Glasgow, the nightmare of my last attempt on Carn na Nathrach converted to a more user-friendly dream of my next bid. I think not. I have photographic evidence. Not of the postie, of course, that would be creepy. I have pictures of the chicken sign and the hill. I was there.

Adders and chickens aside, Carn an Nathrach can present problems. It's a long, knolly ridge with its high point on the far end to the east, and it is guarded on three sides by forestry. Venturing into ranks of fir trees is never a good move so I would like to say a big thank-you to the website Munro Magic for the comprehensive breakdown on describing the chinks in this arboreal armour in such precise detail. It's worth studying this route, a series of moves through four tracks, laid out like dance steps, which culminate in finding a little cairn marking a hidden path on to the open hillside.

Now above the trees I looked back at a hidden valley, a hanging mist midway between treetops and mountain tops, a recreation of a time before the dawn of man. Beinn Resipol was the headline act here, a coppery red iceberg sticking out of a sea of cotton wool. The ridge ahead kept the snake theme going, a long, serpentine way twisting and turning ever onwards round bumps and little crags and, at times, the remains of an old, rusted fence line.

There's a drop into a curious dip just before the final push brings you to the large well-built cairn. Unfortunately by this time the mist had risen so the views had disappeared and it needed a compass reading to make sure I came off the featureless slopes in the right direction. There were steep crags close by on both sides and a wrong turn here could lead to some dodgy situations.

The rest of the descent was simple and I was back down around noon. And there to prove I hadn't been hallucinating earlier was Cara, back from her rounds and walking the dog again.

I arrived back for work at 4pm, having clocked up Corbett No.200 and met a supermodel postie. And I had escaped unpecked from the land of giant chickens.

The two attempts on Carn na Natrach had once again highlighted the topsy-turvy world of the Scottish weather. The snow which had blasted in with such purpose at the start of October had seemed like a harbinger for the rest of the year. But just as furiously as it arrived, it departed as November clocked on.

The first fall had taken everyone by surprise, not least of all me. I was in Torridon to climb Beinn Dearg and decided I needed a short nap in the car park at the foot of Coire Mhic Nobuil. Before I dozed off, the ground was dry and the sky filled with stars, not a cloud in sight. When I roused a couple of hours later in the faint light, I was greeted by heavily snow-capped peaks, a light covering on the trees and a thin sheen on the road and path. It had sneaked in under cover of darkness, the perfect ambush.

Not that I was unhappy. Far from it. The first snows always lift the spirits. They change the hills dramatically, providing a clarity of the air and more defined vision, demarcation lines on the landscape.

At 2,999 ft, Beinn Dearg fails to make Munro height by just one foot and as a result is less well-trodden than Beinn Alligin, Beinn Eighe and Liathach. But it is in no way inferior. It sits proudly in its own space at the heart of the three and its sickle-shaped ridge provides a grand day out with its own set of challenges. The path snakes up through mixed woodland, midge hell in high summer but now with every leaf glistening like tiny mirrors in the sunlight.

It emerges from the wood but still sticks close to the waters of the Abhainn Coire Mhic Nobuil, enlivened by the unexpected reinforcements from the overnight snowfall. And all the time I was surrounded by the bellowing of rutting stags echoing across the hillsides, their perfect camouflage keeping them out of sight but their chainsaw calls reminding everyone of their ambitions.

The path splits at the bridge and I took the left branch, the usual descent route from the west to east passage over Beinn Alligin and its famous Horns. I stuck with it past a series of little waterfalls until it petered out and then I began the steep climb east over bands of pancake rocks on to Stuc Loch na Cabhaig at the northern edge of the ridge. The snow was soft powder, disintegrating under my footfall, and the steep angle necessitated a few diversions round crags but it was short and sweet and I was soon standing ankle-deep in snow on the top of the ridge.

The view was a revelation, the black and white streaked Torridon giants like massive rock zebras stretched out before me, every pinnacle of the Liathach ridge standing starkly in line, a regiment of stone soldiers, every slash along the faces of Beinn Alligin cutting deep, trimmed in white ermine. I didn't want to go down. I considered the full traverse which would involve crossing the rock bastion known as The Castle further along and decided it would be better for a day on dry rock rather than collapsing snow. Besides, time and newspaper deadlines wait for no one, and it was a long way home.

Seven days later and I am taking part in my very own version of The Men Who Stare at Goats. It's 6am on the kind of icy cold morning when your breath can be seen in clouds just before it solidifies in front of your eyes.

I had arrived at the public road end at Killilan, a seven kilometre B-road drive in off the A87 a few miles east of Kyle of Lochalsh. The journey had taken around four hours and I was facing a walk of some 22km over two remote mountains, Sguman Coinntich and Faochaig, deep in the wild country above Glen Elchaig. I was starting to feel weary. This seemed to be the ideal time to try out my new sleeping bag so I settled down for a few hours' rest.

I awoke in that half-light created in part by the lack of sunlight and also by the fact that I wasn't yet fully awake. I was moving like an automoton, sorting out map and compass, putting Vaseline on my pressure points, lacing up my boots and creating the correct body layers. As it was 6am and Baltic this was an easy decision – everything I had would go on.

Ten minutes later and I was off on the smooth black surface of the start of the estate road. As I approached the big house near the gate, I became aware of a dark presence standing on the immaculate lawn to my left. A guard dog becoming spooked by the sudden presence of an intruder with no one else around could be a problem. But this wasn't a dog – it was a goat.

Judging by its expression, it's hard to tell who was more surprised. It stood stock still, its eyes firmly fixed on me, just bending efficiently to grab another mouthful of grass without its eyes leaving their line of sight. I was doing exactly the same, except for chewing the grass, obviously. No sudden movements, no reason to suggest any threat.

We must have reached the same decision at the same time and the staring contest ended. No reason to waste any more time. I had mountains to climb and the goat had grass to mow. I slipped off on a path up the side of the house and left it to its breakfast. It still hadn't moved an inch.

The initial path followed a stream through mixed vegetation before reaching more open ground and switching to a bouldery track up Coire Mor across the side of Ben Killilan. I had only been going around 30 minutes but already the deep powder snow was kicking in. With the ground levelling off a bit, I crossed the stream and headed for the 'mossy peak' of Sguman Coinntich. It's not a big or difficult climb on to the ridge but the intervening ground was holding lots of snow and it was slow going through sometimes waist-deep drifts. It was also bitterly cold, the glen hidden in the shadows out of the reach of the low sun.

The summit was graced with a cairn and a trig pillar whose lower section was missing as if it had been eaten away from the inside. The contrast in colours from here was stark, everything above 300 metres coated white while below the water sparkled blue and the late autumnal shades of the flora jostled for priority. You could pick out every white cap of Skye's Black Cuillin as they sat in line along the clear horizon.

I was sweating, a combination of the effort needed on the final push, the fact that the sun was fully in charge, and because I was wearing so many layers. It was one of those days where you can never be happy with your choice of clothing. And it's on days like these that I wonder why no one has yet come with the idea of edible hill walking gear. It's a simple premise – after all, people used to be able to suck on shoe leather to survive a lack of food. Surely it's not beyond our technologic geniuses to come up with lightweight layers that could double as sustenance?

Imagine the benefits. You could set off on the coldest, most miserable day in comfort and warmth and then as the day got warmer and the clothes needed to be peeled off you could start eating your way through the gear layer by layer. It would also cut down on the need to carry emergency food if you knew you could just cook up a nice stew from your middle layer garments. It would finally make sense of the phrase: I'll eat my hat.

Some folk might not go for it, though. There are those just too attached to their gear and their brand names. I've never cared much about that. I'm a bit of a mountain raccoon: I will rake around in the bargain bins for whatever is on offer. Don't get me wrong. I have good gear. I just don't swear by one or other manufacturer or bother about the co-ordinated look. Anyway, I long ago learned an important lesson when it comes to named products.

I was asked to pick up some Parmesan cheese. Sounds simple enough, but when I got to the supermarket I found there were a dozen different varieties. After about 10 minutes, I settled on one, mainly because its front packaging showed a mouse wearing a smoking jacket and a cravat. My theory was that no mouse is going to bother dressing in a smoking jacket and cravat unless this was really good cheese, so I bought it. What a fool I was. It was rotten. Since then I have never trusted brand names. Or mice for that matter.

The route onwards to Faochaig involves a lot of work, but in clear weather it is obvious. The views down into the wild, northern corries kept me occupied as I wove through a series of knolls and crags and one small intervening top.

Faochaig suggests 'the whelk', a possible reference to the mountain's shape but it could be a spelling corruption and refer to heather. A peak of moss and a peak of heather, neither in much evidence with the deep carpet of snow covering all. The final push up to the summit was simple but again the often thigh-deep snow and the heat of the sun made it seem much harder.

Off to the north-west there's another summit just a couple of metres lower and it is worth a visit, especially for top collectors. You can extend the walk and take in another Corbett, Aonach Buidhe, from here but that was beyond my abilities and timescale on that day.

The descent south soon picks up a good path which, in its latter stages, slaloms its way down a steep wooded section where there were deer foraging for titbits, and then comes out on the track near the shores of Loch na Leitreach at Carnach.

I hadn't seen a soul all day but here I met a few parties, all heading to the Falls of Glomach. Now there was only the small matter of an 11km track walk back to the start. I arrived back at the car footsore, tired but happy. There was no sign of the goat.

The November thaw gave me time to fit in a run round Ben Tirran, the first time I had been up there when it wasn't buried under feet of snow. The crags of Loch Wharral looked so different without their massive gravity-defying overhangs.

Then we moved into December and the snows returned, this time with a meaner disposition. I had a grand winter's day on Ben Lui and Beinn a' Chleibh, when the sky hung with perpetual threat but generally kept its distance, and then a deep freeze in the Cairngorms on one of my favourites, Carn a' Mhaim. The last light burning its way down over the horizon turned out to be a metaphor for the last walk of the year.

Twenty to go – and the chase would begin again in the New Year.

19
North by Northwest

Seasonal greetings from Rudolf and pals;
nine-hour drive for a four-hour climb; the
great escape and a new lease of life;
three maps to climb one mountain

ALFRED HITCHCOCK would have been impressed. The bells had hardly ceased pealing after welcoming in 2009 and I was deep into a chase movie. Cary Grant and the crop-duster I could do without. Eva Marie Saint would have helped the mood, though.

I had set the finish date for my Corbetts round – I never seem to learn – and I now had to knuckle down and start whittling away at the 20 remaining peaks. Trouble was, most of them were in the farthest reaches of the country, including a batch in Sutherland.

The good news was that winter hadn't really arrived. Sure, there had been some wild, stormy and freezing cold days but there was a distinct lack of snow on the mountains and the roads were generally trouble-free.

The sensible way to approach these hills is to find a base and then pick them off day after day. I had the usual problem of having to try to fit them in between work shifts. Anyway, accommodation in this area is as sparse as the landscape during the winter months so it would have to be a series of quickfire raids and damn the mileage.

A cold but clear night early in January and I was out the door at 12, the long and leisurely run up the A9 passing under cloudless skies, an endless carpet of stars lighting the way. I cut across to Lairg and then took the left-hand branch of the circuit which heads for the northern coastline. The roads were dry and I was travelling reasonably fast on this stretch, relying on my usual trick of being able to spot the lights of any oncoming traffic from miles away.

Of course, there's always the chance that someone coming the other way may not have any lights or have them switched off. If you think that's unlikely, I once knew a guy who, when travelling on back country roads, switched his lights off when approaching corners. His theory was that it was then easier to see anything approaching. Unless, of course, the person coming the other way was thinking the same.

He didn't have an answer when I asked what would happen in that situation – he hadn't factored in the idea that there could be another idiot out there. He really should have been in a witless protection programme for his own good.

My stopping point was Loch Merkland, a small body of water sandwiched in between the bigger lochs of Shin and More. From there a good track and then path would take me in to the enclosing arms of Ben Hee. The Christmas spirit was obviously still in full flow here because all the signs along this stretch warning of deer on the road had been vandalised in a fairytale fashion – a small red circle had been placed over the nose of the deer. Reindeer games indeed.

The light was already rising but the landscape was leached of any colour, a palette of greys with the next shade appearing at the last minute with every step. On a good day this hill would provide a nice circuit but there was an icy cold and I was more than happy to reach the trig point and accompanying cairn at the main summit. I was even happier when the sun burst through a huge hole in the cloud to dispel the gloom and provide a view of Ben More Assynt and Conival bathed in a series of golden rays. The next best thing to being in good weather is to see it somewhere further off.

Ben Hee is thought to be one of many fairy hills in Scotland, the name a derivation of the word 'sithean' or 'shidh' but it could also be from 'shith' meaning peace or quiet. It was certainly peaceful today, not another soul in sight or any sound penetrating the blanket of grey, just a few deer looking confused at my presence. It had taken me just three and a half hours to get up and down, compared to around nine hours of driving. These hills were heavy on the fuel bills.

Nevertheless, a few days later I took the opportunity of an earlier than usual finish to head back home for a few hours' sleep before miraculously rising in the middle of the night. I'm sure some of my neighbours may have had suspicions that I was a vampire. The thought did cross my mind to really give them something to talk about by starting to spell my name backwards a la Dracula so that the plate on the door read Nawor.

I drove through the streets populated at this hour only by the undead of club land and set my sights on another long trip to Sutherland. This time I was after Meall Horn, the more neglected of the three hills accessed from the rather aptly named Lone. Foinaven and Arkle are spectacular mountains, twisting, turning ridges peppered with rock towers and narrow sections. Meall Horn, on the other hand, provides a gentler picture, twin humps rising from grassy slopes above a small lochan, as its name suggests, 'meall' being the Gaelic for a rounded hill, and 'horn' a Norse word for a hill. However, there may be more to this than meets the eye – or tongue.

Horn could also be a corruption of 'fhir-eoin', a place where a bird of immense importance could be found and may refer to a sea eagle which were known to nest in the north-west.

The A838 was alive with deer, their eyes piercing the tree cover on both sides of the road. Occasionally, some would spring out of the undergrowth at the last second forcing me into evasive manouevres. It was a painstakingly slow journey for the last half hour or so.

I set off walking in winter darkness at 8am but within minutes the light took over. I was passed on the track by two Land Rovers overflowing with men in camouflage gear with rifles. Either I'd got my directions wrong and I was now in Chechnya or they were stalkers on their way to a shoot. Although it was out of season for the stags, this time of year is when the hinds are culled. They just nodded to me and then disappeared off on a branch track. My chances of catching a stray bullet had just been dramatically reduced.

Arkle's mottled slopes were glowing in coppery hues and the babbling of the Allt Horn was gaining in strength. By the time I reached my eastern ascent point, Foinaven's tops were peeking up over the horizon, while two stags boldly stood their ground on the path further ahead, trying to suss out my intentions. They wouldn't have been so bold had they seen the men with guns. Or perhaps they just knew it was ladies night and they would be okay.

The four and a half hours it took to get in and out with another scalp under my belt was again dwarfed by the nine-hour journey. This was an expensive way to do mountains, but that's what obsession does for you. At least the drive back down to the darkness of the start of my shift at the coal face of news was done in sunshine.

Deep snow curtailed any big trips for a few weeks and I confined myself to my local hills. An outing in Glen Doll had to be abandoned high on the Capel Mounth route, the snow proving just too unstable to battle through. The following day there was disaster on Buachaille Etive Mor. Three people lost their lives when they were caught up in an avalanche in Coire na Tulaich, a reminder of how deadly it can be approaching this headwall in winter conditions. Several others had a lucky escape.

The rain and wind which had helped loosen the snow pack continued and within days the hills were mostly clear again. I decided to head for all points north once again. Unfortunately it was one of those days that could have fallen foul of the Trades Descriptions Act.

Under cover of darkness on the drive up towards Ullapool the true rotten nature of the weather went largely unnoticed. It was the middle of the night in February, it was supposed to be cold and miserable, and I was heading round to Destitution Road. I realised exactly how miserable when I set off on the track along Loch a' Bhraoin.

The wind was whipping down the loch, the drizzle was biting into my face and my feet were struggling to get any rhythm going on the rubble track. It was hard going, and not for the first time I wondered just what the hell I was doing walking hills at this time of night and at this time of year. There had to be easier ways of channelling my madness.

Then there was that moment which makes it all seem worth it. About halfway along the track the clouds and gloom parted and the morning light broke through. Suddenly the water was transformed to a sheer blue sheet of glass, the hills appeared all around and I could see the route ahead. It felt like being at the eye of the storm, perfect calm all round. Then it closed in again. The rest of the morning was spent trudging up grassy slopes against the wind with rain and snow blowing through to a hidden summit. A final bit of teasing at the top of Creag Rainich with threatened glimpses of the Fisherfield giants brought the whole sorry episode to a conclusion.

As I headed back out the track I met two walkers coming in. They never asked where I had come from but I got the usual looks which were a mix of admiration and incredulity.

Two weeks later I got the news I had been hoping for – my application for voluntary severance had been accepted. I had made up my mind two years earlier that my job had become an unacceptable burden but previous bids to leave had been blocked. Now, with the economy in freefall and the company in dire straits it was open season. Anyone who wanted to leave could do so. Reputations and importance to the business counted for nothing as they tried desperately to cut costs. The stampede was in full flow.

Newspapers had failed to adapt quickly enough to changing times. Websites and blogs were now providing instant coverage of events, social media breaking news hours before the papers could catch up. The quality of these sources wasn't as reliable but they still hit the print industry hard. The failure to keep up to speed was hitting home.

Besides, I had felt for many years that all I was doing was fire-fighting. Over the past 10 years we had seen whole departments vanish in the name of progress and all the work was piled on to the remaining few. There was no time for forward planning, and like in so many other industries and professions, everything was cut to the bone.

Good, investigative journalism which involved months of work was rare. Everything had to done by the shortest possible route and good people were being placed in impossible positions. Specialist writers now had to turn their hand to anything. It was collapsing around us – and it was never likely that it would ever recover.

I'd always known I was in a safe place financially if the call came. There was good money on offer for those wanting to depart and I saw this a great opportunity to realign my life and go and do all the things I wanted to.

I now just had two full months left to work. I was also due a lot of time in lieu so I put it to good use. Trips to climb island peaks and getting in to some of the most remote hills suddenly became a whole lot easier. I managed to rack up three or four big Munro days, and a couple of easier jaunts with friends around Loch Lomondside. It felt like a flashback to my early days of walking with Fergus and Malcolm, short trips close to Glasgow so we could get back for work, long before any of the midnight rambling madness had taken hold.

I had one last run at a night mountain. It was a tortuous journey, three sets of roadworks after Glen Coe, then the car overheating and threatening to blow during the long blast up my favourite road – the Loch Arkaig highway to Hell. I was nearly at the end of my Corbett journey but it looked like my car was already preparing for retirement.

After all the excitement, the walk in darkness and mist in Glen Pean was an anti-climax. I had just reached the knobbly ridge of Carn Mor when I got a surprise – two figures loomed out of the mist. They greeted me with the unnecessary revelation that there were no views to be had. I didn't ask their names but Holmes and Watson would be a good guess.

This mountain is home to one of the biggest landslips in the country but the visibility was such that I couldn't verify if this was the case. I will just have to believe the books. Loch Monar was also lost.

The day before I was due to leave work for the last time, I accompanied a friend up to Glen Nevis for an assault on Sgurr Choinnich Mor as I fitted in my last due day before the grand finale. It was late April but the snow was blowing through, the wind was viciously cold and the ridge was icy. As we sat at the small summit cairn taking in the lack of views along the Grey Corries ridge, a ghostly figure loomed out of the mist from the opposite direction. He was covered in hoar frost and looked as if he had spent the night in freezing conditions. Which he had.

He had camped out on the ridge overnight with a tent he had bought for his kids from Toys R Us. Now he looked like he was a walking advert for Frostbite R Us.

Kids, don't try this at home. And definitely don't try it nearly 4000ft up a Scottish mountain in winter conditions.

Winter bit back with a vengeance and our annual walking week in May was reduced to two days by the inclement conditions at our base in Glen Affric. The first day we set off in sunshine and as we rose into the heart of the Mam Sodhail chain it started snowing.

By the time we hit the ridge it was a near white-out and we had to take shelter in the ruins of the old weather station just below the summit for some respite.

It eased a bit as we headed out to Beinn Fhionnlaidh and when the sun did finally make another appearance, the blue skies and thick snow cover brought an Alpine feel to the day, reinforced by our full winter gear and goggles. The next day brought more of the same, and then it went downhill. Horizontal freezing rain, accompanied by gales, meant the mountain week was spent in cafes and pubs.

I may have been away from work but it was hard to kick the midnight habit. So exactly one week after our Arctic adventures, I was standing on the summit of Breabag early in the morning in a heat wave, every drop of snow having melted away. In less than a week Scotland had thrown off its impersonation of the Arctic and now looked more like southern Spain.

Breabag is translated in some books as 'little height' and that makes sense as it is the little brother of the big Assynt pair which stretch out on the horizon to the north and west. But it's probably more accurate as 'little kick' which refers to a cleft on the mountain.

It's a simple ascent which provides great views in every direction and has the added attraction of taking you past a series of caves on the way where bones from bears, reindeer, lynx, Arctic fox and wolves were discovered more than 100 years ago. More recently a skull was identified as that of a polar bear. It can be seen in the National Museum of Scotland.

Some of the reindeer bones date back 47,000 years, proving these animals roamed this area after the last ice age. There are also human bones thought to be 4,500 years old.

There were days when I had been on the hill that I felt 4,500 years old but this wasn't one of them. It took just three hours to circuit Breabag and for once I had no reason to rush back, so I figured I may as well chalk off another Corbett.

I drove round to the Loch Lurgainn road and took the path north to Lochan Fhionnlaidh before tramping east and then up a steep grassy gully to reach the summit ridge of Cul Beag, the 'little back'. This is often done in conjunction with its bigger neighbour, Cul Mor, but bad weather on a previous ascent had meant bailing out halfway round at the summit.

It can be a tricky traverse, more so in thick cloud and freezing winds. From the road this looks like an impressive lump of rock but the route up is easy and quick. The summit perch is a perfect viewpoint; the outrageously-shaped monolith of Stac Pollaidh dominates the skyline to the west, thrusting up between a series of little lochs and boulder-strewn terrain while Cul Mor, Suilven, Canisp and triple-pronged Quinag are stacked one after the other to the north.

One week on and I was back at Loch Merkland after another night-time drive full of whispered radio voices and musical extravaganza. I was now so familiar with this journey that I could probably have had a nap while the car made its own way there. The police tend to frown on this sort of thing however, so I kept my hands on the wheel and my eyes open.

Beinn Leoid, the 'mountain of the slope', was waiting for me.

A good stalkers' path which starts from the north end of the loch takes you up quickly on to open ground and then a short pathless line catches another good path coming in from the right. A short push west brought me to the open summit and views which have a wilderness flavour. (Memo to Walkers Crisps: you may wish to explore this idea. I will only take a small suggestion fee.)

Despite this, the route is simple. The real wilderness approach is off to the west. From here Beinn Leoid is a different animal, a high point lying among a complicated mix of bog, lochs and rock and deep, lonely glens. Any assault is best started by boat from Unapool to be taken to Glencoul. Once ashore, a good path leads past the dramatic Stack of Glencoul, ending just beyond Loch an Eircill and then an uphill push north-east completes a hard day.

Next was a real biggie, in name if not in height. Mullach Liath Coire Mhic Dhughaill has the longest name of any Scottish mountain. It's the 'grey hill of Dugald's son's corrie' and it's a bit of an octopus with spurs and ridges chaotically firing out in every direction. It also provides a mental challenge for walkers by virtue of being spread over three OS maps.

Having said all that, the route is straightforward.

The night drive was accompanied by a buffeting crosswind, the only variation on a trip made so many times in the last few weeks. There were some big hills to come but this would be my last visit to this area for a while.

A track leads round the foot of Loch More where the white horses were galloping in under a blue sky with pointy Ben Stack framed beautifully in the centre distance. A sharp right turn brings you to a good zig zagging stalkers' path, which after one final zig (it may be a zag) cuts back across the hillside. The view back down Loch More is one to savour, so enjoy it before taking to the long heather and rock strewn spur of Meallan Liath Beag which tops out on to the bending summit ridge. A right turn leads to the subsidiary top of Carn Dearg, a left to the tumbled down shelter cairn and trig of Mhic Dhugaill.

The continuing ridges of Sail Rac and Meall Garbh look worth a bit of exploration and eventually drop down to the track heading for Lone but it's a long way back from there to the car. I didn't need any more complication – I had already created plenty of my own by deciding to drop off the ridge earlier and following a shortcut to what I thought would be easier ground. I ended up in a series of bog and giant slabby rocks. I did get down to the road faster, but it wasn't particularly pleasant.

The other surprise was that I met a few separate parties of walkers heading up. Most of the time I'd spent on these north-west hills had been spent alone so it was hard to say why this one was proving so popular. Maybe it was a meeting of the Clan MacDougall.

20
Barn Nights

Ferns and cattle skulls in the Fisherfield
Hilton; a night spent on a bed of nails;
smoked out on a cook-in; the perils
of using communal toilet facilities

IT was a beautiful night but I supposed I should have been more alarmed by the amount of bodies lying out in the open on the beach at the head of the Fionn Loch when there was a perfectly good shelter handy.

The sky was clear but this was the north-west of Scotland and the chances were an open-air sleep-out would result in an unexpected deluge during the night or, even worse, a midge-fest. All these sleeping bags laid out – it was like ringing a dinner gong for the wee beasties.

Then it occurred to me that the nearby barn must be full and these were the unfortunates who had arrived too late to get in. Hmm, if that were the case, I might have to curl up on the sand and become part of the buggers' banquet as well.

I set off over the causeway that divides the light and dark lochs – Fionn and Dubh – walked round towards Carnmore Lodge and the barn which sits nearby and is left open for use by walkers. I needn't have worried about not getting a spot for the night – it was empty. And now I realised why so many people had decided to take their chances by staying outdoors for the night. It wasn't exactly the Hilton. It probably didn't even rate as highly as the infamous Hanoi Hilton.

It has four reasonably solid stone walls and a well-maintained roof but that's where the 'luxury' ends. The floor is bare earth, with an old railway sleeper as a divider/seat in the middle and some pallets lying around. There are a few old single bed frames, but the danger of being corkscrewed by renegade springs during the night is high and the better option is laying out a groundsheet on the floor.

Ferns are growing through the floor in the corners, and the ambience is completed by having a couple of cattle skulls hanging on the end walls. It's not to everyone's taste, but the roof is watertight and on a wet and windy night it would be a welcome haven from the elements. It's the only shelter for miles.

The mountains of Fisherfield are always a challenge, remote hills that lie a long way from the nearest road. Picking them off piecemeal means a lot of long, long days. To tackle them in any number normally means an overnight stay in one of the wettest areas of the country. River crossings can be impossible at times and escape options limited.

I was down to the last days of my Corbett round and had been waiting for good weather to climb two biggies in one expedition. To bag Beinn a' Chasgein Mor means a round trip of about 27 miles, a 12-hour walk from Poolewe. Beinn Lair is 10 hours and 22 miles away. It made sense to combine them with an overnight stop. The plan was to walk in to the barn, dump most of my gear, and then do an evening climb on Chasgein Mor. I would then tackle Beinn Lair early next morning before walking out.

I reached the summit of the 'big forbidding hill' just before sunset, the myriad of little lochs shining out of the darkening landscape to the west, while Loch Ewe took on a fiery glow in the dying embers of the sun. The Dubh Loch meanwhile was living up to its name, a shiny, black, unmoving surface carrying a perfect mirror image of the red crags which overlook it, while pinpricks of light came from the dozens of bivouackers stretched out further along on the shore.

I descended in darkness to find myself still the lone occupant of the barn. I chose what appeared to the best of the bed frames and settled down for the night. Even with my mat and sleeping bag, I would have been as well lying on a bed of nails so it shouldn't come as any surprise to hear that I was up, breakfasted and away by 4am.

It was light but everything lay in shadow and reflection, the mountains identifiable by their outlines, the waters by their mirror sheen. I passed the beach encampment, tents, kayaks and rucksacks dotted around, nothing stirring. It was if they had all been slowly devoured during the night by the midges until nothing was left of them but the colourful husks of their sleeping bags.

I took the good path up to the start of the climb to Beinn Lair and was soon heading into the confines of the Bealach Mheinnidh. Two tiny yellow headlights shone up ahead, a lone female deer surprised by my early incursion.

The walk up the long rising ridge along the edge of the cliffs was constantly disrupted by the need to look back over Beinn Airigh Charr and the Fionn Loch changing with the growing light, and down to the causeway and the tiny speck of the barn where I had tried to sleep and failed miserably just a couple of hours ago.

The walk up Beinn Lair is spectacular, the summit is a little disappointing; a giant beehive cairn is the only bump on a wide plateau whose flat horizon eviscerates the views. This is the 'hill of the mare' and it deserves further exploration, especially out to the east and the rocks known as the mare and the foal which give rise to the mountain's name.

It did provide an unusual vision of the An Teallach ridgeline though, with the jagged tines of The Forge standing to attention on a mountain turned blue by the distant haze.

The Carnmore Barn may not be the ideal place to spend the night but it had served its purpose. I had managed to climb two remote mountains and save myself a lot of grief.

A few years later I led a party of friends in to tackle the Munros A' Mhaighdean and Ruadh Stac Mor. To say they were stunned when they saw their accommodation would be a severe understatement. We tackled the hills the same way, leaving at lunchtime to walk in, dumping our overnight kit and then ascending in the evening. Again we came down in darkness, again there was no one else in the barn despite the many walkers we had met during the day.

It was early May, so despite the fine weather of the day by the time the sun went down it was decidedly chilly. So much so that Crawford, our chef for the night, decided it would be too cold to cook outside so set to work inside the barn.

When it came to food there was no stopping Crawf. This is a man who once devoured eight pork pies during one walk. On a rest day during a trip to Assynt we visited Lochinver. There he discovered his Nirvana – the local pie shop. Every possible variation of filling was there and apart from stocking up his food cabinet for the next few days, he was also snapping away with the camera. No people, just pies.

Suddenly the hill plans for the rest of the week became secondary to the pie shop. He made a return visit later in the week to buy a stock for taking home. Some people get hooked by online betting, Crawf became hooked when he discovered the pie shop website.

Even when we were setting off for the walk in to the barn, food was the main attraction. Everyone else was paring their gear down so they had the lightest possible pack for the long trek in. Not Crawf. He had two rucksacks, one on his back, one on the front.

Having had experience of walking like that in the past I told him he could not take on a hike like this with front and back packs. The likelihood was a lot of stumbling and this was no place to turn an ankle.

Reluctantly, he took them off and started to try to get all his gear in one bag. We couldn't believe the amount of food and drink he had packed. It would have catered for an army for a few days. But then Crawf was a one-man army when it came to food.

It was dark enough at the barn that we were already using head torches but by the time the food was coming to the boil, the barn had filled up with smoke and steam. It brought to mind that scene from *Aliens*, when the marines are stumbling around in an indoor fog, only the shafts of light from their helmets suggesting there is anyone there. We had to leave the door open for a few hours.

Still, on balance, it was probably better than having to eat outside when the midges are gathering. One of the most miserable sights I have ever seen was during a documentary about two guys trying to break the Munros record a few years ago.

They had trained in the Himalayas for six months and had their programme and all the logistics down to a tee. But within a day or two of success disaster struck; one of them was hit by a debilitating stomach bug and couldn't continue. The devastation was plain to see. There they were, two miserable souls sitting outside their tent having something to eat, their dreams in tatters.

A panned-in shot of their food summed it all it up – it was rice pudding but it was black. The air may have been thick with midges but so was their rice pudding. The two guys didn't seem to notice. So downhearted were they by their failure to hit the record and their efforts over the previous six weeks, they just spooned the midge-filled mix into their mouths. At least our food was insect-free.

During the night we heard the rain thundering down on the plastic panels of the roof. No one was complaining about the basic shelter then. When we went outside at first light, the hills were coated with a thin layer of fresh snow. The beach wouldn't have been a good option. You would have needed a crowbar to prise your body from the pebbles on the shore.

The Fisherfield mountains can also be tackled from the other side, from Kinlochewe, and many walkers who choose that option use Shenavall bothy as a base. This is a bit more upmarket than the barn and it has been improved greatly in recent years, but it can be busy, especially at weekends so you need to be prepared to camp out if necessary.

I always love that moment when you get the first glimpse of Shenavall as the path in starts to descend to Strath na Sealga. With its backdrop of the Beinn Deargs, this cottage looks like a homestead from the Old West, a lonely outpost on the plains awaiting an attack by marauding Apaches.

I wasn't planning a stay at Shenavall on my last venture though. It was early March and I was heading for the Dearg twins, Mor and Bheag, setting off after midnight in the hope I could do the circuit and get back out in time for a later start at work. The main problem would be the double river crossing. This is an area of exceptional high rainfall and the waters can rise dangerously in a matter of minutes. But it hadn't rained for days and it was forecast to stay dry so with waders at the ready I set off with from the parking bay at Corrie Hallie with optimism.

A light wind was waving the tree branches and there were a few early birds but they weren't quite at full voice just yet. The main sound was the clacking of rocks on the rubble track as I headed on into the chilly darkness.

Shenavall sat in shadow and silence as I walked down the steep rock staircase ready for the first water hazard of the day, the Abhainn Strath na Sealga. Once over this, it's a half mile or so of boggy ground to the next river, the Abhainn Gleann na Muice.

Beinn Dearg Mor is just a big push straight up from here on slopes of grass and loose earth, the consolation being the sight of An Teallach stretched out across your eyeline. Higher up the ground becomes rockier and a turn into a little hanging corrie leads up to the summit and views over the mountain's Great Prow to the Fisherfield Munros. The route onwards goes along the rim of the circular Toll an Lochain, which cradles a small body of water in the hollow between the hills, and then up to the cairn on a rocky promontory which provides even better views than its bigger neighbour.

I dropped back to the col and then down past the lochan, eventually being spit out of the corrie at the shores of Loch na Sealga. The two troublesome rivers have joined forces here, but the water was calm and low enough to give me the bonus of one crossing and negating the need for a reprise of the inward bog trot.

Shenavall still seemed to be in lockdown mode, although there was a lone figure on a nearby hillock with a shovel. Burying a dead man, no doubt. I had to keep reminding myself it was March as I plodded heavily back up the stairway in the heat, two hours from the start of the long road back to purgatory.

Anyone who is out regularly on the hills will have spent at least couple of nights in a bothy. Even if the idea of spending the night in a basic shelter in the middle of nowhere throws you into a fit of apoplexy, you will have had to bite the bullet at some point. They become a necessity if you want to avoid a 15-hour tramp across hostile territory in one go.

There are many who enjoy the whole experience; the crackling wood in the open fire, the constant brew-ups, the spontaneous camaraderie and, of course, the sounds of a variety of wildlife eating their way through your possessions.

The range of accommodation is immense. Some of these buildings are old estate cottages and are still used at certain times of the year by deer stalkers. Many have been taken under the wing of the Mountain Bothies Association. This voluntary group works with the estates to help maintain these shelters and they do a fine job. It's an alliance which, on the whole, works well. Many of the thousands of members often give up days of their own time to join work parties and carry out essential repairs and maintenance.

Some of these rudimentary refuges have two or even three rooms, some just the one. Some have two floors and many have bedding shelves. Some even have working toilets. Some of the bothies are that not far removed from the old youth hostels. But the hostels market has been reborn in the past 10 years or so and the level of comfort and facilities has changed dramatically. No more turning up with your sleeping bag and having to sweep floors before you leave – now it's hot showers, clean sheets and sometimes even meals if required.

There's still that whole thing about the possibility of having to bunk up with strangers though, with up to 12 to a room. Shenavall in peak season can make the Black Hole of Calcutta seem spacious. And if you are a solo walker or in a small group you just have to grin and bear it and hope your new room-mate is not an escapee from a secure unit.

It can be irritating to have 10 folk bedded down for the night and then have two latecomers arriving at two in the morning, having to turn on the lights and then spending the next hour or so unpacking noisily and muttering in stage whispers to one another. Despite their best efforts, it's always disturbing.

Once when we were in a mixed dorm of 12 in Aviemore, we had a disturbed night. Some of the occupants in the room above had arrived late and sounding somewhat the worse for wear. Ten minutes after settling down, there was a huge crash, what sounded like furniture being moved and then some moaning. It all quietened down again.

Ten minutes late, more thumping. Another ten minutes, the same again. A deputation was sent upstairs to sort it out. It turned out one of the guys had had a bit too much to drink, and when he had leaned out of his top bunk for something, he'd overbalanced and the whole thing went crashing. The rest of the noise was his pals trying to rebuild the bed and get him back into it, while he kept collapsing. His sober mates were mortified. The noise just sounded so much worse because of the thin ceiling and walls. Eventually they managed to strap him into his bed and he passed out.

But that wasn't the end of our sleep disruption that night.

Our toilet facilities were in a small cubicle attached to the room, not ideal with the thin walls and the close proximity to a group of strangers. In the middle of the night, I saw a small figure getting out of bed and padding off to the toilet.

After a few minutes there was a lone squeaky sound from that room. A few ears pricked up. A few minutes later, came a longer sliding parp like someone playing a trombone. This was the sound of someone desperately trying not to make a noise in the bathroom and failing miserably. There were a few snickers now.

After a few more notes in the same fashion, the culprit must have decided that his soundproofing efforts were failing and he'd be better off just going for broke and getting out quicker. Cue a series of squeaks, screeches and deep bass notes, building in intensity, frequency and speed until it was as if a brass band had moved in next door.

One sleepy female voice asked: "What in God's name is that?"

"I think it's 'Shite of the Bumble Bee'," came a reply from across the room.

A round of applause was all that could be expected when this Miles Davis of the toilet pan emerged red-faced, either through shame or the exertion, to head back to his bed.

Then there are the basic shelters, howffs, often just a well-arranged pile of boulders with a tin roof, but they be a life-saver for someone lost in a blizzard. They are not meant to be occupied for any length of time, just in case you thought of swapping your two weeks in Benidorm for a cheaper option. They are survival shelters, pure and simple.

Sometimes the line between bothy and hostel can be blurred, like the wee Hiker's Bothy at the farm at Camasluinie, near Killilan. Formerly known as Whitefalls Retreat, it has a cosy double room on the ground floor, a good shower, a kitchen and a small sitting room. Upstairs there is room for four more.

The only other guests when I arrived were a young couple who had claimed the honeymoon suite. I had the upstairs all to myself, a choice of bed frames for the night.

It has been upgraded since my last visit but is still described as no-frills accommodation. It is however a handy base for tackling the hills in Glen Elchaig. Fresh eggs are provided every morning for breakfast, but I was up before the cock crowed so my chances of an early omelette were clucked. I followed the track up the glen to Iron Lodge then left the path beyond and took a direct line north-east on grassy slopes. The wind was at my back and the rain threatened but never got beyond a few spits that would have shamed that infamous gobshite El-Hadj Diouf.

A few days later I was at a bothy at the higher end of the comfort scale in the heart of the Attadale Forest. Bendronaig has wooden floors and a working toilet but I used it mainly as a lunch spot out of the wind during a long day on Ben Dronaig.

Many people take a look at the track on the map and decide to bike in. But it's not all easy pedalling. There are two big climbs in and out and one woman I met was dreading the return journey. She ended up pushing the bike more than riding it. I at least suffered on my own two feet.

21
The Isle High Club

A night in the castle and a beer with a
deer wearing shades; shadowed by a
sea eagle; stormbound on Arran; white
beaches, dark cliffs from an island peak

I WAS sitting in a huge, soft armchair, drink in hand, the only customer in the bar, staring at the stag's head on the wall and wondering when it was going to start talking to me. I'd only had the one pint but the strangeness of the setting was getting to me.

The last time I had been on an April sunshine break where animal heads lined the wall and talked to the customers was at the Country Bears Jamboree in DisneyWorld. But this was Rum, not Florida. The weather was similar, blazing sun, blue skies and hardly a breath of wind, but this was an anomaly. This was an often rain and gale lashed island off the west coast of Scotland. This was Di snaenormallylooklikethisWorld.

A day on the Scottish mountains should always feel like an adventure but there's an added edge when you are heading for the islands. The feeling of remoteness, the military-style planning and the variables of the journey itself all add to up to something extra special.

You feel like Robinson Crusoe in reverse as you happily watch the ferry pull away from shore leaving you stranded in a strange land for a few days.

Rum's Cuillin mountains provide one of the best ridge walks in Scotland. But to reach them and complete the circuit in time to fit in with the ferries requires a bit of planning. Whereas the likes of Arran and Mull have a regular ferry service, Rum is not so straightforward, with boats only crossing on certain days and at varying times.

The ideal way to do the hills is to stay over for a few days but if you are pushed for time then Saturday provides the only chance to get in and back in a day. That gives you nearly 11 hours on the island. The mountain circuit and coastal walk back can take around 11 hours. One minute late and you're there until Monday.

Rum is a national nature reserve and until fairly recently you had to have written permission from Scottish Natural Heritage to visit. There are only about 50 people on the island and it's an important base for research on the red deer population. It's also home to the most voracious midges in the country. It's like all the worst ones were rounded up and sent into exile from the mainland. Just think of an insect penal colony, the Australia of the bug world. Camping is permitted but in the midge season it must be horrendous. I am careful with my visiting hours.

There's also a village store which seems to have as many chickens as customers and a post office, and there's a telephone box with a lifebelt propped up against it, probably handy in times of heavy rain. I haven't heard of anyone drowning in a phone box but that's not to say it couldn't happen. Better safe than sorry.

You can't take a car to Rum but there are a few four-wheel vehicles on the island, and for those who don't fancy the 15-minute walk from the ferry to the castle or just want their gear taken on it's handy.

I travelled over on the Friday ferry, having spent the day before climbing Carn Mor, from the head of Loch Arkaig. I had spent the night at Lochailort and woke to find the clag had burnt away and even the sun was wearing Raybans. The Cuillin were in sight the whole sailing, starting off as little bumps on the distant horizon, getting bigger all the time until they towered over the boat as we sailed into the harbour.

I turned down the offer of a lift to Kinloch Castle and instead did the short walk in the sunshine. Being off season, there were only a few other souls staying and I had an eight-bed room to myself. There were rooms for every price range, some with four-poster beds. I had a few hours exploring, watching the sun go down over Loch Scresort and then retired to the castle.

There was a small restaurant – half a dozen tables and waiter service – and a lovely wee bar which I had to myself. Apart from the stag on the wall, that is. He wasn't saying anything but he was wearing a nifty hat and a cool pair of sunglasses.

Now there's a spanking new hostel beside the castle with a modern kitchen but, alas, no four-poster beds like the castle. There's also a good campsite with wooden igloos for those who fancy roughing it but not too much.

I was up and away at 5am on a stunning Saturday morning on the Coire Dubh path up to the Bealach Bairc-mheall and soon I was on my first summit, Hallival. Purists will say the ridge begins with Barkeval, the smaller peak on your right, but my eyes were firmly on the clock and I would rather have time to spare at the finish. As I reached the bealach below Askival, the highest point on the round, I could see the morning ferry gliding into the bay, bringing in its day trippers. I was a few steps ahead by arriving the day before.

Hallival was now just a pointed top sticking out of a low layer of wispy cloud, a monk's tonsure with a ring of white hair, as I made my way up the ridge. Soon you come to the Askival Pinnacle but if you don't fancy the challenge it is easily turned on the left. You also notice lots of holes in the ground. These are nesting burrows of the Manx shearwater, but unless you are here around dusk it's unlikely you will see any activity as the chicks stay tucked away deep under the surface.

As I made my way to the summit I had the feeling I was being watched. I looked up. High above, on the rocks of the pinnacle route, was a little black goat intently studying my progress. It needn't have looked so worried – no way could I get to where he was. When I reached the summit he had vanished, no doubt perfectly camouflaged, he and all his mates blending in with their rocky surroundings.

The twin rocky peaks of Trallval are next and they provide an easy scramble in spectacular terrain, a field of boulders all shapes and sizes to be negotiated, some used as stepping stones, some clambered over in a variety of ungainly styles. A careful descent leads to Ainshval and a cunning path cutting through the seemingly impossible scree and boulder mess which litters this side of the hill. The final peak of the round is Sgurr nan Gillean, and as I made this now grassy ridge, a sea eagle circled, a black speck shadowing my progress.

A drop down over rough ground brought me out at Dibidil Bothy, and then there was only the small matter of the three-hour coastal path walk back. The isles of Eigg and Muck had been constant companions on the round, and although they started to fade as I got closer to the pier, you can rest assured a day in the Cuillin doesn't fade fast from the memory.

Even as the ferry sailed back to Mallaig, Rum put on one final show. As the boat slipped through the calm evening waters, the Cuillin sat in a perfect example of shadow art, lit from behind by a muted sky of orange, yellow, pink and purple. You could almost hear the collective sigh of contentment from the passengers who had massed on the rear deck to say goodbye.

The plain sailing continued with a speedy visit to Mull and a circuit of Dun da Ghaoithe, the 'fort of the two winds', and then Arran and its highest peak, Goatfell. This was the one that got away on a previous visit, but this trip went like clockwork, the combined ferry and bus timings blending seamlessly for a relaxed day, even if the view from the top was missing.

The contrast to my last visit to Arran could have hardly have been greater. This was a reminder of how the weather can suddenly tear the best-laid plans to shreds. Storm force winds forced the cancellation of the ferry home and that meant an extra day on the island.

Doesn't sound like a great hardship but my boss at the time didn't agree. When I called to say I would not be in on the Monday because the weather had left me stranded on Arran, he didn't seem to quite grasp the situation.

"Is there no other way you can get back in time?" he asked.

I didn't have enough money for a helicopter and I thought the swim was a bit far so unless we could snag a passing submarine, the answer was no. Even then, you could hear the cogs working in his mind as he pondered these ideas. I offered to work Saturday instead and killed the call before he could ask me to least try the swimming option.

There was no hint of any weather problems as we sailed over on a beautiful morning in early February. It was icy and cold but wall to wall blue sky and sunshine suggested spring rather than winter. We were staying with Malcolm's brother, Ian and his wife, Sally, and had two days of superb walking and scrambling ahead. Our host was in charge of routes, it was his home ground.

The ferry pulled in around lunchtime and with no time to stand on ceremony, it was a quick hello and straight on to the hills. It would be dark in about four hours. We walked up Glen Rosa, then climbed on to Beinn Nuis and over to Beinn Tharsuinn before taking a look at the impressive A'Chir ridge and heading round to close the circuit of Coire a'Bhreadain.

Our visibility was now impeded by an thick icy mist and the approaching darkness. On top of that our host was getting worried that his favourite watering hole was on winter hours and our slow descent and then the long road walk back would mean a dry evening. This is where local knowledge came to the fore – Ian called a taxi from the top of the hill. This was the thirsty man's equivalent of a 999 call and as soon as we hit the road, the local Michael Schumacher recognised the scale of the emergency and had us in the pub within minutes.

I've seen walkers using taxis to arrive at the start of a walk and have often thought of doing it myself at times, but then have always thought it seems too much like cheating. Hitching or begging a lift from other walkers always seems to work well enough.

The next day was also car co-ordinated. We were driven round to Glen Sannox a phone call from the ridge would arrange a pick-up time. We climbed Cir Mhor and Caisteal Abhail, dodged round the Witch's Step – nearly coming a cropper, my slide only halted by a foot becoming wedged between two boulders – and then finished on Suidhe Fhearghas before retracing our steps a little and dropping down to the north.

We were running late again due to the icy conditions but our driver, Sally, was picking up the lights from our head torches, and we could see the car headlights moving up the road to meet us. It all seemed so civilised. We celebrated for the rest of that Sunday night, not realising that the forecast storm was arriving 24 hours earlier than predicted. The only hurricane we noticed was the one inside our heads.

We spent a frustrating day pinned indoors, unable to even enjoy the consolation of a hair of the dog because there was no guarantee when I would be called upon to drive. The winds eased in the evening and the ferry finally ventured out into the choppy waters heading for Ardrossan.

About halfway through the journey, there was a huge bang that had everyone on their feet. Then Malcolm said: "We've turned round." I wouldn't have noticed the change in direction but he was a sailor. The boat had been struggling against the wind and the decision was made to head for the more sheltered harbour of Gourock. The journey home was extended: we would have to be bussed from Gourock to Ardrossan to pick up our cars.

We finally made it back sometime before midnight, but at least we were now back on the mainland. I'm happy to report my swimming trunks were not called into action.

My deadline was looming but I only had three more to do and I had two weeks in which to do them before the final party in Knoydart. Granted, one was on Harris and another on Jura, so there was still a bit of planning needed, although now I had left my job time was on my side. I also had the advantage of having a friend who could help out with the logistics. Katie had left the newspaper business in the same wave as myself and had gone back to her roots in Lewis to live and work.

My first instinct was to sail from Ullapool to Stornoway, but that would involve staying over and I was hoping to get back to the mainland and take in the remaining Corbett, Beinn Dronaig, on the way home. The better option was to catch the 5.30am ferry from Uig in Skye which sails into Tarbert in Harris. Katie would then pick me up, drive round to Clisham and climb the hill with me.

If I missed this boat the trip was scuppered, and probably plans for the big finish as well. This nagging feeling of unpredictability saw me leaving home about 8pm, driving through the night via Fort William and Kyle of Lochalsh and up through Skye to Uig, on the north-west tip of the island. Driving anywhere at this time of night makes you feel strangely detached from the rest of the world. You are chilled out, nothing much on the road, your own choice of music inside this bubble providing the soundtrack for your very own road movie.

Every so often you emerge from the darkness to pass through the lights a small town or village, mostly silent, sometimes some revellers still finding their way home, and then, within seconds, the lights are left behind and you are swallowed by the darkness again.

After Portree the feeling of solitude grows ever deeper, the road now a thin, winding, grey trail travelling over featureless moorland. Then a pair of headlights appeared in my rear window. I was just ticking along but they stayed with me, no attempt to overtake as they could have on a few occasions. After a few miles, the blue light started flashing and I pulled over. My first thought was that something had fallen off the car or had been about fall off – a regular occurrence with the type of punishment my cars took – or that one of my lights was out. I certainly hadn't been breaking any speed laws.

Then the road movie thoughts kicked in. Maybe this was like one of these of these nightmares you see in films about the deep south of the USA. I would be framed for some crime and locked up. I would be beaten black and blue and hosed down. Worse, I would miss the ferry.

Both occupants got out of the car and approached. I stayed where I was and let them have their customary sniff of the inside of the car. No drink, no drugs. Damn, that was their evening ruined. You could feel their interest dissipating.

They kept it polite then saying there had been a number of car thefts recently and they were just doing a spot check. That was the best they could think of.

Really – who the hell would steal a car like this and drive all the way to Skye keeping within the speed limits? I had always lived in hope that someone would do such a thing just to take this car off my hands but it was a pipedream. Car thieves nick good cars guys, not mobile pig styes.

They asked a few questions to justify the intrusion, could I tell them the registration of the vehicle, where was I going etc. I said I was heading for the ferry but they didn't even seem to know there was a ferry. Local knowledge, eh? Then they wished me a good night and a safe trip and went off to beat their heads off the side of their car with frustration.

The brilliant white glow from arc lights along with the alternative orange flashing lights of a road crew provided a minor hold-up further on but I had reached the ferry port with hours to spare. A few hours' rest in the car and then I joined all the utilities vans, HGVs, posties and fellow bleary-eyed travellers in the flat grey morning light for boarding.

I had avoided breakfast on the boat – 5.30am just seemed indecently early although it didn't seem to staunch the rush. I made do with a cup of tea, which puzzled Bob, my server. His patter was good.

He introduced himself: "The name's Bob, Calmac Bob. Server double-O 3, licensed to sell hot drinks and food." I immediately felt guilty about not wanting more than a cup of tea. But what better name could there be for someone working on a boat than Bob? Far better than Drowny or Sinky, for instance.

The ferry looms large over Tarbert when it docks in what seems an impossibly small harbour for vessels this size. The breakfast vacuum was filled after I disembarked, Katie driving me round to the Harris Hotel for some food. She had also had an early start, driving down from Lewis. We then headed up the A859 for the start of walk up Clisham. An hour and a half later and we were sitting at the massive summit cairn.

The island peaks have a feeling of being islands themselves. Wherever you look there is water. The name Clisham is derived from the Norse for rocky cliff, and the mountain provides a dividing line for the competing views; the west and south presenting a bold rocky landscape dotted with beaches of sparkling white sands, while to the north and east is the more rolling landscape of Lewis, bog and moor pockmarked by thousands of lochs of every shape and size. Up that way lay Katie's new life, a complete contrast to the one she had recently given up in Glasgow.

If Stornoway can be considered the back of beyond then where Katie was living was the back of the back of beyond. Her husband, Jason, is a ghillie and their house was on the estate where he worked. It sat in isolation beside a river just off the road in the middle of miles and miles of nothing. I have to admit that when I first saw it, Wuthering Heights sprang to mind. I pictured Katie as Cathy, running across the peatland and heather, searching for Heathcliff. And then I couldn't get that song out of my head.

In good weather it's a beautiful location, but in bad weather it would certainly present a few logistical challenges. The year after our Clisham day out, we were hit with one of the worst winters of recent times. By this time Katie had a young son, and she told us that because of the snow she never managed to get of the house for two weeks.

I can't imagine what that fortnight must have been like, housebound with a baby crying and Kate Bush warbling away constantly. You're a better man than I, Katie/Cathy/Kate.

Our day on Clisham was a welcome diversion, a chance to catch up with an old friend from a life consigned to the past, and Katie made sure I got a decent tour of Harris before it was time to head back for the boat.

We strolled along the beach at Luskentyre, one of the finest on the planet, miles and miles of fine, pale sand and shell, the water lapping gently on a horizontal plate, the dark mountains forming a backdrop few other places can replicate. I stayed in Skye that night then headed down to Attadale for a long day climbing Beinn Dronaig, thus completing a grand tour with no snags.

A week later and I was starring in a new version of Speed, a journey of smoking cars, multiple ferry trips and having to shower in a cupboard as I reached the summit of Beinn an Oir in Jura without the help of Sandra Bullock.

Epilogue
Dolphin Salute

Fin – and an escort home in style; an
insect menace that put midges in the
shade; V for victory on the final peak;
sailing away on sheets of glass

WE SET sail from Inverie on a sheet of glass, the sun lighting up the water to the horizon, the heat already building. The line of white buildings along the shoreline that mark the nucleus of the remote peninsula of Knoydart was blinding in the fierce light. It's never easy saying goodbye and doubly so if you are saying goodbye to one of the most special places in the country.

It was the morning after my big finish on the Corbetts and the celebrations of the evening and night before had been replaced by moments of contemplation for the boat trip back round the coastline into the Sound of Sleat and then into Kinloch Hourn. There was six of us plus four other passengers and it was a fitting end to a mountain chase which had led me all over the country for some 15 years in the middle of the night.

The initial chatter as we set off was quickly stifled as the beauty of the voyage kicked in. It seemed there was an unspoken decision taken collectively that what we were experiencing was simply too beautiful to be disturbed by words.

Then the first fin broke the surface of the water on the port side. A dolphin, then another on the starboard side, getting bolder as they raced the boat, playing a game of chase that only they would ever win.

I was being escorted home in style.

I had made the cut-off, my trip to Jura leaving just the two Corbetts to climb, as planned, during a weekend away in Knoydart with friends. No night walks this time, just an enjoyable three days in which to climb the final two mountains. Even the weather played ball, wall to wall sunshine and blue, clear skies forecast for the entire trip.

We loaded up with porridge on the Friday morning at the Little Chef at Spean Bridge before driving down to the end of the road at Kinloch Hourn. We took the Barrisdale Path to the head of the bay, then, after a short lunch stop at the bothy, began the beautiful but punishing climb from Coire Dhorcaill up and over mighty Ladhar Bheinn.

We dropped down the long, grassy slopes to the south-west and then began the track walk out to Inverie and our base for the weekend, the upscale b&b, The Gathering. No slumming it at the bunkhouse – we were here for a celebration and after all the years and months of toil I had endured on the Corbetts, I wanted to finish in style and comfort. Strangely enough, there were no voices of dissent.

The evening was spent in the country's remotest pub, The Old Forge, a meal accompanied by an inpromptu music session and then it was off to bed ready for the task ahead.

I was heading out to Beinn na Caillich the next day, while Robert, Crawford and Katie went for the Munro Luinne Bheinn and Rebecca and Susan decided to have a rest day after their exertions on Ladhar Bheinn the day before. It seemed fitting that I was going solo, as most of my Corbett excursions had been undertaken alone.

Beinn na Caillich is a remote and craggy mountain in the north-west of this rough land. It is one of three hills in this part of the country which bear the name 'hill of the old woman'. The other two are in Skye and refer to tales of Norse princesses, fabled giantesses and hoards of treasure. The likelihood is there may have been a similar link here.

The strong sunshine and the breeze meant that the midges, so often a scourge here, were posted missing. However, as I took the path up towards the Mam Li pass, I felt a sharp sting on my shoulder. My first thought was a wasp but then I felt another, and another. Horse flies, the worst I had ever encountered. They were everywhere, and despite my wearing two layers, they were able to bite right through.

At least they managed to speed my progress up to the pass and then a short, left turn at the top brought me out at the summit where I found an unusual view of Ladhar Bheinn and met a kindred spirit. Sitting at the cairn was a couple, the female half of which had only five Corbetts left to climb. We were able to mutually disperse some wisdom about what we had left to complete and then take each other's photo for posterity.

I exited via the south-west ridge and the subsidiary summit of Meall Coire an t-Searraich and was back to the pub three hours before the Munro baggers. The final day loomed and a date with Beinn Bhuidhe.

We all left together next morning, walking into Gleann Medail where we parted company for a few hours. Susan decided to join me for the final summit while the others headed up the glen for Meall Buidhe. We would be on opposite arms of the corrie.

As so often seems the case, the final push appeared to be the hardest yet. The 'yellow mountain' was more a lush green and its complex slopes provided plenty of detours to get on to the ridge, all the time accompanied by yelps of pain as the horse flies struck.

Then I saw the rounded trig point and the pace quickened. Susan stood back to let me enjoy the glory of a first-placed finish, snapping away all the while.

I set my poles in a V for victory sign in the trig and took pictures in every direction. Then I lay down for the most appropriate pose. I felt I finally deserved a rest after all the nights spent giving up sleep in pursuit of my target.

We found a more direct – and much steeper – way down which involved plunging into deep vegetation which immediately saw a volcanic puff of beasties exploding up in a mushroom cloud to assault your eyes, nose and mouth every time.

Eventually we reached clearer ground and saw the others making their way into the glen. We met at the bridge and Crawford couldn't resist the urge to get his kit off and dive in the river. The strong sun was keeping the midges at bay.

The adrenaline was well and truly flowing when we hit the pub. The seats and benches outside were filled to overflowing, everyone taking advantage of the late afternoon sun.

There were guitars, fiddles and a variety of other string instruments, snare drums and pipes. The drink was flowing well into the night. They know how to have a party here. After all, this is where they once had an impromptu fancy dress party and got round the problem of last-minute costume hunting by merely going along dressed as each other. That must have been a tad alarming if you weren't in on the joke.

We had the option of walking back out along the Barrisdale Path but it had been suggested we could hire a private boat to take us round the coast if we could rustle up 10 or 12 people to share the cost.

We left Inverie Bay heading west at first then turning north away from the ferry route past Sandaig Bay, round the headland off the Sound of Sleat, past the outposts of Doune and Airor.

As we curved east round the north shores of the peninsula, the dolphins appeared and we watched in silence, transfixed as this unusual guard of honour went through their array of aquatic tricks.

When we started heading further into Loch Hourn, the dolphins left us and we were aware of the passage narrowing, Arnisdale and Corran over on our left and the giant spires of Ladhar Bheinn's towering over the cavern-like corries underneath.

Deeper into the loch we went, the boat's sonar showing the depth of water starting to diminish. We pulled over to rocks near the shore to let two of our fellow travellers off so that they could walk back to Inverie. It took some careful work from our captain to get the boat in so close and then some careful work from the departing duo to leap over to the rock.

Once they were safely ashore, we continued the voyage east, passing through the narrowest point of the loch at Caolas Mor. Now we were crawling along, watching the screen showing the water depth going down, down, down.

Then, just as it seemed we were at the limit of our clearance, we saw the slipway. From here we had a two kilometre walk to the cars. We waved our skipper and his remaining passengers off. We were home and dry.

The chase was over, the Corbetts had been done, but that's not the end of the story. Not yet anyway. There's always another mountain, another list, another day, and hopefully that will go on for a long time yet.

My first Corbett had been climbed in 1993, my last in 2009. But again that doesn't tell the whole story. For the early years of my first Munro round, the Corbetts were just a sideshow, hills that often had to be climbed when the weather on the higher peaks was too wild or when I needed to get out for my fix and I didn't fancy a big journey.

It was only around 1998 that I looked at them more closely, and even then they still remained a clear second choice. But after my Munro finish in 2000, I turned my guns fully on them. Doing them in tandem with a second Munro round was far more economical.

In 2011 I 'compleated' for the second time on Beinn Eibhinn in the Alders range and then again in 2015 on Ben More in Mull in the middle of a wet and windy night. Age and fitness will dictate whether there will be another, but the progress so far has been heartening.

There definitely won't be another Corbett round. That's done and dusted, and there's no need for a repeat. They have taken me to many new places and provided some startling memories and sure, I will make a point of revisiting the best ones but there are other targets. A revisit of the whole gamut is definitely not on my bucket list.

I started my mountain career relatively late, and I am aware I am increasingly on borrowed time. I have been lucky with injuries but one big setback at this stage would spell the end for the big mountain days.

The night walks are fewer and further between now, the necessity of using the hours of darkness for the chase no longer valid. That all happened in a certain time and space and it was the way to go at that point. Now, any night walk I do is more down to nostalgia, a trip down memory lane, a novelty as opposed to the routine midnight trips in pursuit of a name on a list. It already seems like a lifetime ago.

I realise I am fortunate to still have the choice. There have been tears, traumas and tragedy, pleasure, laughter and accomplishment.

I have lost three friends who were taken far too soon, and there has been a whole cast of characters who have wandered through this mountain life bringing their own brand of madness and friendship.

Whenever I sit alone at the summit of a mountain watching the sun coming up, it becomes a sanctuary. I soak in every moment and wish that more of the people who have enriched my life could be there to see it. I hope that in years to come, those who have joined me at some point in this great adventure will be able to do likewise.

Glossary

A

ABHAINN (PRONOUNCED: AVIN) – river

ACHADH (ACH) – field

ALLT (OWLT) – steam

AONACH (OE-NACH) – ridge

ARETE (ARET) – sharp ridge

B

BAC – bank

BAN (BAAN) – pale, white

BEAG (BEG) – small

BEALACH (BYALACH) – mountain pass

BEN / BEINN / BHEINN – mountain

BHREAC / BREAC (VRECHK, BRECHK) – speckled

BIDEAN (BEEJAN) – small pointed top

BIOD (BEET) – pointed top

BINNEIN (BEEN-YAN) – pinnacle, pointed summit

BRAIGH (BRAY) – slope

BRUACH (BROO-ACH) – slope

BUIDHE (BOO-YA) – yellow

C

CADHA – steep slope, pass

CAIRN / CARN / CHARN (CAARN) – rocky hill

CAISTEAL (CASH-TYAL) – castle

CAM – bent, crooked

CEANN (KIN)– head

CIOCH / CICHE (KEECHA) – breast

CLACH – stone

CNOC (CROCK) – knoll

COILLE (COL-YEA) – wood

COIRE / CHOIRE – corrie, hollow

COL – mountain pass

CREAG (CRAIG) – crag

CRUACH (CROO-ACH) – heap, stack

D

DAMH – deer

DEARG (JERRAK) – red

DIOLLAID (JEE-ALITCH) – saddle, pass

DOIRE – copse

DROCHAID (DROCHITCH) – bridge

DRUIM (DRUM) – spine, ridge

DUBH (DOO) – black

DUN – fort

E

EACH / EICH (YECH) – horse

EAG (AIK) – cleft or notch

EAS (ASS) – waterfall

EILEEN (I-LEEN) – island

EUN (EEYAN) – bird

F

FADA, FHADA (ATTA) – long

FEADAN (FED-DAN) – small valley
FIACAIL (FEE-ACHKILL) – tooth
FIONN (FYOON) – fair
FRAOCH (FROECH) – heather
FUAR (FOO-AR) – cold
FUARAN (FOO-ARAN) – spring

G

GABHAR (GHOWER) – goat
GAOITH (GOO-Y) – wind
GARBH (GARRAV) – rough, stony
GEAL (GYAL) – white
GEARR (GY-ARR) – short
GLAS (GLASS) – grey green
GLEN / GLEANN – valley
GORM (GORRAM) – blue
GREIGH (GRAY) – herd

I

INBHIR / INVER – river mouth
IOLAIR (U-LIR) – eagle

L

LAIRIG (LAHRIK) – pass
LIATH (LEE-A) – grey
LOCHAN / LOCHAIN – small lake

M

MAM – breast
MAOL (MOEL) – bare
MEADHOIN (MEE-AN) – middle
MEALL (MYOWL) – lump
MOINE – moss, bog
MONADH (MONNA) – mountain
MOR / MORE / MHOR (MOAR, VOAR) – big
MULLACH – height, summit

O

ODHAR / ODHAIR (OA-AR) – dun-coloured, tawny

R

RUADH (ROO-A) – reddish

S

SAIL (SAHL) – heel
SLOC / SLOCHD – hollow
SGOR / SGORR (SKORR) – rocky-topped hill
SGORAN (SKORRAN) – little rock
SGURR (SKOOR) – rocky peak
SOCACH (SOCH-CACH) – snout
SPIDEAN (SPEEJAN) – high point above corrie
SRON (STRAWN) – nose
STAC (STACK) – conical hill
STOB (STOP) – peak
STRATH – valley
STUC (STU-(KH)K) – steep conical hill
SUIDHE (SEE-A) – seat

T

TOLL / THOLL (TOAL, HOAL) – hollow
TOM (TOAM) – hillock, knoll

U

UAINE (OO-AN-YA) – green
UAMH (OO-ARV) – cave
UISGE (OOSH-GA) – water

V

VANE – middle

Acknowledgements

MOONWALKER covered my first round of Munros, and ended in September, 2000. But the story continued. My constant night wanderings on Scotland's mountains went on for another nine years until I took early retirement from my newspaper career. I still walk at night but now it is less of a mission, just fun and reminiscence. I can walk at any time of day – no more need for mad dashes to far-off places and an equally mad dash back in time for work.

Although *Moonwalker* is perfectly fine as a standalone book, I always saw it as a two-parter. Well, this is the second and concluding part, another nine years of night adventures chasing Corbetts and Munros. And, just like on so many of these nocturnal walks, I have decided to go it alone with this book.

The boys at BackPage Press. Martin Greig and Neil White, were a dream to work with on the first book, but for reasons too complex to explain they were unable to go with this one and it didn't make sense to take a Part Two to another publisher. Martin and Neil have still been a great help to me on this solo effort.

I have tried to stick with their tried and tested – and very successful – formula, so the look and the format of the book is similar, a true companion piece.

Once again I have to thank the Herald's legendary sportswriter Hugh MacDonald for his support and sterling editing work, Laura Kincaid for her knowledge and skill in putting the book together, and Gary Duncan for being my tech wizard across all medias.

Once again I have to thank everyone who has walked with me during all these adventures, whether you are name-checked or not, everyone who has bought or supported the books and everyone who has turned up at book festivals, mountain festivals and various talks all around the country.

And once again I have to thank my wife Alison, daughters Claire and Lucy, and granddaughters Ava and Lily, mini-Moonwalkers in the making.

MOONWALKER
ADVENTURES OF A MIDNIGHT MOUNTAINEER

ALAN ROWAN

Have you read *Moonwalker* yet?
Here's a taste of what's between the covers.

1
Treig and Intrigue

MY NAME IS ALAN and I'm an alpaholic. I am addicted to mountains. I need them. I have to get out at least once a fortnight. If I don't, I get bad-tempered, fidgety and my concentration starts to wander. All I can think about is my next fix.

For the last 20 years or so, the priority every week has been to climb a hill. No sooner has it been conquered than the planning must start for the next one. And the next. And the next.

It consumes you piece by piece, like a snake swallowing its tail. The more I did, the more I wanted – no, needed – to do. The planning became just as important as the climbing, hours spent working out the logistics of getting there, the best route up, both aesthetical and practical, and exactly how much would be too much to take on.

Which is why I was now slogging my way up a rising ramp of grass and scattered boulders towards two peaks in the wild region east of Fort William as the morning light was starting to filter through.

I should have been in bed, asleep, recovering from a hard day at the office. Instead, here I was, heading for the twin pyramids of Stob a'Choire Mheadhoin and Stob Coire Easain. It was not yet 4am and this was my first night assault on the Munros.

I had already racked up 53 peaks in just over a year in my quest to do the Munros. Most of these had been done with my buddies Fergus and Malcolm, but I just could not get enough and was becoming frustrated at the thought of all these hills that were outside our usual time limits. When I pitched the idea of overnight climbs to the pair of them, I was met with: "Yeah, right." That was the end of the conversation. They thought my proposal was just a whim.

But once an idea forms in my head, it is hard to shift. At the very least, it would be worth experimenting. One trip could not hurt.

So here I was striding up a three-mile rising ridge, alone. My body was still adjusting to this alien experience as I pushed on. The first hour of any climb is always tough as your body fights to adjust to the sudden shock. When you are doing it before dawn, it seems doubly hard.

Your legs feel like they have lead weights attached. Your breathing is heavy. Your head is telling you that this is wrong, wrong, wrong. And yet you move on step by step, making what is often referred to as controlled progression. That is just a fancy way of saying it's a slog.

There is no path. I weave in and out of rocky outcrops and undulating grassy terrain to find the best line. The only thing that matters is the next horizon. It is like an uphill slalom. All this time the morning is rising with me, changing the colours of the terrain with every step.

Then there is the magic moment when I break the back of the climb. The gradient eases and the ground becomes firmer. I move towards my target faster, like a rocket jettisoning its heavy, bottom section. And finally there is the feeling of elation when the summit is in sight. The thought that I still have to cover the same distance to get home hardly ever figures. It is all about the moment.

I am lying out above 3,000 feet in the early-morning sunshine. My wife, Alison, and daughters, Claire and Lucy, are blissfully unaware of where I am and what I have been doing. It is not a case of telling lies, more a sin of omission. There is no point telling them in advance what I am planning to do, no point in them having a sleepless night worrying about me.

They have often played second fiddle to my obsession. They also know that life is much sweeter this way. Better a happy, satisfied husband and father most of the week than a grumpy one all of the week. Besides, Superman is not the only one who needs a fortress of solitude. This was my secret, my me-time, a regular slot to chat with myself and find solutions to any troubles.

As for work? Well, I've always regarded it as merely a means to support my hobby. I take pride in doing my job well but it is a job, not a lifestyle. One should work to live, not live to work. I always felt immense sadness when I heard colleagues say they would not know what to do with themselves if they did not work.

I was lucky with my career. I worked for a national newspaper in Glasgow, which meant doing backshift for most of the last 20 years. Starting times ranged from 2.30pm to 7.30pm, finishing times from 9.30pm to 3am, and the rolling rota was over six days so that some weeks you were off Mondays, some Tuesdays, and so on. The only day I did not have to work was Saturday, which was sacrosanct. I never walked or climbed on a Saturday. That was a day for the family.

My home is on the east coast and, as Alison and my girls were settled there, I lived in Glasgow during working spells and returned home for my days off. It was unusual to have to work five days straight through, but sometimes you could have five days off in a row.

I spent down time between working by going to the cinema, meeting friends for lunch and wandering around book stores, but I needed to keep fit. I am not a fan of gyms. It had to be the outdoors. But it is hard to find team sports taking place during the day, so it had to be something I could do solo.

I started taking my lunch in the great outdoors. I would hike for a couple of hours, find a spot and then settle down for a bite to eat and some sunbathing. It would be the ideal antidote to the pressures of the office.

From simple beginnings come great things. The need to get out grew, the targets became bigger, more elusive, more prized. Mountains would become my sport and my fulfilment.

This was my personal triumph, something that set me apart from my colleagues. A round of golf or a walk in the park was often the limit for many of them, no six, seven or eight hours of constant uphill movement in the middle of the night.

Gazing out of the office windows on a lovely day, it was easy to imagine myself scaling a mountain, but when the dark cloak of night had descended and the weariness of the day had set in, that was the real test. The hardest part of going climbing at night was winning the battle of will with a body that naturally wanted to shut down. And it was a constant fight. Every time I went out I had this inner struggle, but most of the time I won.

The ability to turn my back on my natural instincts would lead to this moment, the struggle up a faraway slope in the middle of the night.

The first two forays into nocturnal walking gave me the ideal grounding for the many trips that would lie ahead. The first went like clockwork. The weather was superb, the timings were spot on and it was a huge success. The second was exactly the opposite. The clinging cloud never lifted, the visibility was non-existent and it was not a particularly pleasurable night out. The experience of both sides of the coin was to prove invaluable. When I set out for the Easains, the mountains were still shedding their winter garb, and the temperature was rising by the day. But that was only one consideration in my choice of day and hill.

I did not want to have to travel too far the first time. I had no idea how I would react to the lack of sleep and the journey, no idea how I would fare tackling a 3,000-feet plus climb in the middle of the night when I would normally be sleeping, and no idea how I would manage the drive back and then do a long shift at work.

The hills had to be sufficiently far away. There was no point in an overnight journey and climb to a peak I could do comfortably during any normal day. Also, if I was going to make a long journey, I would be as well climbing a couple of peaks rather than just one.

The twin peaks which rise above Loch Treig were perfect. They are similar in appearance and shape and are joined together by a high bealach. The legendary mountaineer Hamish Brown once jokingly referred to them as This Yin and That Yin, a sobriquet which has stuck.

To reach the starting point meant making the familiar 100-plus mile run up the A82 to Fort William and then on to Spean Bridge. From there I would take the A86 east before turning down the narrow public road to Fersit, which sits on the line of the West Highland Railway.

The drive time would be about three hours. I reckoned if I left work at midnight, I would be there for about 3am. That would give me time enough for a nap if required before climbing the hills and returning with time to spare for a 5pm start in the office.

I packed a sleeping bag and travel pillow, and made sure I had plenty of energy snacks and fruit. I also had a caffeine lake with me, cans of Coke in the car for the journey back and a flask of coffee. My route had been posted with several colleagues – which they noted with some disbelief – and I was clear for take-off.

Travelling long distances at night is usually a case of quiet roads and whispered radio voices. I enjoy driving, and although there is not much to see on the outward journey, there is the anticipation of the return when everything you have only imagined in the darkness will become clear. In the years that followed I found myself catching up on whole back catalogues of music I had missed.

If the weather was fine and it was a clear night, I counted down the journey by ticking off the dark shapes of the familiar landmarks along the route. On overcast nights with no visibility above a few hundred feet, I felt I was in a road movie, headlights picking the way through an unseen landscape and, if the heavens opened, the music was turned up to drown out the drumming on the roof.

On my first night the sky was clear, and my mood was euphoric. Four days earlier I had finally seen Dundee United, my team, win the Scottish Cup, a fitting reward after six previous failed attempts, and I was still on a high.

My drive progressed with a selection of mellow and wild music. Talking Heads were a constant companion and John Martyn kept me chilled after the radio contact in the first part of the journey was lost; then a bit of Led Zep and other heavy metal in the latter stages to get me pumped up for the task ahead. Stairway to Heaven? I could only hope. But as I passed through Spean Bridge and started looking for the turn-off for the few miles down to Fersit, the music was switched off. I always prefer a few moments of silence before the hard work starts.

The twisting, narrow road south to the head of Loch Treig is only a couple of miles long but it passes over an old bridge and then through beautifully wooded areas before ending at a small quarry where I parked. It was down this quiet road that Hitler's right-hand man Rudolf Hess was held for a spell after his wartime flight to Scotland in 1941.

Hess had crash-landed in a field near East Kilbride, supposedly while flying in to make a peace offer, and was moved around the country. One of his 'holiday' homes while in Scotland was Inverlair Lodge, which is tucked in just off the road to the left. It is always disappointing to tell people that to see the house where Hess was held, you have to take a first left: it would be much better if it was third Reich.

There was no sign of any life as I stopped at the edge of An Dubh Lochan, 'the little black loch'. The moonlight shimmering on the dark water had turned the scene into a beautifully stark, black-and-white image. I had been weary in the latter stages of the drive but, at 3.15am with the light reflecting brilliantly off the still water and a cacophony of newly roused birds starting to pierce the silence, sleep was out of the question. The adrenaline was pumping.

When solo, it takes just five minutes from arrival at the destination to actually setting off. A few moments of quiet contemplation, eyes shut and head on the seat rest, is all that is required.

With the help of my head torch, a short walk over a level, grassy meadow took me over the line of an old mining tramway and then I rose on to the broad ridge for the ascent. With the early rising light starting to pick out the way, I was soon on steeper ground at Meall Cian Dearg, a minor rocky section on the way to my first Munro of the day, Stob a'Choire Mheadhoin.

Off to my left were the remains of the massive cornices that had smothered the cliff walls above Loch Treig but which were now cracking and slewing off in great slabs, ready to collapse down the mountainside, eventually to melt into the water and complete the wet fall to earth which began months before.

By 6.30am I was on the stony top of Stob a'Choire Mheadhoin, 'the peak of the middle corrie', to be greeted by a fluttering red flag planted in the summit cairn. My first nocturnal Munro and the flags were out to salute my achievement. Treig Heil, if you like.

Stob Coire Easain is one of the few mountains whose English translation – 'the peak of the corrie of the little cascade' – trumps the beauty of its Gaelic name. It is only about half a mile further on, a steep half-hour walk over stony terrain, up a graceful, curving ridge with the snow lines of the cornice providing a metaphorical handrail.

With the steepness of the ascent, the summit cairn cannot be seen from below, and it was here that I had my first taste of the mind playing tricks, a phenomenon that was to become a recurring feature of walking in the wee, small hours. As I approached the final push, a huge bank of snow stood in front of me, a giant lip in front of a cairn which I still could not see.

I stopped. All I could see was snow. Maybe there wasn't any more ground ahead. I could step over this snow and plummet into thousands of feet of thin air.

No, this was daft. Of course there was solid ground – I had seen the cairn from the other peak. Pushing my doubts aside, I stepped in and then over the snow. I was standing at the second summit.

With a snow wall all around the cairn, the crown of this peak was like an eyrie, a beautiful spot for breakfast. Sitting there at 7am with the snow-capped Grey Corries and the Nevis Range prominent in the morning sunshine, I wondered why anyone would want to climb at any other time. Everybody else was out of step, not me.

As I was sitting back at the car, basking in the glow of self-satisfaction, my socks off as I massaged my weary feet, another vehicle drew up. After a few minutes the driver got out, all kitted out for a day in the hills, and strolled over to where I was sitting.

"Are you going up the hills?" he asked.

"No, I've already been up."

It was the first time I had seen that look, a combination of puzzlement and almost fear. He retreated to his car. It was another first, but it would not be the last.

My journey back to Glasgow was slow, with constant pit stops for caffeine and snacks and, at one point, a nap. The sun was out, it was a glorious day and the Munro hotspots were packed with cars and walkers preparing to start their day. The night shift had finished, the day shift was beginning.

I managed to get through my shift at work without dozing off. The nocturnal adventure had been a resounding success. My hunch had paid off. This was the way I would conquer the Munros.

The chance of a second bite at the cherry did not arise for another six weeks. During this spell I had managed to tick off another 20 Munros in just six outings, including a big weekend away, taking my total up to 75. I was on a roll, and I decided to keep it going by upping the ante on my next night fling.

I was going to head into the Mamores to try to do at least three, maybe more. The journey to the village of Kinlochleven takes just a couple of hours and, being early July, the light should have been good enough for a very early start. The last three outings had been in exceptionally fine weather, and the forecast for this day looked like being the same again.

The Mamores are a chain of mountains to the south of Ben Nevis and it is possible to do all 10 Munros there in one big round. It is a long day, certainly too much if you factor in the car journey and lack of sleep, but I figured that with the good tracks into these hills and a superb path network, I could get going in the dark and conquer a few at least. But, to paraphrase Burns, the best-laid schemes o' mice an' madmen gang aft a-gley.

It had been a good night at work. At the 1994 World Cup, Bulgaria had pulled off a massive shock by beating Germany 2-1 and the buzz you get from a genuinely thrilling football match was still reverberating in my head as I headed off into the night. Rather than start from sea level, I parked at the Mamore Lodge hotel, a few hundred feet higher up, a nice wee starter for the day. It would be a slightly longer walk from there but I had reckoned trading distance for a small height gain was worth it. By 2.30am I was on the move, heading north on a good track into Coire na Ba, 'the corrie of the cattle'.

My first objective was to reach the col between Stob Coire a'Chairn and Na Gruagaichean. Then I would head south-east on to the twin summits, before continuing on the main ridge round to Binnein Mor, down one of its long arms and over to Binnein Beag and then sweep up Sgurr Eilde Mor on the way out. It was ambitious for a night walk but I did not foresee any difficulties. But I had been banking on the thick, early morning cloud blowing away sooner rather than later. And it was not showing any sign of doing so.

The damp was creeping through my layers and the ferns and grasses that had been soaking into my feet and legs earlier had left a wet overcoat that was not shifting as I plodded upwards on a muddy path into the corrie with nothing to see ahead of me. I was walking in a strange, half-lit gloom that was more akin to a day in December than July.

On my left was the massive Am Bodach, all dark cliffs and slashed gullies with white sheets of water roaring and tumbling down out of the greyness, moisture oozing and dripping from every orifice. It is a mountain with the power to intimidate, a brute looming threateningly out of the mist with seemingly no chinks in its armour. Somewhere up ahead on my right, smothered under the wall of cloud, were the twin summits of Na Gruagaichean but for now all I could see was long, wet grass in the limited horizon available.

An unexpected flash of colour briefly broke the monotony; a lone foxglove off to the right, cerise bells being pulled down by the weight of the water. Then it was back to the green and the grey as the flower was swallowed by the cloud and I continued upwards to my first target.

Eventually the path's long, contorted approach led me over the steep slopes which pulled up to the col, but there was still no sign of the cloud dispersing. In mornings like these, the myth of the silence and solitude of the great outdoors is easily dispelled. With the stillness around me, every movement of water sounded like a raging torrent. The sound of each laboured step seemed to be amplified tenfold, even above the heavy breathing of a man who realised that he should really be at home, tucked up in bed like every other sane human being. It ought to be all beautiful views bathed in yellow and orange light, not some trudge up the rock-strewn gloom of Mount Anywhere.

This was not pleasure. This was revenge for the smugness of my last outing. It was as if some greater power was saying: "That'll teach you."

The first of the two towers of Na Gruagaichean loomed. It is an impressive lump of rock, even more so when you make your way down the other side among lots of loose earth and rock to be confronted with the equally steep pull up its twin, the main summit.

According to Gaelic legend, this mountain got its name, which translates as 'The Damsels', from two young ladies who met a hunter on these slopes and gave him a hunting dog. There were no strange women here today, however, and the only dog was the climb.

I was shuffling along like a zombie; this was indeed the night of the living dead. I needed a view to lift the spirits but, by the time I reached the boulder field at the summit, I was beaten. No sign of anything ahead, no sign of anything behind. My heart was not in this any more. I just wanted to get back to the car. And that probably led to what happened next.

What should have been a simple walk over to the next peak became a confused effort in the mist and boulders. I ended up dropping down too low off the ridge and then the compass went crazy.

I suddenly had no true idea of exactly where I was. I was wandering around at 6am on a heather and boulder clad slope, having lost my bearings and with no visibility. I had lost the plot.

I knew the bulk of Binnein Mor was somewhere above me. That was logical, but logic seemed to be going out of the window.

After about half an hour of aimless and weary movement, I decided enough was enough. Heading down the corrie would take me out of the cloud and hopefully give me some idea of my whereabouts.

After a battle to get through some sofa-size boulders, real ankle snappers, I could see a path below.

At last I knew where I was. I could have resumed the walk from here – Binnein Mor was back up the ridge on my left – but I did not have the mental strength for any more. I just wanted to lie down and sleep. It was time to accept defeat and head down from the hills.

The cloud lifted when I was driving back down the road and it turned into a beautiful day. I could have been dancing round these peaks had I started walking at a sensible time. I was deflated. This night had been a disaster, and I was not sure I could handle night walking if the weather was unfavourable. I would either have to toughen up or forget this whole idea.